Praise for *American Catholics in Transition*

"Assumptions and assertions about 'Catholics,' 'the Church,' or 'the Catholic vote' need to be, but often are not, backed by the facts. Facts are what *American Catholics in Transition* supplies in abundance, with sometimes surprising results. The authors' clearly stated and provocative interpretations of data yield an invaluable window onto U.S. Catholicism, past, present, and to come. This is an engrossing and important book for scholars, people working in or on Catholic institutions and culture, and for anyone who wants to follow the role of Roman Catholicism in U.S. society and politics."

—Lisa Sowle Cahill, Boston College

"In *American Catholics in Transition* survey and analysis confirms that Catholics remain consistently committed to core doctrinal teachings but increasingly distance themselves from moral teachings and institutional structures. The two most disturbing trends are women's decreasing identification with the Church and the millennial generation's independence from Catholicism in particular and organized religion in general."

—Chester Gillis, Georgetown University

"Professor D'Antonio and various collaborators have conducted the only regular series of national surveys that collectively illuminate changes and continuities among American Catholics over the past quarter century. I was especially pleased to see that this fifth volume in the series appropriately presents the most extensive treatment of Hispanic Catholics to date."

—Timothy Matovina, University of Notre Dame,
author of *Latino Catholicism: Transformation in America's Largest Church*

American Catholics in Transition

American Catholics in Transition

William V. D'Antonio, Michele Dillon
and Mary L. Gautier

ROWMAN & LITTLEFIELD PUBLISHERS, INC.
Lanham • Boulder • New York • Toronto • Plymouth, UK

Published by Rowman & Littlefield Publishers, Inc.
A wholly owned subsidiary of The Rowman & Littlefield Publishing Group, Inc.
4501 Forbes Boulevard, Suite 200, Lanham, Maryland 20706
www.rowman.com

10 Thornbury Road, Plymouth PL6 7PP, United Kingdom

British Library Cataloguing in Publication Information Available

Library of Congress Cataloging-in-Publication Data

American Catholics in transition / William V. D'Antonio, Michele Dillon, and Mary L.
Gautier.
    pages cm
  Includes bibliographical references and index.
   ISBN 978-1-4422-1991-5 (cloth : alk. paper)—ISBN 978-1-4422-1992-2 (pbk. : alk.
paper)—ISBN 978-1-4422-1993-9 (electronic)
  1. Catholic Church—United States—History—21st century. I. D'Antonio, William V.,
editor of compilation.
  BX1406.3.A44 2013
  282'.7309051—dc23

                                                                    2013046948

♾™ The paper used in this publication meets the minimum requirements of American
National Standard for Information Sciences—Permanence of Paper for Printed Library
Materials, ANSI/NISO Z39.48-1992.

Printed in the United States of America

~

Table of Contents

Preface

In the 25 years since our first survey, much has changed in the Church. This is especially true if we focus on Catholics themselves and their lived understanding of Catholicism. Consider the case of Betty and her daughter Beth. Betty is an upper-class white woman who grew up in comfortable circumstances in New England, and now in her early 60s, she is a member of what we call the Vatican II generation. Her earliest memories are of attending Mass in a suburban parish every morning before Kindergarten at St. Michael's school, and how it hurt to have to kneel so much on the hard wood. She remembers it as a painful experience that she did not like at all. For her, daily Mass was then and still is today a distraction.

Early on, she had trouble with the church and Catechism rules that seemed to loom over so much of her daily activities. She recalls classmates who would question the nuns at school about various elements of Church doctrine and how one of her friends was dismissed from class for arguing that just because some American Indians did not believe in the Catholic religion this should not mean that they could not get in to Heaven. She recalls well how some of the things she was taught as being rigidly unchangeable did in fact change after Vatican II—and her gradual realization during her teenage years that she could figure things out for herself. After attending Catholic schools for 12 years, her experiences at a small liberal arts college challenged her faith. Meeting young people of different religions and even of no religion, she gradually became what she calls a "Smorgasbord Catholic," though she attended Mass fairly regularly, especially because she liked the priest.

Betty likes the idea of sharing in the Lord's Supper, the Eucharistic breaking of the bread, but she is unsure about transubstantiation and the idea that at the consecration, the bread and wine is transformed into the Body and Blood of Christ. She misses the priests who ran the local Newman Center at the university campus, a good 25 minutes away from their home; she prefers to go to Mass there than to the parish church nearby. She doesn't like the current leadership in the Vatican or locally in her diocese and pretty much ignores what the bishops have to say. She recognizes the need for a formal institution but rejects what she sees as a narrowly focused leadership. All in all, she feels comfortable with her version of Catholicism and is proud of her role in the Sanctuary Movement some years back when she joined with others in making their church a sanctuary for illegal immigrants from Latin America.

As for her oldest daughter Beth, Betty feels that the poor quality of the Sunday school teaching led her daughter to have lots of doubts about Biblical stories and miracles at an early age. She admits that she herself did not do much to address those doubts, given her own doubts and disagreements with official teachings. Betty did, however, decide to volunteer as a catechist at the Newman Center for a couple of years, where she taught a fifth grade class. What prompted her to stop was her feeling that she was not prepared to teach the faith the same way the nuns had taught her. Besides, one hour a week was just not enough, she felt, to help these children, and the materials provided for teaching Sunday school seemed so superficial that she doubted the kids were learning anything of value about their faith.

Her daughter Beth, who is now in her early 30s, went to Mass every Sunday up until she was college-bound because that is what the family did, but she resented the expectation and was bored by the religious education classes. She attended public schools through high school, and she developed more and more doubts about her faith as her friends talked about religion, especially her evangelical friends who seemed very convinced about their beliefs. Nevertheless, she went to a Catholic college. She loved the spiritual atmosphere of the campus, including the gentle and respectful way the priests and monks treated each other and the students. After she graduated, she drifted away from church, and her faith became more diffuse. Nonetheless, she married a Catholic, and they had their son, Thomas, baptized. Beth found the ritual uplifting, but it did not bring her back to the Church. Her husband is a much more active Catholic than she is, but she makes an effort to go to Mass with Thomas, now age 4, a few times a year. She thinks it's likely she will go more often, at least to the Children's Mass, once he starts school.

Beth thinks of herself as spiritual but not religious. She finds the nearby Catholic college campus where she attended college a spiritual place, and its quiet, peaceful beauty appeals to her—she still runs there several times a week. She is striving for a balanced life, just as she observed in the behavior of the monks when she was a student there. She teaches biology in high school and still appreciates the fact that her teachers always made clear that there is no conflict between religion and science. Would she recommend her Catholic alma mater to one of her students? Yes, she most definitely would, and has in fact done so—one of her students is currently a student there.

So what does it mean to identify as a Catholic in the United States today? How are these two women, and families like theirs, living out their faith? What difference does Catholicism make in their lives? We explore these questions with our survey data throughout this book.

~

Acknowledgments

This book is now the fifth in a series of studies of U.S. Catholics. The series began with an initial study in 1987, followed by similar studies spaced in six-year intervals. We are grateful to the *National Catholic Reporter*, which funded the first two studies and have published special supplements of the initial findings from all five studies in *NCR* (the most recent on October 28, 2011). We are especially grateful to Tom Fox who, as editor of *NCR* in 1987 and now as publisher, has seen the value of these studies over time. We appreciate his continued support and help in making the findings widely available to *NCR* readers. We are also grateful to Tom Roberts, *NCR* editor at large, for his interest, support, and oversight of the October 28 feature.

Funding for this survey, conducted in 2011, came from a grant from an anonymous Catholic foundation as well as additional support provided by *NCR*, the Institute for Policy Research and Catholic Studies at The Catholic University of America, the Rotondaro Family Foundation, the Rudolf Family Foundation, the Donegal Foundation, and the Luger Family Foundation. We also want to thank the Church in the 21st Century Project at Boston College for hosting a symposium in November 2011 at which we presented some of the preliminary findings from the 2011 survey. Additionally, Michele Dillon is grateful to have had the opportunity to present some of the survey findings to audiences at the 11th Annual Anne Drummey O'Callaghan Lecture at Fairfield University; at the JE and Lillian Byrne Tipton Distinguished Lecture hosted by the University of California Santa Barbara Department of Religious Studies and the Walter H. Capps Center for the Study of Ethics,

Religion, and Public Life; and at the Institute for Advanced Catholic Studies at the University of Southern California.

We thank William McCready and the technical support staff of Knowledge Networks, Inc. (now a subsidiary of GfK Custom Research, LLC) for assistance with the research design, for selecting a panel of Catholics representative of the U.S. Catholic population, carrying out the online survey, and getting the results to us in good order. We thank our colleagues at our respective institutions—Dr. Stephen Schneck, director; Woinishet Negash, office manager; and Lydia Andrews, research assistant at the Institute for Policy Research and Catholic Studies at The Catholic University of America; the Center for Applied Research in the Apostolate (CARA) at Georgetown University; and the Department of Sociology at the University of New Hampshire—for their advice and support throughout this project.

During the research process we were assisted in the development of the questionnaire by Tony Pogorelc, Greg Smith, and James Davidson. Research and technical assistance were provided by Andrew Schaefer, Carolyne Saunders, and Josh Henly.

We thank the editors at Rowman & Littlefield, especially Sarah Stanton, who has been an enthusiastic supporter of our research and who, with the able assistance of Kathryn Knigge, Laura Grzybowski, and Elaine McGarraugh, guided our manuscript through the production process.

We also owe a debt of gratitude to our colleagues who researched and contributed to the previous studies in this series. In particular, we are indebted to our colleague Dean Hoge, who died in 2008, and to our colleague James Davidson for their contributions to the first four volumes on American Catholics. We are also grateful to Ruth Wallace and Kathleen Meyer, coauthors on previous studies in this series. Finally, we thank our families for their encouragement as we moved this book from an idea to a story about a quarter century of American Catholics, persisting and changing.

INTRODUCTION

~

Twenty-Five Years of Observing Catholic Life

At the time we carried out our first survey of American Catholics in 1987, several events of the previous five years showed Church leaders writing two pastoral letters, one on *Peace* (1983) and a second on the *Economy* (1986) that received considerable input from the laity on both sides of the political spectrum. We found the letters noteworthy for two reasons: The way in which they were prepared (over 100 experts were interviewed for each letter, the media were invited to listen to the bishops' discussions of the drafts, and lay people were invited to send in written responses to early drafts), and the fact that the relatively liberal letters were published during a very conservative period in American history (D'Antonio et al. 1989: 164).

Time magazine called the *Peace* pastoral "a sweeping critique of nuclear deterrence strategy at the very time that Reagan was caught up in tense international struggle over the issue" (April 8, 1983: 82). *Newsweek* called the *Economy* letter "a thorough-going, thought-provoking repudiation of the Reagan administration's supply side economics and a call to reexamine economic priorities in light of the Church's preferential option for the poor" (November 19, 1986: 97, 165).

These letters were also well received by mainline Protestant leaders who had long fostered their own "social gospel" approach to the problems of poverty, wages, and general welfare. The bishops then began to work on a pastoral letter on the role of women in the Church, with no shortage of input from Catholic women and women's groups. During this time also, Cardinal Joseph Bernardin of Chicago proposed a national debate on what he termed

"A Consistent Ethic of Life," that is, "demonstrating the sacredness of life from conception to death." A group of conservative bishops insisted that a public debate had to exclude any discussion of conception and abortion; they declared their anti-abortion position non-negotiable. It soon became apparent that the abortion issue and the way it was handled would become a public issue. We did not know it at the time, but our surveys were to become a focal point for observing the laity's attitudes toward many parts of Bernardin's proposed "Ethic."

Some 25 years later, we are still struggling over military budgets versus budgets designed to help those most in need in our society. But this time, the focus is on a budget proposed by the Republican head of the U.S. House Budget Committee. Rep. Paul Ryan (R-WI) is a Catholic who claims his Catholic faith guides his principles. We look in more detail at the Ryan budget in chapter 7, where we will also note the attitudes of American Catholics to several of the key issues raised by the *Peace* and *Economy* pastorals. Meanwhile, the most important outcome of the pastoral on women was that there was no pastoral, as the bishops were unable to find common ground among the women's groups reflecting their broad spectrum of beliefs and attitudes about what a pastoral might say. In this case, no pastoral may be seen as a victory of sorts. Little did we know that these pastorals and the interaction they produced between laity and Church leaders were coming to an end with the maturing papacy of John Paul II.

The second visit of Pope John Paul II to the United States in the fall of 1987 was anticipated with high expectations. His stalwart opposition to Communism and his determination to lead the Catholic Church into a new era of world leadership created a situation of dynamic tension. He was in the 9th year of his reign as pope, a charismatic leader who spoke out against the evils of contraception and abortion, rejected the request from several bishops to allow divorced and remarried couples to receive communion, but also spoke out for protection of the environment and concern for the poor. Within 20 years of the end of Vatican Council II, it was becoming evident that he was going to rule with a strong hand.

It was in this context that our surveys of American Catholics took place. The first survey originated in informal discussions between William D'Antonio, a member in the 1980s of the Board of Trustees of the *National Catholic Reporter* (NCR) of Kansas City, Missouri, and the paper's editor and publisher, Tom Fox and Bill McSweeney respectively. "The discussions focused on the upcoming Synod of Bishops in the fall of 1987 to examine the role of the laity in the Church. The Synod [was] to take place just after the second visit of Pope John Paul II to the United States" (D'Antonio et al. 1989: 1). Fox and McSweeney believed the survey would provide information that would help the bishops during their synodic deliberations. D'Antonio agreed to lead the project and selected three colleagues (Dean Hoge, Ruth Wallace, and James Davidson) to work with him in developing the survey instrument. They then prepared a report based on a national sample of American Catholics that would be published in the NCR in the fall of 1987 in anticipation of the Pope's visit and the bishops' synod. The NCR provided the funds for the first survey, enabling the coauthors to hire the Gallup Organization to carry out the survey. The results of the first survey were published in the NCR issue of September 11, 1987. A book followed in 1989, entitled *American Catholic Laity in a Changing Church*.

It may seem naïve now to think that the bishops—much less the pope—would be interested in the laity's Catholic beliefs, attitudes, and practices, but "the signs of the times" then seemed to suggest otherwise. What is certain now is that the Catholic population in the United States has remained around 25 percent, in part due to sizable immigration of Catholics from Latin America, Africa, and Asia. Meanwhile, some 16 million to 20 million Americans who were born Catholic no longer identify as such. Our five surveys cover an important part of the time period during which this decline in the self-identified Catholic population took place.

The first survey was designed to find out how American Catholics, age 18 and older, were continuing to respond to the social, political, and cultural changes of the 1960s, 1970s, and 1980s. These Catholics had begun their lives in a Church in which the laity's prime role was to kneel, "pray, pay, and obey." By 1987 they were living in a period when more and more of the laity found that role not in keeping with the spirit and writings of Vatican Council II. Our 1987 survey was designed to probe the degree to which Catholics had changed their image of themselves and of their roles in the Church. It also explored their changing perception of the moral and teaching authority of the Church and its leaders. That is, some survey questions focused on who they thought should have the moral authority to decide whether actions like using contraceptives were sinful or not, and whether the laity should have the right to participate in church decision-making that affected their lives. A summary of the major findings from the first survey provides the context for the surveys that followed:

- Personal autonomy and concern for the common good were compatible values.
- The laity should have the right to participate in a wide range of decision-making at the parish and diocesan levels.

- Urban ethnic ghettoes were giving way to suburbia and all segments of the American marketplace; at the same time, Hispanics were becoming a significant presence in the Catholic Church, with estimates at the time running from 15 to 20 percent.
- "Pray, pay, and obey" no longer defined the "good Catholic." A more tolerant image of the good Catholic was emerging. Regular Sunday Mass attendance was no longer a *sine qua non.*
- No more than one in three Catholics thought the bishops alone should be the locus of moral authority on the five sexuality issues that the pope and the bishops had been declaring to be their proper province. More laity looked to themselves and their consciences as the proper locus of moral authority on these issues.
- The laity wanted more active roles in the governing of the Church, working with the bishops on decision-making not involving doctrines. Thus, the laity were separating core beliefs (e.g., the Resurrection of Jesus) from moral issues (e.g., the use of contraceptives), the latter of which were to be resolved by reason.
- Catholic financial contributions were declining, a first indicator of the continuing decline in financial support as we moved toward and into the 21st century.
- Only a minority of American Catholics (less than 25 percent) was aware of the pastoral letters on *Peace* (1983) and the *Economy* (1986), and their appraisal of them depended on their political ideology. Nevertheless, we saw in the letters a potential new model for laity and hierarchy participation in decision-making on issues crucial to the lives of millions of people. Catholics on both sides of the political spectrum had participated in the development of these letters. At that time it was hoped that this model would lead to an effective and well-received pastoral letter on the role of women in the Church. But the failure of that letter to survive the process brought an end to this experiment in lay/ecclesial dialogue in the 20th century.

When the bishops met in November of 1987, their actual agenda did not include the role of the laity in the Church. They published "A Gospel Response to the Many Faces of AIDS"; reviewed "certain aspects of molestation cases from the perspective of Canon Law"; and authorized the General Counsel to prepare a statement acknowledging the scope and extent of the molestation crisis (USCCB, Conference of 1987). While there was no acknowledgment from the bishops that the 1987 survey data helped their deliberations about the role of the laity in the Church, the findings of the survey were found to be of such interest to Catholics and others that *NCR* agreed to support and publish the basic findings of a second survey. This survey was to be carried out in the weeks immediately after Easter of 1993, making possible a trend analysis that would indicate how much the Catholic laity might have changed during that time.

With insights from the findings of the first survey, our focus turned more to "the questions of individual freedom versus obedience to Church leaders, the locus of moral authority, and democratic versus autocratic decision-making in the Catholic church" (D'Antonio et al. 1996). At the same time, John Paul II continued to call Catholics to work for peace, to protect the environment, to promote more interfaith understanding, and to end all forms of anti-Semitism. His rally before 150,000 young people in Denver in August 1993 helped promote him as something of a charismatic hero to young people, who clearly supported his peace and environmental concerns, while paying little or no attention to his preaching on what he called intrinsically evil sexual acts, contraception, and abortion.

We also noted at the time that our findings "placed our study in the broader context of the struggle between the American/integrationist and the European/restorationist conception of the Church that [had] festered during the last third of the 19th and earlier part of the 20th centuries" (Ibid: vii). We found many members of the laity still looking to the documents of Vatican II as a way that would lead to a new era in church history, "one that would include not only the bishops in closer dialogue with the Vatican on matters of Church teachings, but would also include the laity." We cited a paragraph from chapter 12 in *Lumen Gentium* (*Light of All Nations*) one of Vatican II's important documents, as a reason to expect change in that direction: "The body of the faithful as a whole, anointed as they are by the Holy One (Cf. Jn. 2:20, 27) cannot err in matters of belief. Thanks to a supernatural sense of the faith which characterizes the People as a whole, it manifests this unerring quality when, 'from the bishops down to the last member of the laity,' it shows universal agreement in matters of faith and morals," (Abbott, 1966: 29). The reality, however, was a Vatican determined to restore its authority on the worldwide Church, and an American Catholic population picking and choosing what teachings and rituals it would conform to or ignore. On one side, integrationist groups like Call to Action led the movement to implement the documents of Vatican II, while on the other side restorationist groups like Catholics United for the Faith rallied in support of the hierarchy and papal supremacy.

In comparing the 1987 and 1993 surveys, we found that a majority of American Catholics were moving in the direction of wanting a more democratic church in which the laity participated at all levels (including the Vatican). "In the chapters on authority, human sexuality, changes across three generations, the role of women, the Church's most committed, and Latino Catholics, we found that growing numbers of the laity were abandoning the traditional positions demanded by the Magisterium" (D'Antonio et al. 1996: 160).

Even as they urged more democratic decision-making at all levels of Church structure, the ordination of women, the reactivation of married priests, and a more nuanced sexual morality, only a small minority of all Catholics (less than 20 percent) said they were thinking of leaving the Church. They insisted they were part of the People of God, that this was their church, too, and that it could and must be reformed. Our research findings were consonant with other research conclusions of the past few years.[1]

The Louisville Institute provided financial support for the third survey, in 1999, again with some financial aid from *NCR*, and its publication of our findings in an attractive 10-page supplement, October 29, 1999. The survey was carried out for us by the Gallup Organization.

Our focus in the third volume was influenced by our determination to select the variables that were most strongly associated with Catholics' views of faith and morals. Three variables stood out: gender, generation, and commitment to the Church. These three variables became the foci of our analysis. Other factors, such as race and ethnicity, parishioner status, Catholic schooling, and income were found to exert selected influence on beliefs, attitudes, and behavior, and we summarized them in two appendices.

We found a small, but statistically significant relationship between gender and generation. This relationship indicated that there were more women than men in the pre–Vatican II generation. Second, generation affected commitment, with women being more attached to the Church than men. Thus, some of the effects that gender and generation had on Catholics' beliefs and practices were indirect through their impact on commitment. We also found that gender and generation had direct effects of their own. In other words, men and women with similar levels of commitment to the Church still had somewhat different beliefs and practices. Likewise, pre–Vatican II, Vatican II, and post–Vatican II Catholics with similar levels of commitment were still different from one another in some respects. Overall, being a woman and belonging to the pre–Vatican II generation increased the likelihood that one would have rather traditional beliefs and practices, whereas being a man and belonging to the post–Vatican II generation increased the likelihood that one would disagree with church teachings. Finally, commitment to the Church had the strongest, most direct, and most consistent effect on the beliefs and practices we had studied. The more committed a Catholic was to the Church, the more likely he or she was to embrace Church teachings. The less committed one was to the Church, the more one was inclined toward beliefs and practices that did not conform to Church norms.

There was general agreement across gender and generations about the importance to their Catholic identity of Jesus' life, death, and resurrection; the sacraments; Mary as the Mother of God; and concern for the poor. Finally, the findings of the third survey provided clear evidence of the trends away from regular Mass attendance and other practices, and away from obedience to traditional teachings in favor of conscience. It was clear that the Church was no longer the focal point in the lives of the majority of Catholics. It had become one of many commitments that people make in their lives. They were becoming more and more Catholics who "observed, judged, and then acted." That fact showed up strongly when we looked at specific items across generations. For example, while 72 percent of pre–Vatican II Catholics said there was something special about Catholicism that one could not find in other religions, only 54 percent of post–Vatican II Catholics held that belief. Only 28 percent of the pre–Vatican II generation said they could be just as happy in some other religion, while 45 percent of the post–Vatican II generation said they could. The trend lines seemed clear, and we expected to find them sharpened in the years ahead.

By the time of our third survey in 1999, two important things had happened. An increasingly educated, post–Vatican II American Catholic laity was deciding what it considered to be the core elements of the Catholic faith; it was not leaving this determination up to the magisterium as much as less educated pre–Vatican II Catholics once did. It was also limiting the authority of the magisterium to what they considered were core matters of faith and morals. It led us to predict, for example, that Church leaders would have only limited success in their campaign to change Catholics' views on the death penalty unless and until they developed programs that included serious discussions that included the laity in the decision-making process that must include the gradual evolution of the Church's teachings on this issue. We looked forward to what our 2005 survey would tell us.

In the interim between 1999 and 2005, several issues added new dimensions to our survey: the Boston Globe exposé of "The Sex Abuse Scandal and the Cover-up by the Bishops," the nomination of John F. Kerry for President by the Democratic Party, and the emergence of the first signs of a new Catholic generation, called the millennial Catholics because they were the first generation of Catholics to come of age in the 21st century, with beliefs and practices that were strikingly different from the older generations. We asked specific questions about the impact of the sex abuse scandal on Catholics and included political party affiliation to get our own reading on the political leanings of American Catholics. We also added Millennials as a fourth generation of American Catholics. Just before the Gallup Organization went into the field to obtain a representative sample size of 875 interviews, including a subsample of Hispanics, Pope John Paul II died—the most tradition-minded of the popes who had reigned during the lives of the Catholics of our surveys. We also witnessed the elevation of Cardinal Ratzinger to the papacy as Benedict XVI.

We wondered how these events might have affected Catholics' views of their faith and their Church. Would generation and gender play increasingly important roles in distinguishing between faith and Church? As in our previous study, we sought and obtained funding from the Louisville Institute, with a matching grant from an anonymous foundation, and from the *National Catholic Reporter*, including its special supplement of September 30, 2005, based on our comparative findings over four surveys.

In 2005 we reported on survey trends over 18 years. We continued to find differences across generations, with the gap between pre–Vatican II Catholics and the new Millennials being most notable. The steadily increasing decline in numbers of pre–Vatican II Catholics also brought with it a decline in the percent of highly committed Catholics. At the same time, the generations continued to be in agreement on issues that they considered to be central elements of their faith, such as the resurrection of Jesus, the sacraments, the right to be more active in decision-making affecting parish and diocesan life, and the right of women to be ordained and of married priests to return to active ministry.

The big picture was that most Catholics remained Catholic, even if they were unhappy with the leadership, some of the moral teachings, and the way they were imposed. Mass attendance rates continued to decline, but not dramatically. But Catholic identity remained strong on the four variables that had been identified by them in earlier surveys, namely Jesus' life, death, and resurrection; the sacraments; Mary as the Mother of God; and concern for the poor. These have remained the core of the faith for them.

The long-term trend in level of commitment continued its slow decline, based mostly on the growing mortality rate among the pre–Vatican II Catholics, who have consistently been the most regular church-goers and who saw the Church as among the most important influences on their lives. While Catholic identity was closely correlated with commitment, we found that Catholics were more highly aligned with their faith than with the Church, thus leading to the finding that Catholic identity was more stable than was commitment to the Church.

Trends in commitment are important because commitment is a strong predictor of Catholics' views on a variety of other religious issues. For example, high-commitment Catholics adhere more to creedal beliefs and devotions than do other Catholics. Likewise, they are more likely to participate in and have traditional views of the sacraments. And they are less likely to support the death penalty than are less committed Catholics. At the same time we found that highly committed Catholics are not opposed to changes in such church policies as ordination of women and lay involvement in parish and diocesan decision-making.

One of the more noteworthy changes in practice of the sacraments has been the percentage of Catholics who receive Communion when they go to Mass. In the years of pre–Vatican II, only a small percentage of Catholics who attended Mass received Communion; today, while the percentage of regular Mass-goers has declined dramatically from 75 percent to 30 percent, a great majority of those who attend Mass *do* receive Communion. One may wonder about the relationship between the use of contraception before 1968 and now, and the laity's rejection of the anti-contraception teaching in the 1968 Encyclical *Humanae Vitae*.

Three problems that stood out in our findings were the sexual abuse crisis and cover-up, the shortage of priests and women religious, and the lack of young people in the Church. The impact of the sexual abuse crisis was somewhat muted: its impact was mainly on the laity's attitudes toward bishops and to Church authority and how it was used. Mass attendance continued a slow but steady decline, and so did financial support for the dioceses.

Catholics continued their strong support for returning married priests to active ministry, with 60 percent also supporting the ordination of women, although the hierarchy has declared this discussion off the table. And since women religious are not showing signs of returning to traditional roles within the parish, there is not much reason to expect any change in this direction.

The data from the Millennials suggested that this generation would be more interested in activities that served the environment and reached out to the poor than they would in regular Church attendance and religious devotions. They were the least likely to look to the bishops for guidance on any of the five sexuality issues or to pay much attention to any teachings in which they have not had an opportunity to express themselves. However, as with the other generations, they continued to see as the core of their Catholicism the teachings about Jesus, his life, death and resurrection; the sacraments; Mary as the Mother of God; and concern for the poor.

American society has had its influence on each generation's commitment to the Church. Anti-Catholicism, immigrant and second-generation status, and lack of education are no longer factors that might keep the white European Catholics closely bound to their parishes. At the same time, the Church faces new opportunities and challenges in the waves of new immigrants, especially from Latin America, and from Asia and Africa to a lesser extent. With the old ethnic parishes disappearing and a shortage of priests who can meet the new immigrants on a meaningful sociocultural level, the challenge is to find ways that would attract the newest immigrants and their elders into a stronger commitment to the Church. At this time we wondered what approach church leaders might take to reach out to Latinos, Asians, and other new immigrants. We knew that the laity wanted dialogue on most of the issues involving parish governance; a growing minority wanted to dialogue on issues involving the Church's teaching on human sexuality, while a majority had determined to rely on their conscience. Looking ahead to 2011, it was not clear what approach the bishops would or could take that might have a positive impact on the Catholic laity's commitment to the Church. The strongest consolation was that the majority of Catholics were comfortable with being Catholic on their own terms.

The 6-year interim between the fourth and fifth surveys of American Catholics did little to change the structural relationships between the bishops and the laity. On the political front, 80 bishops took issue with and protested Notre Dame University's decision to have newly elected President Barack Obama as 2009 Commencement speaker. That was soon followed by the bishops' overriding concern that the proposed new Health Care Bill would somehow be more friendly to abortion providers. Their concern grew despite efforts by President Obama to assure them that the bill would not add any new support to abortion rights or funding. Nonetheless, opposition to abortion remained a non-negotiable political problem that seemed to have precedence over the Church's social teachings.

There were notable examples of bishops who reached out to, listened to, and incorporated priests and laity into diocesan planning, but such examples were in the minority. More common were the voices of bishops and cardinals proclaiming that Catholics who wished to be seen as in good standing with the Church were those who understood "acting in good conscience" to mean acting in accord with the official teachings from the bishops.

The tension between bishops and the laity was exacerbated by the fact that the sex abuse scandal, which had appeared to be ebbing at the time of the 2005 survey, suddenly burst anew across all parts of the United States and Europe, with some evidence that the Vatican and then Cardinal Ratzinger, now pope Benedict XVI, were involved in the cover-up. This fifth survey, completed in 2011 during the sixth year of the reign of Pope Benedict, provides a portrait of American Catholics showing both persistence and change in the beliefs, attitudes, and practices of Catholics as they head into the second decade of the 21st century.

In addition to the sexual abuse scandal and abortion politics, there are the strains caused by the continuing priest shortage, funding and/or closing of older parishes in decline in urban neighborhoods, gender politics, and the role of women religious, which was under review by a commission appointed by the Vatican. These raised new questions about the bishops' overriding "concern for the poor and the least of these" and their efforts to find a way to protect the millions of immigrants present in the United States legally or not, and the rights of workers to organize, all in a time of an economic recession.

The June 2008 *Pew Forum Report* on the state of religion in American society indicated a net loss of 7.5 percent in the number of Americans who were born Catholic but who no longer see themselves as Catholic, compared to a net loss of 3.7 percent among Baptists, the largest Protestant denominational family in the United States. As was true across all denominations, the departures appeared to be especially heavy among the younger generations. And, of course, there was the inexorable mortality factor of the oldest generation in every denomination. That the Catholic share of the American population has remained steady at just under 25 percent was largely a result of continuing immigration of Hispanic Catholics from Latin America. Our 2011 survey promised to provide the first in-depth analysis of the possible impact of Hispanic Catholics on the trends found in the fourth and earlier surveys.

We designed the fifth survey to continue tracking trends among generations, across gender lines, and among differing levels of commitment and Catholic identity. The continued growth in the Hispanic portion of the Catholic population, and the importance of the youngest generation (the Millennials, those born 1979–1993), led us to enlarge the size of the survey sample to enable more detailed analysis controlling for ethnicity within and across generations. We also added new questions about why people do or do not go to Mass, the personal meaningfulness of Catholicism, spirituality in their lives, and same-sex marriage.

Catholic identity, no longer a matter of simply knowing the old Baltimore Catechism, or of accepting the new one without having even seen it, has become part of the national dialogue between those with a more conservative vision who would undo most if not all of Vatican Council II and those who define the Church more in terms of the Second Vatican Council and its documents. We look briefly at Catholic identity as it has been lived and expressed by those we have called the pre–Vatican II Catholics, those who in our first survey in 1987 constituted one-third of all adult Catholics. In this our fifth survey they constituted barely 10 percent, as mortality takes its inevitable toll. Chapter 1 is not meant simply as a last "hurrah" for the people Tom Brokaw has called "The Greatest Generation." Rather, it is an attempt to capture the essence of what made the generation just before Vatican II so important in American society, its strengths, and its limitations. Perhaps more than anything, it reminds us how people are so shaped by the particular historical time into which they are born and live.

The 25-year period covered by our five surveys provides an opportunity to review trends of change and continuity among American Catholics. This book marks the legacy of pre-Vatican II Catholics, the Church's most loyal members during the 20th century. We begin by looking back at the church they knew and the conditions that generated their particular culture of Catholicism (chapter 1). We then examine the changing demography and geography of American Catholics and their implications for parish life and Catholic socialization (chapter 2), and review the patterns of persistence and change in Catholic identity and commitment, how they are related to each other, and to the Church as institution (chapter 3).

Church leaders have defended their authority to speak out and determine the morality of five key features of sexual morality. Chapter 4 reports the laity's views on the locus of authority on these moral issues, and chapter 5 examines Catholic women's changing relationship to Catholicism. We also explore the changing patterns of Catholic practices in chapter 6 and probe Catholic political affiliations and their relationship to Catholic beliefs, attitudes, and practices in chapter 7. Chapter 8 turns the spotlight on the new generation of Catholics: Millennial and Hispanic. Finally, in chapter 9 we look ahead to possible new directions as American Catholics head into the next decade of the 21st century.

CHAPTER ONE

~

The Legacy of
Pre–Vatican II Catholics

We refer to Catholics born in 1940 and earlier as the pre–Vatican II generation. At the time of our first survey, in 1987, they ranged in age from 47 to
over 90, and they constituted one-third of all adult Catholics. They were
the second and third generations of white European ethnic background, and
most of them resided in major urban areas. They came of age in the Church
of the Latin Mass, with the priest reciting the liturgy with his back to the
congregation. The altar boys recited the appropriate responses in Latin, and
the congregation watched, kneeling and standing as appropriate.

Prior to the Second Vatican Council (1962–1965), Catholics were known
for their willingness to kneel, pray, pay, and obey, which they did every
Sunday, Holy Day, and on special feast days. The theology of salvation was
simple and straightforward: go to Mass every Sunday and Holy Day of Obligation, go to Confession and Communion at least once a year, and say an
act of contrition before death. Purgatory, if not Heaven, was assured; fail the
above and Hell was most likely. Most Catholics chose going to Mass, occa-
sional Confession and Communion, and prayed to have a final opportunity
for a last confession before death. Evidence for that prudential judgment is
substantiated by a Gallup poll conducted in 1958 that reported 75 percent of
Catholics said they went to Mass that week.

This brief description provides a superficial picture of pre–Vatican II
American Catholics, a generation who experienced the Great Depression
and World War II, as well as the immediate postwar changes associated with
the GI Bill, the baby boom, and suburbanization. A closer look reveals that

the period from the 1920s through the early 1960s was also an era of transition in which Catholicism increased its public visibility. It saw the growth of large urban parishes, many of them ethnic like Boston's Our Lady of Mt. Carmel, which had more than 1,000 families, mostly of Italian and Irish descent, during its high point in the 1930s and 40s. The Catholic parochial and high school population also reached its peak during this period (Froehle and Gautier 2000: 68–75).

During this same era, popular movies with Catholic themes were sources of pride for Catholics and provided non-Catholics with positive glimpses of Catholicism. For example, *Boys' Town* earned Spencer Tracy, a Catholic, the 1938 Oscar for his portrayal of Fr. Flanagan, and *The Bells of Saint Mary's* (1945), starring Ingrid Bergman and Bing Crosby as nun and priest, respectively, earned eight Academy Award nominations and one Oscar (Morris 1997: 196–97). Additionally, the Sunday TV show of Bishop Fulton J. Sheen brought a polished vision of Catholicism to millions of American homes; Thomas Merton's *Seven Story Mountain* (1952) was a best seller; and the weekly magazine, *Commonweal*, a journal of religion, politics, and culture, founded in 1924, brought the writings of European Catholic intellectuals like Jacques Maritain, Etienne Gilson, G.K. Chesterton, Lady Jackson (Barbara Ward), Maisie Ward, and others to a growing American readership.

The Legacy of Pope Pius XII

The pre–Vatican II generation also experienced the 20-year papacy of Pius XII (1939–1958), previously known as Cardinal Eugenio Pacelli, the Vatican secretary of state. In contrast to Pope John Paul II, Pius XII was seen only from a distance: a tall, lean ascetic who seemed to run the Church quietly and effectively. The Church was in the hands of Italian bishops and cardinals, and Rome was the point of reference. If there were issues brewing below the surface, the laity was not aware of them. This was especially true of the Nazis' determination to eliminate Jews in every country that they conquered, beginning in Germany in the early 1930s and spreading rapidly to Poland, Czechoslovakia, and eventually even to Italy. Historical documents would later show that Pius XII was opposed to Nazism, but he was also convinced that Soviet Communism would be a greater danger to the Church than Nazism. Thus, his efforts to save Jews from Nazi concentration camps were limited and more personal than communal, and he did not write an encyclical condemning Nazi atrocities against the Jews. In his 1942 Christmas Eve message, he "lamented the fate of 'hundreds of thousands who, through no fault of their own, and sometimes only because of their nationality or race,

[had] been consigned to death or slow decline.'" However, he offered "no explicit mention of either Jews or Germans" (Duffy 2011: 13).

One of Pius XII's most important encyclicals, *Divino Afflante Spiritu* (*Inspired by the Holy Spirit*, September 1943), had little effect in the short term, but its long-term consequences for the Catholic hermeneutic study of scripture have been dramatic. According to Michael Walsh, the librarian of Heythrop College, University of London, "Not only had a pope approved the scholarship of Catholic exegetes, but he had encouraged their endeavors and removed the threat of condemnation by the Church because of their use of modern exegetical method. Its whole tenor was positive with particular stress being put upon the need to return to the original languages in which the sacred texts had been composed" (Walsh 1991: 22). Its importance was that it freed scriptural scholars "to pursue their researches without having to look over their shoulders at the Holy Office." Moreover, said Walsh, "The principles of historical criticism could now be applied to religious disciplines other than biblical ones, most noticeably to the development of doctrine" (Ibid).

Another important contribution of Pius XII impacted the nature of the church hierarchy. It was his decision to internationalize the College of Cardinals. Early in 1946, he appointed 32 cardinals from around the world, and 24 more in 1953. Italians still dominated more than any other national group, but as a result of his foreign appointees, Italians comprised only one-third of the whole body of cardinals (Walsh 1991: 21).

Pius XII's papacy is also noteworthy for its efforts to encourage reforms in the lives of the women religious. In his 1951 address to the first International Congress of Teaching Sisters, he praised them for their many good schools while urging that all should strive to "become excellent" (Pius XII 1951). Subsequently, in 1952, he called for an *aggiornamento*, an openness to reassess and update the various aspects of the sisters' religious and community life. Pius stated that "when it is a question of education, pedagogy, care of the sick, artistic activities or others, a sister should have this assurance: 'My superior is giving me the opportunity of a formation that places me on an equal footing with my secular colleagues.'" And he added that the sisters should also be given "the means of keeping their professional knowledge up to date" (Quinonez and Turner 1993: 12).

The pope's encouraging words coincided with steps being taken by the women religious in the United States. Following preparations in 1951, they convened the First National Congress of Religious of the U.S.A. in 1952. In 1956, with continued encouragement from the Vatican, the women religious formally voted unanimously to form the Conference of Major Superiors of

Women (CMSW). Their goals were to (1) promote the spiritual welfare of the women religious of the United States; (2) ensure increasing efficacy in their apostolate; and (3) foster closer fraternal cooperation with all religious of the United States, the hierarchy, the clergy, and Catholic associations (Quinonez and Turner 1993).

The women religious took Pius XII at his word, and with the added impetus provided by Vatican II, they not only brought their educational levels up to those of their secular colleagues, but they also became renowned for their labors in inner-city slums, in hospital building and care, and in general providing leadership in the promotion of the Church's social teachings to the larger American society. These initiatives by Pius XII seem more than a bit ironic today given the actions announced by the Vatican in the spring of 2012 toward the Leadership Conference of Women Religious (LCWR). Specifically, the Vatican's Congregation for the Doctrine of the Faith reprimanded the LCWR and placed it under the control of three American bishops. The Vatican cited three major concerns for its actions against the LCWR, including the content of speakers' addresses at its annual assemblies; alleged "corporate dissent" in the LCWR regarding the Church's sexual teachings; and the prevalence in its programs and presentations of what it deemed radical feminist themes incompatible with the Catholic faith. The document cites an address by Dominican Sr. Laurie Brink, given at the 2007 LCWR assembly and says that certain passages in it addressing how some members of religious congregations view their vocations indicated a "serious source of scandal." The document notes specifically "the absence of initiatives" by LCWR members to promote the reception of the Church's teaching, including Pope John Paul II's apostolic letter (*Ordinatio Sacerdotalis*) reaffirming Church opposition to the ordination of women (McElwee 2012: 8).

Pius XII was also responsible for a number of "user friendly" liturgical reforms. These reforms are taken for granted by most Catholics today, but they were important steps in the transition from the conservatism of Pius XI to the reform movement that emerged with much success at Vatican Council II. These reforms included the institutionalization of evening Masses. Pius XII had permitted them during World War II out of necessity, but because they proved to be very popular, he permitted them to continue, and further, he also permitted Saturday evening services to fulfill the Sunday obligation. With the addition of evening Masses, Pius XII also modified the regulations regarding the Eucharistic fast. In 1953, the fasting period was fixed at three hours for solid foods and one hour for liquids, with water at any time. Prior to this change, fasting was from Saturday midnight for Sunday Mass, and from midnight at other times.

Pius XII also increased the use of the vernacular language, especially in countries with expanding mission activities, and he permitted the use of the vernacular in rituals and sacraments outside of the Mass. This sensitivity to the importance of native or vernacular language in Catholic worship thus helped to pave the way for the more wide-ranging liturgical changes approved by Vatican II. Pius XII also made important changes to the Easter Vigil ceremonies, culminating in 1955 with a New Rite for the ceremonies of Holy Week. These changes were, again, highly pragmatic. For example, before the change, the Easter Vigil had become so long with so many readings and baptisms that the Mass itself would take several hours, lasting from Saturday evening into early Sunday morning. Pius XII streamlined the procedural details (e.g., simplifying the process for lighting the Easter Candle and processing into the church) and reduced the length of the Mass.

On several occasions during his papacy, Pius XII condemned artificial contraception. Most notably in his 1951commentary on Pius XI's 1930 encyclical on Christian marriage, *Casti Connubii*, Pius XII reaffirmed the sinfulness of artificial contraception; at the same time, he confirmed the legitimacy of the use of the rhythm method (natural family planning). A growing number of Catholics became aware of the rhythm method in the 1930s and were using it with varying degrees of success (Adams 2012: 2). It required a considerable amount of commitment, knowledge about menstrual cycles and temperature changes, and a determination to accept calendar restrictions on a couple's sexual lives. Studies showed that millions of Catholic couples had tried it. By the mid-1960s, 32 percent of non-Hispanic women aged 15–44 reported using the rhythm method (Goldscheider and Mosher 1991: 104). The Papal Birth Control Commission, appointed by Pope Paul VI in the 1960s, pointed to the widespread use of the rhythm method among members of the Christian Family Movement. Submissions to the commission, including detailed personal statements, showed that many Catholics who used the method found it unrealistic, frustrating, and in many ways, a threat to marital stability (McClory 1995: 58, 64, 72–74). These findings concerning Catholics' views of the negative aspects of the rhythm method were important to the deliberations of the commission (Ibid). By 1968, as a result of Catholic conferences (organized, for example, by the University of Notre Dame) and extensive coverage in Catholic periodicals and other media, the American Catholic public had become aware of the broad consensus within the Birth Control Commission for change that would accept the use of contraceptives. This consensus appeared to move Catholics toward increased use of the Pill, and when Pope Paul VI issued *Humanae Vitae* (1968) and ignored the commission's recommendations, the response to the encyclical was all the more negative.

An untold number of Catholics were also using condoms during these pre–Vatican II decades. But it was not until 1965, when the Supreme Court, citing the right to privacy, struck down the laws prohibiting artificial contraception, that Catholics and Americans began to avail themselves more readily of the Pill and of other forms of artificial contraception (Burns 2005; Goldscheider and Mosher, 1991; Luker 1984).

Order and Tensions in the Pre–Vatican II Church

What is striking in looking back at the pre–Vatican II era is that the Church was such a well-ordered and orderly institution. There was little public discussion among Catholics of church teachings, and no open debates took place about the Latin Mass or the new Easter Rite instituted by Pius XII. When Catholics did disagree with papal pronouncements, they did so privately and quietly. As Leslie Tentler (2004) documents, notwithstanding *Casti Connubii* (1930), many married Catholic couples used artificial birth control in the 1930s and 1940s, but they did not discuss it in public. Even though the Anglican Church had given a cautious blessing to the use of contraceptives at its Lambeth Conference of 1930, and the morality of artificial birth control was variously accepted by Mainline Protestant churches in America, the Catholic laity remained quiet in public, even as fertility records showed that during this period the Catholic completed fertility rates were only slightly higher than those of mainline Protestants.

Despite the appearance of order, however, there were also tensions within the Church in the 1950s and 60s. In the 1950s, Catholic scholars (e.g., Ellis 1956; O'Dea 1958) raised serious questions about the vibrancy of Catholic intellectual life in the United States. The tension in the Church between obedience and autonomy, for example, was revealed in the Church's suppression of the third volume of the Southern Parish Series by Jesuit sociologist Joseph Fichter in 1953. The New Orleans pastor of the church that served as the subject of the study had tried unsuccessfully to have the first two volumes removed from the market. The archbishop of New Orleans had originally supported the research, but the church's pastor claimed that the book had defamed him as well as his parish. Even though the archbishop had approved the three books for publication, he assented to the pastor's demands that the third volume be suppressed. Fichter was unsuccessful in his attempts to convince his Jesuit superiors to defend his work as good social science research and eventually acceded to the call for obedience. Fifteen years later, however, he reflected that he had been wrong to accede (Fichter 1973).

This suppression lent support to critics who said that the Catholic commitment to obedience stultified intellectual life. During this same period, the tension between science and obedience to church teachings was tested in another way in Gerhard Lenski's classic study of religion in American life (1963). In 1958, Lenski surveyed Catholics, Protestants, and Jews in the Detroit area, the first modern scientific survey with religion as its main focus. On a number of important behavioral, value, and attitudinal characteristics, he found that Detroit-area Catholics were sharply distinguished from Protestants and Jews. As expected, Catholics had a higher fertility rate, lower divorce rates, greater focus on family life, less interest in voluntary associations, much higher church attendance, and lower achievement aspirations. He also found that Jews and Protestants were much more likely than Catholics to choose intellectual autonomy (thinking for oneself) as the most important thing for a child to learn to prepare for life. It was not that Catholics rejected personal autonomy, but they were more likely to see obedience as the primary value for children to learn.

In line with the modernization paradigm (Parsons 1971; Smelser 1968) then dominant in American sociology, Lenski related his findings on value differences directly to upward mobility: those who valued autonomy were more likely to be vertically mobile in society, since modern American society required and rewarded achievement orientation in school and in work. In terms of income and occupational attainment, the data supported his hypothesis. The emphasis on personal autonomy was a key finding for Lenski, as he saw it as a vital element in defense of democracy. As first observed by Alexis de Tocqueville (1835/1984) when he visited America in the 1830s, respect for individual freedom also fostered support for voluntary associations. Early generations of largely Protestant Americans not only valued freedom for themselves as individuals, but also the right to organize themselves into associations that owed allegiance to no higher authority, religious or political. Thus, rightly understood, individual autonomy meant thoughtful, reasoned participation in, rather than withdrawal from, the life of the community. A reliance on obedience, on the other hand, would correlate with restraints on individual freedom, as well as on the individual's capacity to be competitive in school and the professional world.

Lenski was tapping into a central dilemma of Catholic life at a time when many Catholics were still first and second generation immigrants tied closely to ethnic churches and neighborhoods, less educated, and more commonly blue-collar than white-collar workers compared to Protestants and Jews. In 1958, there was no reason to think that the Church would not be the same a decade or even two decades later. But, in fact, while Lenski was writing his book on the importance of religion in social life, more and more American Catholics were completing college degrees and going to graduate school (Greeley 1989) and making an impact across scientific and political arenas. For example, it was a Catholic scientist and daily communicant, Dr. John Rock, who at this time was leading scientific experiments that would ultimately produce the birth control pill, a scientific innovation whose impact was and still is central to the transformation in women's roles and gender equality. Church opposition to the Pill's use among Catholics was also, of course, the watershed that publicly ruptured the hierarchy's moral authority among Catholics, a reverberating issue that we discuss in detail in chapter 4. Moreover, Dr. Rock's Catholic colleague, Dr. Luigi Mastroianni was simultaneously pursuing research that would lead to in vitro fertilization and translating this basic knowledge in reproductive biology into clinical care. In the political sphere, meanwhile, John F. Kennedy was soon to become the first Catholic U.S. president, and the Church itself, unknowingly, was on the verge of a transformative period with the election of Cardinal Roncalli to the papacy as John XXIII in the late Fall of 1958.

In retrospect, one of the most important of Pius XII's actions was the appointment of bishops and cardinals who would later anchor and participate in the deliberations of Vatican II. The response of the bishops to his successor Pope John XXIII's convening of Vatican II revealed a worldwide list of cardinals and bishops as well as theologians and canon lawyers who were sufficiently open to John XXIII's call to open the windows and let in some fresh air (Albergo 2006). The deliberations of the bishops at Vatican II showed that they were able to overcome the efforts of the conservative Curia within the Vatican to oppose any changes (Wilde 2007). Many of the clergy had been working quietly for years in anticipation of doctrinal changes, while others, especially within the Vatican bureaucracy, had assumed that the Church was above change and tried to ensure that the council would be under their control (Hastings 1991: 27–33). Waiting in the wings were forward-thinking theologians including the American Jesuit John Courtney Murray, the French Dominican Yves Congar, Hans Kung from Switzerland, Bernard Haring of Germany, the Canadian Gregory Baum, and many others whose progressive ideas penetrated into the changes to be found in the documents of Vatican II, approved by more than 2,000 bishops from all parts of the world.

John XXIII may only be a vague historical note for Millennial Catholics in 2012, but he was and continues to be significantly more than that for pre–Vatican II and Vatican II Catholics. When he succeeded Pius XII in late 1958, it was assumed that he would be only an interim caretaker pope. But his convening of Vatican II startled both the Church and its critics and set the Church on a path that sought to make itself a revitalized and relevant force in the modern world—for Catholics and non-Catholics alike. Before Vatican II, the Church appeared to its members and critics as a monolith in its religious beliefs and practices. However accurate that image of an earlier time, the doctrinal and institutional reforms instituted by Vatican II greatly shattered the image of an immutable Church and transformed the ways in which Catholics were Catholic. And although pre–Vatican II Catholics had inherited and grew up in a very different church and society, they enthusiastically embraced the changes of Vatican II and melded them into a remarkably open and robust Catholicism. They were the descendants of the great migration wave that came from Europe between 1870 and 1925; and they were 96 percent non-Hispanic white, in contrast to the millennial generation, which was 50 percent non-Hispanic white. In 1987, they comprised one-third of all adult Catholics, now in their twilight years (ages 71 and older), they were only 10 percent of adult Catholics: 57 percent were women, and 43 percent men. It is to their beliefs, attitudes, and practices that we now turn. The aging of the pre–Vatican II Catholics over time attenuates not only the presence of this generation in the Church, but it also impacts the complexion of American Catholicism in general.

Pre–Vatican II Catholics: Church Participation and Commitment

Pre–Vatican II Catholics have been the most highly committed Catholics in the four previous surveys, and they remain so, even as their numbers are diminished. They have maintained a regular Mass attendance rate of between 54 percent and 64 percent over the 25 years of our surveys, from 1987 to 2011. Nevertheless, twice as many (35 percent) seldom or never attend Mass now as did 25 years ago (18 percent). Three in 10 cite family responsibilities and health problems as important reasons why they do not attend Mass. On the other hand, those who go regularly to Mass cite experiencing the liturgy (95 percent) and feeling the need for Eucharist (94 percent) as the two most important reasons why they go to church. Their felt need for Eucharist is significantly higher than that of any of the other three generations.

Table 1.1: Level of Commitment to the Catholic Church, 1987–2011, Pre–Vatican II Catholics

	1987 %	2011 %
1. Apart from weddings and funerals, how often do you attend Mass?		
a. At least once a week	57	54
b. At least once a month	24	11
c. Seldom/Never	18	35
2. How important is the Catholic Church to you personally?		
a. The most important part of my life	24	15
b. Among the most important parts of my life	39	34
c. Quite important, as are other parts	29	34
d. Not terribly or not very important	8	17
3. Imagine a scale of 1 to 7. Point 1 being "I would never leave the Church"; point 7 being, "yes, I might leave the Church," Where would you place yourself on this scale?		
a. Points 1 and 2	80	74
b. Points 3, 4, and 5	16	16
c. Point 6 and 7	4	10

One of the important contributions that the generation variable makes to our understanding of the Church in our time is that we are able to use it to point to patterned differences in habits and worldviews between generations. Because each generation comes of age at a particular historical and sociocultural moment and embodies the spirit of that time and of those unique lived experiences, distinct generational habits tend to move with a particular generation as they age. These differences can be used to look ahead and back to discern trends in Catholic practices, beliefs, and attitudes. Thus in 1987, for example, while 44 percent of Catholics as a whole reported weekly Mass attendance, there were distinct generational differences underlying this trend. Six in 10 (57 percent) pre–Vatican II Catholics went to weekly Mass, whereas this was true of 4 in 10 (41 percent) Vatican II Catholics and true of less than a third (28 percent) of post–Vatican II Catholics. These generational gaps persisted over time such that the overall percentage of Catholics reporting weekly Mass attendance in 2011 had declined to 31 percent. Although the same proportion of pre–Vatican II Catholics goes to weekly Mass today (56 percent) as was true 25 years ago, their generational attendance habits do not have as much impact on Catholics' overall rate of attendance because these Catholics now account for only 10 percent of the total Catholic population. At the same time, it is likely that Catholics' Mass attendance will continue to decline because the millennial generation currently has the lowest weekly Mass attendance rate (23 percent). This rate is likely to remain low as they age and add to their numbers unless factors other than generational influences occasion a substantial increase in their future Mass attendance.

Generational differences are also apparent in the importance that Catholics attach to the place of the Church in their lives. Again, while half of all Catholics (49 percent) in 1987 said that the Church was the most or among the most important parts of their lives, there was considerable variation between the older and younger generations. This view was expressed by 3 out of 5 (61 percent) of the oldest generation (i.e., pre–Vatican II Catholics) but only 4 out of 10 (42 percent) of younger Vatican II and post–Vatican II Catholics. In retrospect, these generational differences foreshadowed a more general decline in the importance of the Church among all cohorts of Catholics. In 2011, there was, in fact, a decline of 12 percentage points (from 61 percent to 49 percent) among pre–Vatican II Catholics and a decline, too, among Vatican II and post–Vatican II Catholics in the proportion who said that the Church was among the most important parts of their lives. Despite this decline in the importance of the Church in the lives of pre–Vatican II Catholics over time, the overwhelming majority (74 percent) continued to say that they would never leave the Church. Although the proportion who indicated that they might leave doubled in the 25-year interval between 1987 and 2011, the total was still only 10 percent (see Table 1.1).

Pre–Vatican II Catholics' Construal of Catholicism

In addition to their high level of commitment to the Church, pre–Vatican II Catholics show consistency in what they consider the aspects of Catholicism that are most important to them personally. The question (see Table 1.2), first included in our 2005 survey, asked respondents to select the aspects of Catholicism that were very important to them. As in 2005, the four aspects that received more than 60 percent support from pre–Vatican II Catholics in 2011 as very important to them personally as Catholics were Jesus's resurrection (82 percent), the sacraments (70 percent), Mary as the Mother of God (73 percent), and helping the poor (69 percent). There was a significant decline in the 6-year interval in the proportions affirming two of the elements (e.g., the sacraments and helping the poor). The three aspects that pre–Vatican II Catholics gave least support to in both surveys were (1) the teaching authority claimed by the Vatican, (2) the Church's teaching opposing the death penalty, and (3) a celibate male clergy. Support for the teaching authority claimed by the Vatican declined from 42 percent in 2005 to 29 percent in 2011. Those who see a celibate male clergy as very important to them declined from 29 percent to 16 percent. In sum, pre–Vatican II Catholics, the most loyal to the Church's teachings, make clear distinctions between those aspects they see as core and those they see as less important to them.

United States Catholics have long talked about who is a "good Catholic" and what this entails. We have traced their attitudes on an ever-growing list going back to 1987. Here we consider the six items that appeared on both the 1987 and 2011 surveys (see Table 1.3). On 5 of the 6 items, the attitudes of pre–Vatican II Catholics became more accepting of a position that is independent of the official teachings of the Church. Acceptance of the idea that one can be a good Catholic without going to Mass every weekend spread even to the most "Mass going" of our Catholic generations with 78 percent currently accepting this idea compared to 64 percent in 1987.

Substantial majorities now also agreed that one can be a good Catholic without accepting the Church's teaching on birth control (87 percent vs. 50 percent in 1987), divorce and remarriage without an annulment (60 percent now versus 44 percent in 1987), and without one's marriage being approved by the Church (61 percent now versus 43 percent in 1987). With regard to abortion, still the most divisive issue among Catholics, close to half (47 percent) of pre–Vatican II Catholics in 2011 said that one can

Table 1.2: The Persistence of Core Beliefs over Time among Pre-Vatican Catholics (Percentage responding "very important")

	2005 %	2011 %
Belief in Jesus's resurrection	85	82
The sacraments, such as the Eucharist	82	70
Church's teachings about Mary	79	73
Helping the poor	84	69
Having a regular prayer life	54	52
Participating in devotions (Eucharist, Adoration, Rosary)	50	36
Catholic Church teachings opposing same-sex marriage	47	45
Church activities directed toward social justice	47	32
Catholic Church's teachings that oppose abortion	44	52
Teaching authority claimed by the Vatican	42	29
Catholic Church's teachings that oppose the death penalty	35	29
A celibate male clergy	29	16

Table 1.3: Pre-Vatican II Catholics Who Agree That One Can Be a Good Catholic Without . . .

	1987 %	2011 %
Going to Mass every weekend	64	78
Obeying the Church's teaching on birth control	50	87
Getting an annulment after divorce/remarriage	44	60
Obeying Church's teaching on abortion	27	47
Without one's marriage being approved by the Church	43	61
Without giving time/money to help the poor	45	50

be a good Catholic without obeying the Church's teaching on abortion. This view was expressed by only 27 percent of that generation in 1987.

Pre–Vatican II Catholics' views of moral authority

By 1987, Pope John Paul II had made clear his intention to reassert the Church's traditional teachings about human sexuality. For that reason, as well as our sociological interest in assessing the extent to which lay Catholics are constrained by the Vatican's teaching authority, we constructed a series of questions to learn where American Catholics stood with regard to sociosexual teachings. Keeping in mind Vatican II's affirmation of the importance of personal conscience and its recognition of lay expertise in the life of the Church and society, as well as the importance of the church hierarchy as the magisterial teaching authority in the Church, we inquired as to where the Catholic laity believed the locus of moral authority should rest regarding Catholics' decision-making in the sociosexual domain. We focused on five separate decision contexts: contraception, divorce and remarriage without an annulment, abortion, sex outside of marriage, and homosexuality.

In 1987, pre–Vatican II Catholics looked to church leaders as the ultimate source of moral authority on three of these five issues (see Table 1.4). There was much variation, however, across the specific issues. Pre–Vatican II Catholics' support for church leaders' authority ranged from a low of 19 percent regarding contraception to a high of 47 percent regarding non-marital sex. Only on birth control did a majority support the moral authority of individuals alone as the proper locus of authority. Over the course of the next three surveys (data not shown), pre–Vatican II Catholics gradually moved away from the bishops' singular authority toward either the individual and her/his

Table 1.4: The Locus of Moral Authority: Percentages of Pre-Vatican II Catholics Saying "It should rest with..."

	1987 %	2011 %
1. Divorce, remarriage w/out annulment		
a. Church leaders	32	15
b. Individuals	28	50
c. Both	36	36
2. Contraceptive birth control		
a. Church leaders	19	7
b. Individuals	52	68
c. Both	23	24
3. Choice regarding abortion		
a. Church leaders	39	30
b. Individuals	37	52
c. Both	17	16
4. Homosexual behavior		
a. Church leaders	43	24
b. Individuals	23	50
c. Both	20	26
5. Nonmarital sex		
a. Church leaders	47	24
b. Individuals	31	39
c. Both	15	37

conscience or toward a dialogue between the bishops and the laity to work out a resolution that would be meaningful.

By 2011 (see Table 1.4), 3 in 10 (30 percent) pre–Vatican II Catholics continued to look to church leaders as the proper locus of authority on abortion. Nonetheless, over half (52 percent) saw the individual as the locus of authority on abortion, and half did so regarding remarriage after divorce and homosexuality. Two-thirds (68 percent) of this generation said that individuals taking church teachings into account should make the final decision regarding contraception, but just 2 in 5 (39 percent) said so with respect to sex outside of marriage. In sum, the generation most closely identified with the pre–Vatican II Church, and whose weekly Mass attendance rate continued over time to range above 50 percent, moved away from seeing church leaders as the primary locus of moral authority on these sociosexual issues. This was so despite the fact that the Church's leaders from Pope John Paul II to Benedict XVI had been unreserved in stating that the church hierarchy is the sole authentic teacher of morality on these and other issues, a stance to which the American bishops have given unwavering support.

Pre–Vatican II Catholics' Views of Church Structure and Participation

Finally, we turn to consider whether pre–Vatican II Catholics, the generation who came of age at a time when the laity had a highly restricted role in the Church, show much change in their attitudes toward the Church's structure and lay participation. (See Table 1.5) Over the 25-year span of our surveys, the proportions of pre–Vatican II Catholics who expressed support for the idea that the laity should have the right to participate in how parish income is spent (76 percent in 1987; 80 percent in 2011) and that the laity should have a say in selecting priests for their parishes (50 percent in 1987; 53 percent in 2011) have remained the same. On matters of church structure, however, there has been an attitudinal shift. In 1987, only 34 percent of pre–Vatican II Catholics supported the idea of women being ordained, but 55 percent endorsed this view in 2011. There has been an even more pronounced increase in the proportion who favors the idea of married priests. Only a third (35 percent) of pre–Vatican II Catholics expressed this view in 1987, whereas over three-quarters (79 percent) do so currently. As noted earlier, only 16 percent of pre–Vatican II Catholics in 2011 said that a celibate male clergy was personally very important to them as Catholics, whereas 29 percent said so in 1987.

Table 1.5:   Percentages of Pre–Vatican II Catholics Who Said They Should Have the Right to Participate in Certain Parish Activities, 1987 and 2011 (Percentages responding yes)

	1987 %	2011 %
Catholics should have the right to...		
Decide how parish income is spent	76	80
Select priests for their parish	50	53
Decide whether women should be ordained	34	55
Decide whether priests should be allowed to marry	35	79

Conclusion

Pre–Vatican II Catholics, the older of whom are part of what Tom Brokaw has called "The Greatest Generation," are dwindling in number. Their lives have spanned a broad range of significant historical and cultural events, and as Catholics, their experiences encompass a time of enormous change within the Church. As we have noted, although it is easy to exaggerate the conservatism and order of the pre–Vatican II Church, the papacy of Pius XII (1939–1958) was a time of transition. The reforms implemented by Pius XII and strands of cultural and intellectual ferment among Catholics helped pave the way from the very conservative Church of Pius XI (1922–1939) to the watershed of Vatican II (1962–1965) and its marker of the Church as a Church in, and for, the modern world. Vatican II revisited many doctrinal and institutional matters and raised the question and challenge of the place of reason and faith in the modern world.

CHAPTER TWO

~

Catholics in the United States: A Quarter Century of Change

I was born in Mexico, my sisters still live there, and I am very proud of the Mexican love for life and family and faith that first turned my heart toward God.

> —Archbishop José Gómez, upon his appointment in April 2010 as the archbishop of Los Angeles, the largest Catholic diocese in the United States

We have 22,000 members . . . four Masses every weekend in Spanish (all on Sunday) and three in English. . . . Latinos represent 86 percent of the registered parishioners. . . . I have tried over the past two years or so to unite the communities when I can. . . . In 1997 we only had a little more than 400 families; now we have more than 5,900 registered families. We have between 15 and 20 baptisms every Saturday, except during Advent and Lent. This year more than 500 children will make their First Communion and more than 160 will be confirmed.

> —Father John Connell, pastor of St. Raphael Catholic Church in Springdale, Arkansas (as cited in *U.S. Catholic*, June 2012)

In the 25 years since we began this series on American Catholic laity, the Catholic population in the United States has increased by more than a fifth to more than 75 million[1] adults who identify themselves as Roman Catholic. Of course, the U.S. population is also growing, but Catholics are still about a quarter of the total population. The Catholic population continues to grow at about 1 percent a year, and even conservative estimates project that Catholics will top 100 million by the middle of the 21st century (Gray et al. 2011).

Catholics are also more dispersed geographically than they were in 1987, continuing the patterns of migration that emerged at the end of World War II. As the children and grandchildren of immigrant Catholics assimilated into U.S. mainstream culture, they gradually moved out of the inner city ethnic neighborhoods of the "Catholic ghettos" and into the suburbs; out of the traditional Catholic strongholds in the Northeast and the Upper Midwest and into the rapidly growing Sunbelt cities and suburbs in the South and the Southwest. This migration has been so thorough that Catholics are now nearly equally distributed among the four U.S. Census regions.

Changes in Catholic Population

Not only is the Catholic population steadily increasing, but it is also becoming more culturally and linguistically diverse, influenced by immigration from predominantly Catholic countries around the world. Just as the mostly white waves of European Catholic immigrants of the 19th and early 20th centuries assimilated into and transformed the Catholic Church in the United States, new waves of Catholic immigrants from Africa, Asia, and Latin America are adding a new diversity to the Church of the 21st century. The new challenge for the Church, however, is to create structures for assimilating these groups even as they add to the broad culture that manifests itself as American Catholicism. Unlike the European immigrants of the pre–Vatican II Church,

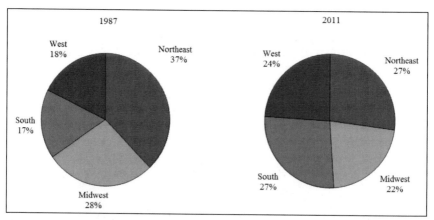

Figure 2.1   Changes in Catholic Population, 1987 and 2011.

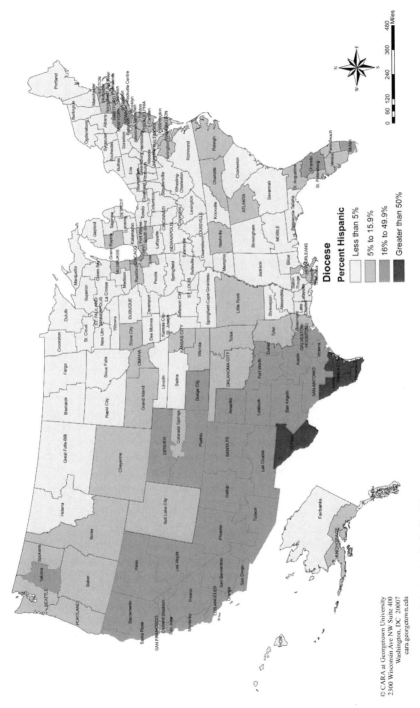

© CARA at Georgetown University
2300 Wisconsin Ave NW Suite 400
Washington, DC 20007
cara.georgetown.edu

2010 Hispanic Polulation in Catholic Dioceses

Diocese

Percent Hispanic

Less than 5%

5% to 15.9%

16% to 49.9%

Greater than 50%

0 60 120   240   360   480
⌐—⌐—⌐————————————————— Miles

these immigrants do not have the Latin Mass as a unifying element. They do not usually arrive in such large numbers that they bring priests with them, as did many of the European immigrants, and they are no longer encouraged to create nonterritorial, "national" parishes. Instead, these immigrants must find their way into existing parishes, and those who do so successfully are adding to the color, culture, and texture that today is described as multicultural parish life (Gray et al. 2011).

The most readily apparent influence in U.S. parishes has been the large numbers of immigrants from Latin America and the Caribbean, in particular Mexico, Cuba, the Dominican Republic, and El Salvador. In the 1980 census, persons born in Latin America or the Caribbean and living in the United States made up not quite 2 percent of the U.S. population.[2] By 2010, they were 6.7 percent of the population. Research consistently reports that at least half to two-thirds of Hispanics in the United States (including these immigrants as well as U.S.-born Hispanics) self-identify as Catholic (Perl et al. 2006; Pew Forum on Religion & Public Life 2007). And these immigrants, like other immigrants before them, tend to settle in areas where they find others who have preceded them, often from the same village or area of the country that they left behind. They form supportive networks based on language and culture. Thus, parishes that may have had just a handful of Hispanic families in the 1980s in some parts of the South now have a third or more of their parishioners who are Hispanic (Gray et al. 2011).

Increasing numbers of immigrants from predominantly Catholic countries in Asia, such as the Philippines and Vietnam, as well as Catholic immigrants from African and Afro-Caribbean countries such as Haiti, Nigeria, Cote d'Ivoire, Ethiopia, and Eritrea are also adding to the new diversity of the Catholic Church in the United States. Although the numbers of African or African American and Asian or Asian American Catholics are still too small to capture accurately in a national random sample for a reasonable cost, Hispanic Catholics are now sizable enough to form a statistically valid subgroup.[3] Because we want to explore how characteristics, behaviors, and attitudes differ between Hispanic and non-Hispanic Catholics, we provided the 2011 survey in both English and Spanish. We also surveyed additional Hispanic Catholics and used statistical weights to correct for that oversample so that the proportions presented accurately approximated the true proportions in the U.S. Catholic population as a whole.

While our 1987 study is not an ideal measure of the race and ethnicity of Catholics since it was conducted only in English, at that time 85 percent of Catholics surveyed were non-Hispanic white and 10 percent were Hispanic. For comparability, we can look at the race and ethnicity of only those who took the survey in English in our 2011 survey. Among that restricted group, 3 in 4 were non-Hispanic white and 17 percent were Hispanic. Even in this restricted comparison among those who responded in English on both surveys, an increase of 7 percentage points in just 25 years is important. Throughout the remainder of this book we make direct comparisons between Hispanic and non-Hispanic Catholics to demonstrate the impact of increasing racial and ethnic diversity on Catholics' behaviors and attitudes.

In addition to the increased racial and ethnic diversity described above, Catholic generations are also more complex since 1987 as the oldest generation, which we named "pre–Vatican II" Catholics, are being succeeded by millennial Catholics, the youngest generation of adult Catholics in 2011. As noted in chapter 1, pre–Vatican II Catholics (born in 1940 or earlier), who were 31 percent of Catholics in 1987, were just 10 percent in 2011. Vatican II generation (born between 1941 and 1960) made up 47 percent of adult Catholics in 1987 and are now 33 percent. Post–Vatican II Catholics (born between 1961 and 1978) were just coming on the scene in 1987. Those who were 18 and older were 22 percent of adult Catholics in 1987. By 2011, this generation equaled the Vatican II generation in size, at 34 percent. And in 2011, a new generation of Catholics (born 1979 to 1993), which we introduced in the 2005 survey with the name "Millennials" are now 23 percent of adult Catholics in our sample. This generation will continue to grow as more of its members reach adulthood, but its

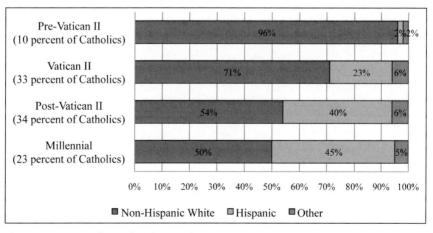

Figure 2.2 Race/Ethnic Identification by Generation, 2011.

influence is already being felt, particularly because of the large proportion of this generation that is Hispanic.

Because an increasing share of the Catholic population is younger, with no lived experience of the Church before Vatican II, and because about half of the younger Church is Hispanic, we will make comparisons by generation and by ethnicity throughout this book, to explore how these characteristics are shaping how the faith is lived and practiced.

Changes in Parishes

An unintended consequence of the growth and migration of the Catholic population since the mid-20th century has been a mismatch between Catholic institutions and the Catholic population. (See Table 2.1) Increasingly, large, once-beautiful urban parishes and elementary schools in traditionally Catholic urban population centers such as Cleveland and Boston struggle under the burden of too few Catholics to provide financially for their maintenance or to keep them vibrant communities of faith. In contrast, Catholics in southern cities such as Atlanta and Austin are lobbying their bishops for new parishes and schools to accommodate the growth.

Catholic churches in the South and in the West are, on average, 10 years newer and accommodate 150 more parishioners over the course of a weekend than those in the Northeast and the Midwest (Gray et al. 2011). As smaller, older churches have been closing and merging in the urban core of the Rust-belt and the rural areas of the Midwest, the Church has been hard-pressed to keep up with demand in the suburbs and in the Sunbelt.

In 1987, there were about 19,600 parishes for 54 million Catholics,[4] or about 2,700 Catholics for every parish. By 2011, the number of parishes had been reduced to about 17,800, a net decline of more than 7 percent. Even though most of the parish mergers and closures occurred in the Northeast and the Upper Midwest, areas that have lost Catholic population, the areas of the country that are experiencing the most growth have not been able to build enough new parishes to meet the increased demand. Thus, the ratio nationally is now more than 3,600 Catholics per parish.

Pastoral Leadership

At the same time that the numbers of Catholics have been growing, the numbers of priests and sisters, who provided the bulk of parish ministry in 1987, continue to decline. (See Table 2.2) This places additional pressure on parish life, which revolves around the sacraments and requires a priest for most of them.

Table 2.1: Catholic Population and Parishes, 1950 to 2010

	1950	1960	1970	1980	1990	2000	2010
Catholics	28,634,878	42,104,899	48,214,729	50,449,842	55,646,713	60,639,168	65,299,219
% of U.S. population	19%	23%	24%	23%	22%	22%	21%
Parishes	15,533	16,996	18,244	18,829	19,559	19,143	17,784
Catholics per parish	1,843	2,477	2,643	2,679	2,845	3,168	3,672

Source: The Official Catholic Directory, 1951–2011

Table 2.2: Catholic Population and Pastoral Leadership, 1950 to 2010

	1950	1960	1970	1980	1990	2000	2010
Catholics	28,634,878	42,104,899	48,214,729	50,449,842	55,646,713	60,639,168	65,299,219
Total priests	43,889	54,682	58,161	58,398	52,126	45,188	39,502
Deacons	N/A	N/A	N/A	4,725	9,723	12,851	16,934
Sisters/brothers	159,798	181,366	163,801	130,619	107,169	83,603	60,652
Catholics per priest	652	770	829	864	1,068	1,342	1,653

Source: The Official Catholic Directory, 1951–2011

In fact, there was only a brief period in American history—in the 1940s and 1950s—when U.S. Catholics produced enough native clergy to meet the needs of the population (Morris 1997; Hoge and Okure 2006; Gautier et al. 2012). Since the 1980s, the shortage of priests has intensified. In 1987, there were about 1,000 parish-identified Catholics for every priest; in 2011, there were more than 1,600 per priest—an increase of more than 60 percent. The number of priests serving in the United States has declined by a quarter since 1987, and the number of religious sisters has declined by almost half. This shortfall has been compensated, to an extent, by an increase in the number of permanent deacons and lay ecclesial ministers serving in parishes. Both of these pastoral leadership positions, which emerged largely out of the discussions during Vatican II, were relatively new in 1987 but are an increasingly accepted part of parish life today (Gray 2012).

Attitudes about Parish Leadership

In general, we see from the trends that Catholics remain attached to parish life. Most Catholics *disagreed* that Catholic parishes are too big and impersonal, despite the fact that half of all parishes today have more than 750 attending over the course of a typical weekend (Gray et al. 2011). Hispanics, who are more likely to attend larger rather than smaller parishes, were a little more likely than non-Hispanics to agree that parishes are too big and impersonal.

Catholics still feel strongly that parish priests are doing a good job. Overall, 9 in 10 agreed with that statement, although Hispanics are a little less likely than non-Hispanics to agree.

We do see, however, some increasing signs of indifference or ambiguity about the role of laity in parish leadership. Despite the fact that opportunities for lay leadership have increased as parishes get larger and more complex, lay Catholics seem somewhat reluctant to step up to the plate. Ten years ago, when we first asked the question, fewer than half of Catholics

Table 2.3: Trends in Attitudes about Church Leaders and Parish Life, 1999-2011
(Percentage responding "somewhat agree" or "strongly agree")

	1999 %	2005 %	2011 %
On the whole, parish priests do a good job.	91	91	88
Most Catholics don't want to take on leadership roles in their parish.	—	—	65
Most priests don't expect the laity to be leaders, just followers.	44	53	58
Catholic parishes are too big and impersonal.	46	40	43

(44 percent) agreed with the statement, "Most priests don't expect the laity to be leaders, just followers." Today, about 6 in 10 agree, and Hispanics are just as likely as non-Hispanics to share that opinion. That sentiment is reinforced by a new question we asked for the first time in 2011. Two-thirds of Catholics agree that "Most Catholics don't want to take on leadership roles in their parish." Again, Hispanics are just as likely as non-Hispanics to agree with the statement.

At the same time, Catholics are still uniformly in agreement that they should have the right to participate in decisions about parish life that affect them. Overall, 3 in 4 agree that they should be able to participate in selecting the priests for their parish and in deciding about parish closings. Even more, 8 in 10 say they should have the right to participate in deciding how to spend parish income. (See Table 2.4)

For the most part, these opinions are shared across the generations. However, the oldest generation is less likely than younger Catholics to agree that laity should have the right to participate in selecting priests for their parish. Just over half of pre–Vatican II Catholics agree with that statement, compared to between 70 and 75 percent of the younger generations.

Hispanic Catholics are less likely than non-Hispanic Catholics to agree that they should have a right to participate in these parish decisions. Two-thirds of Hispanic Catholics, compared to 85 percent of non-Hispanic Catholics, agree that they should have a say in deciding how parish income should be spent. Hispanics and non-Hispanics are mostly in agreement that they should have a say in selecting the priests for their parish, but Hispanics are less likely (63 percent) than non-Hispanics (78 percent) to agree that they should participate in decisions about parish closings.

Alternatives in Light of the Priest Shortage

Most priests who serve in parish ministry are diocesan priests. Religious order priests, like the Jesuits or the Franciscans, are fewer in number, older on average, and less likely than diocesan priests to be in parish ministry.

Table 2.4: Should Catholic Laity Have the Right to Participate in...?
(Percentage responding "should")

	1987 %	1993 %	1999 %	2005 %	2011 %
Deciding how parish income should be spent	81	83	86	89	80
Deciding about parish closings	—	—	—	80	75
Selecting the priests for their parish	57	74	73	71	75

About a third of religious order priests are pastors in parishes, and the rest serve in a variety of other apostolates or in administration of their order (Gautier et al. 2012).

The average U.S. diocesan priest is about 60 years old. Half of the diocesan priests currently serving in parish ministry expect to be entering retirement by the end of this decade (Gautier et al. 2008). The number of men in postgraduate seminaries preparing to become Catholic priests has been relatively stable for the past quarter century, but the number being ordained to priesthood each year is only about a third as many as are needed to compensate for those who are retiring, dying, or leaving the priesthood. CARA asked lay Catholics in 2000 and again in 2008 if they had noticed a declining number of priests in recent decades. Although 2 in 3 say they had noticed a decline, about half of those who noticed a decline said they have *not* been personally affected by this (Perl and Gray 2000, Gray and Perl 2008). Bishops have been diligent and creative in exploring ways to compensate for this shortage, but any discussions of broadening the priesthood have been strictly off the table (i.e., Schoenherr and Young 1993, Schoenherr and Yamane 2002).

Nevertheless, in our five surveys, we have been asking the opinion of Catholics about a variety of options, including allowing married men to be ordained, inviting priests who have been married to return to active ministry, and allowing women religious or even married women to be ordained. In all cases, at least half of the Catholics in each of our surveys agree that it would be a good thing if these options were allowed. A smaller majority of Hispanics (56 percent) than non-Hispanics (80 percent) agree that it would be a good thing if priests who have married were allowed to return to active ministry or to favor ordaining married men (53 percent compared to 76 percent). Fewer than half of Hispanics (47 percent) compared to more than half of non-Hispanics (57 percent) favor ordaining celibate women (including women religious) or married women (38 percent compared to 56 percent).

We also noted that a majority of both Vatican II and post–Vatican II generation Catholics favor each of these alternatives. A majority of millennial Catholics favors each of the alternatives except allowing married women to be ordained as priests; just 44 percent of Millennials support that option, which is similar to the 42 percent of pre–Vatican II generation Catholics who support ordaining married women. In fact, pre–Vatican II Catholics do not favor either of the options regarding ordaining women, but they strongly support allowing priests who have married to return to active ministry (77 percent) and allowing married men to be ordained (73 percent).

Catholics also have relatively strong and consistent opinions about the variety of alternatives that dioceses are using to address the priest shortage and the demographic changes described at the beginning of this chapter. As the numbers of priests available to pastor a parish declines and the Catholic population moves away from traditional Catholic neighborhoods, bishops are exploring a variety of options to reorganize parish life and ministry. We asked Catholics about several of these alternatives, and we found that their attitudes about each alternative remain quite consistent over time. (See Table 2.5)

For example, the three alternatives that Catholics find most acceptable include sharing a priest with one or more other parishes, merging two or more nearby parishes into one, and bringing in a priest from another country to lead the parish. Each of these alternatives is at least somewhat acceptable to about 9 in 10 Catholics. Strong majorities of each generation (85 percent or more) favor each of these alternatives. Hispanics and non-Hispanics are also equally accepting of these three alternatives.

There is another alternative, spelled out in canon 517.2 of the *Code of Canon Law*, that allows a bishop to "entrust a share in the exercise of the pastoral care of a parish" to "a deacon, or some other person who is not a priest." In practice, this means that the bishop appoints a deacon, a religious, or a lay person to assume the day-to-day administrative and

Table 2.5:   Trends in Acceptance of Parish Leadership Alternatives, 1987–2011
(Percentage responding "very acceptable" or "somewhat acceptable")

	1987 %	1993 %	1999 %	2005 %	2011 %
Sharing a priest with one or more other parishes	—	—	—	92	93
Merging two or more nearby parishes into one parish	—	—	—	88	88
Bringing in a priest from another country to lead the parish	—	—	—	89	87
Having a deacon or lay person run the parish, with visiting priests for sacraments	—	—	—	—	76
Not having a resident priest in the parish but only a lay parish administrator and visiting priests	39	56	51	54	—
Reducing the number of Saturday evening and Sunday Masses	—	—	—	—	71
Reducing the number of Masses to fewer than once a week	28	41	41	40	—
Having a Communion service instead of a Mass some of the time	—	—	68	60	66
Not having a priest available for visiting the sick	24	41	34	37	39
Closing the parish	—	—	—	30	36
Not having a priest available for administering the last rites for the dying	15	30	20	20	26

pastoral responsibility for a parish with one or more priests (who often are in residence at another parish) to handle the sacramental and canonical responsibilities for the parish. This is a difficult concept to explain in just a few words on a survey question, and when we phrased the option as "Not having a resident priest in the parish but only a lay parish administrator and visiting priests," no more than about half found that alternative even somewhat acceptable. However, when we rephrased the question in 2011 to read "Having a deacon or lay person run the parish, with visiting priests for sacraments" three in four said that would be at least somewhat acceptable, with pre–Vatican II Catholics slightly more favorable to this option (81 percent).

Most Catholics would find it at least somewhat acceptable to reduce the number of weekend Masses or to have a Communion service instead of a Mass some of the time, but only about a third agree that closing the parish is even somewhat acceptable. Interestingly, millennial Catholics are least agreeable to reducing the number of weekend Masses (66 percent) while pre–Vatican II Catholics are most agreeable to this alternative (82 percent). On the other hand, close to half of Millennials (46 percent) favor closing the parish, compared to a third or less in the other generations. Hispanics are less accepting than non-Hispanics of each of these alternatives.

Finally, while about 4 in 10 would find it at least somewhat acceptable if there was no priest available for visiting the sick—which is a ministry that can be performed by a lay person—not having a priest available for administering the Last Rites for the dying is "not at all acceptable" for 3 in 4 Catholics.

Changes in Catholic Schools

Catholic schools are affected by the same demographic changes that are so impacting parishes. Most Catholic elementary schools were built on the grounds of Catholic parishes and drew nearly all their enrollment from parish families. The same process of gradual assimilation of European Catholics into the American mainstream and the ensuing migration of their children and grandchildren out of the ethnic neighborhoods that emptied parishes of the inner cities of the Northeast and the towns and villages of the Midwest had the same effect on those parish schools. New parishes in the Sunbelt and in the suburbs had a hard time keeping up with the demand for schools as the post–World War II baby boom emerged.

Catholic elementary and high school enrollment reached its peak in the 1960s, with roughly 5.5 million students (about 45 percent of all Catholic school-aged children) enrolled in over 13,000 schools in 1965 (Froehle and Gautier, 2000). Since that time, however, Catholic schools have struggled to maintain enrollments and stay open. Many schools tried to augment their declining Catholic enrollment with non-Catholic students, but the rising cost of tuition was a barrier to many of the urban poor who displaced the Catholics in inner-city neighborhoods where many Catholic schools were located.

The rising cost of tuition in Catholic schools during the second half of the 20th century was also partly a function of changing Catholic demographics. A major reason why so many poor ethnic Catholics of the first half of the 20th century were able to grow the parochial school system was because they had the benefit of women religious, who staffed the schools at very low wages and with few or no benefits. As ministry opportunities for women religious broadened after Vatican II and as the numbers of new vocations to consecrated life plummeted, the sisters were gradually replaced by other lay persons, who expected a living wage and benefits. In 1950, more than three-quarters of the teachers in Catholic elementary and high schools were women religious (Froehle and Gautier, 2000). Today, well over 9 in 10 are lay teachers, and women religious are all but gone from the scene.

Since 1987, when our surveys of American Catholics began, the total number of Catholic elementary schools and elementary school enrollments have declined by more than a quarter. According to data reported by dioceses to *The Official Catholic Directory*, the number of Catholic elementary schools dropped by more than 2,000, from just over 7,700 in 1987 to just over 5,700 in 2011. In the mid-1980s, Catholic elementary schools enrolled[5] just over 2 million children, compared to not quite 1.5 million children in 2011 (out of a total Catholic elementary school–age population of approximately 8.8 million, according to sacramental data published in *The Official Catholic Directory*). This means that today no more than about 17 percent of Catholic elementary school–age children attend Catholic schools.

Catholic high schools have fared a little better, in part because their welfare is typically less directly tied to a parish. Many Catholic high schools were founded by religious orders, such as the Christian Brothers or the Sisters of St. Joseph. Other high schools were built by a diocese or archdiocese or by a group of parishes as a regional school. In the mid-1980s, there were just over 1,400 Catholic high schools, of which a little more than 1,200 remain today (a net decline of just over 15 percent). The number of high school–age children enrolled has declined by a quarter, from 775,000 to 575,000 (out of a total Catholic high school-age population of

Table 2.6: Catholic Elementary and High Schools, 1950 to 2010

	1950	1960	1970	1980	1990	2000	2010
Elementary age Catholics	5,874,435	8,851,456	11,804,084	9,423,457	8,396,211	8,903,244	8,796,964
Enrollment in Catholic schools	2,561,000	4,373,000	3,359,000	2,293,000	1,983,000	2,013,084	1,507,618
Elementary schools	8,589	10,501	9,366	8,100	7,395	6,923	5,889
High school age Catholics	2,054,158	2,839,085	4,538,342	5,230,049	3,662,933	3,841,057	4,003,417
Enrollment in Catholic schools	506,000	880,000	1,008,000	846,000	606,000	639,954	611,723
High schools	2,189	2,392	1,986	1,540	1,324	1,221	1,205
Sisters/Brothers teaching	84,925	112,029	80,615	42,732	20,020	11,011	5,749
Lay teachers	9,370	39,873	85,873	104,562	116,880	146,123	148,567

Sources: *The Official Catholic Directory, 1951 to 2011*, and McDonald, 2012

approximately 4 million). Even if we make the necessarily false assumption that all children enrolled in Catholic high schools are themselves Catholic,[6] only about 1 in 7 Catholic high school–age children are enrolled in a Catholic high school.

The reasons for these declines in schools and enrollments are many and complex, such as the relationship between rising tuition costs associated with fewer sisters teaching in the schools that was alluded to above, but the demographic change in Catholic population and the decline in Catholic parishes described above are also important contributing factors. Building and staffing new schools is a very expensive and risky project; few pastors and even fewer bishops see this as a priority for limited parish and diocesan resources.

In general, pre–Vatican II Catholics had relatively good access to Catholic education. About 4 in 10 pre–Vatican II Catholics attended a Catholic elementary school, 1 in 4 attended a Catholic high school, and 1 in 10 attended a Catholic college. Similarly, Vatican II Catholics also had good access to Catholic schools. About 50 percent attended a Catholic elementary school, 25 percent attended a Catholic high school, and 10 percent attended a Catholic college or university.

Post–Vatican II and millennial Catholics, however, are less likely to have attended Catholic schools, particularly at the elementary level. They are a little less likely than the older generations to have attended a Catholic high school, but they are just as likely to attend a Catholic college or university.

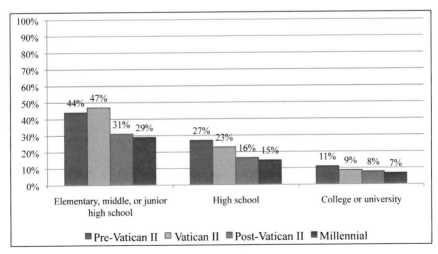

Figure 2.3 Did You Ever Attend a Catholic School for Any of Your Education?

Overall, 37 percent of Catholics in this survey attended a Catholic elementary school, and half of them attended for at least 8 years. One in 5 attended a Catholic high school, on average for 4 years, and 8 percent attended a Catholic college or university, with half attending 4 years or more.

Catholic Schooling and Hispanic Catholics

Hispanic Catholics experience a very different reality than non-Hispanics when it comes to Catholic schooling. Economics, demographics, and culture all play a part, but the end result is that Hispanic Catholics of each generation are only about half as likely to attend a Catholic school at any level. In economic terms, history tells us that immigrants earn less than native-born, gradually improving their lot as they assimilate. Hispanic Catholic immigrants entered the United States in large numbers at the time that Catholic schools were transitioning from sisters' stipends to lay salaries, and tuitions were rapidly increasing to make up for the difference. Demographics enter the picture because Hispanic Catholics disproportionately settled in the South and the Southwest as well as in the suburbs around major cities rather than in the old ethnic neighborhoods that were losing Catholic population. Thus, they were less likely to find available Catholic schools for their children, even if they could afford to pay the tuition. Finally, culture also plays its part, in that there is less expectation among Hispanic Catholics that their children should attend Catholic schools. Catholic schools exist for the benefit of the wealthy elite, primarily, in the Latin American cultures from which many of these Hispanic Catholics came (Grace and O'Keefe 2007).

Unlike the European Catholic immigrants of the 19th and early 20th century, who struggled to send their children to Catholic schools to escape the often severe anti-Catholic sentiment in the public schools, Hispanic Catholic immigrants today have access to free public schools that may also provide accommodations, such as bilingual teachers, which are less likely to be available in Catholic schools.

Perhaps it is not important that so few Hispanic Catholics attend Catholic schools in the United States. After all, Hispanic Catholics have a strong sense of their Catholic identity and, except for parish registration, appear to be as strongly attached to the Church as non-Hispanic Catholics (although research suggests that second generation Hispanic Catholics are less likely than their parents to remain Catholic; see Navarro-Rivera, Kosmin, and Keysar 2010). For example, 84 percent of Hispanic Catholics, compared to 71 percent of non-Hispanic Catholics, agreed that being Catholic is a very important part of who they are. Likewise, 84 percent of Hispanic Catholics, compared to 65 percent of non-Hispanic Catholics, agreed that the sacraments of the Church are essential to their relationship with God, and Hispanic Catholics were even more likely than non-Hispanic Catholics to say that it is important to them that younger generations of their family grow up as Catholics (85 percent compared to 70 percent).

Catholic schools are associated with socioeconomic success among Hispanic Catholics, however, and the relationship is stronger for this group than it is for non-Hispanic Catholics. For example, Hispanic Catholics who attended a Catholic elementary school are twice as likely to graduate from college as those who did not. Hispanic Catholics who attended a Catholic high school are two and a half times as likely to graduate from college. Non-Hispanic Catholics who attended Catholic schools are also more likely to have graduated college than those who did not attend Catholic schools, but the association is not as strong. We are not suggesting that attending a Catholic school causes success later in life, but Catholic schools do provide a college preparatory curriculum, and 85 percent of the graduates of Catholic high schools go on to attend college.

Catholic schools are also associated with income success for Hispanic Catholics but not for non-Hispanic Catholics. Hispanic Catholics who attended Catholic elementary schools are twice as likely as those who did not to have annual household income in excess of $75,000, and those who attended a Catholic high school are three times as likely to have this income. This relationship does not hold for non-Hispanic Catholics. Those who attended Catholic schools, at either level, are no more likely than those who did not to achieve an annual household income over $75,000. Again, we are not speculating that there is a causal relationship between Catholic education and socioeconomic success later in life—certainly there are many other intervening factors that are beyond the scope of this simple correlation—but the data shown here indicate that Catholic schooling does make a difference for Hispanics.

Table 2.7: Catholic Schooling and Markers of Socioeconomic Success
(Percentage in each group who graduated college or have household income over $75,000)

	Hispanics				Non-Hispanics			
	Catholic Elementary		Catholic High School		Catholic Elementary		Catholic High School	
	YES %	NO %	YES %	NO %	YES %	NO %	YES %	NO %
College graduate	21	10	26	10	40	30	43	31
Income over $75,000	23	11	33	11	46	44	52	42

Conclusion

Much has changed in the Catholic Church in the United States since we began this series of surveys in 1987—Catholics are more numerous, more culturally diverse, more dispersed, better educated, and more affluent—yet much remains the same. Catholics still primarily identify with a parish, even though parish life has changed in some rather significant ways. More than half of lay Catholics still disagree that parishes are too big and impersonal, even as Catholic parishes are rivaling evangelical megachurches in size. They still agree that parish priests do a good job, even when the pastor comes from another country or has sole responsibility for several parishes. They are still very willing to accept a variety of compromises to keep parishes open as the numbers of available priests continue to decline. Parishioners would like to have more say in the decisions that affect parish life, but they seem committed to the model even as it is evolving.

Catholic schools have also evolved, adapting to some of the same demographic, economic, and cultural pressures that are redefining Catholic life in the United States. Catholic schools are less available now than they were 50 years ago, and fewer Catholics are sending their children to a Catholic school. Catholics remain conflicted about their value, expense, necessity, and efficacy. Nevertheless, the data show that for Hispanic Catholics in particular, Catholic schooling may make a difference in socioeconomic success.

In the next chapter, we explore Catholic identity and changes in Catholics' commitment to the faith. We look at what is central to the beliefs of Catholics as well as what they feel is entailed in being a "good Catholic." We also examine what aspects of Catholicism they find personally meaningful and what aspects are less meaningful to them personally. In particular, we explore the similarities and differences between Hispanic and non-Hispanic Catholics on key aspects of identity and commitment.

CHAPTER THREE

~

Catholic Identity and Commitment

The term "Cafeteria Catholic" is commonly used to refer to the fact that Catholics tend to selectively value certain aspects of Catholic theology and tradition while seeing other strands as less important to their practice of Catholicism. Many Catholics themselves reject this typically dismissive characterization of their faith and of their practice of Catholicism (e.g., Baggett 2009). The doctrinal selectivity that lies beneath it, however, prompts condemnation from church leaders and nonreligious critics alike. Pope Benedict XVI himself commented that a smaller Church but one whose members would be "more ardent in faith" might be a more effective bulwark against the forces of secularism (Donadio 2009: A6). At the other end of the spectrum, the atheist Richard Dawkins (2008), while highly critical of religion, also argues that those who identify as religious should adhere to its full orthodoxy. Thus he maintains that Catholics who describe themselves as Catholics but who do not believe in the Church's teachings should be honest, admit that they no longer belong to the faith, nor should they call themselves Catholic (Humphreys 2012). Both of these perspectives, though articulated by two very different figures who embrace radically different and polarized understandings of the nature of reality, share an underlying view of the overarching purity and authority of dogma.

The sociological reality, however, is far more complicated. Catholicism is not a fundamentalist tradition whose "deposit of faith" is static or consolidated in a literalist biblical cage. It is rather a living theological tradition that blends faith and reason and whose doctrinal interpretations reflexively evolve over time. Thus Catholic orthodoxy is itself heavily encrusted with doctrinal shifts, institutional changes, and theological nuance. Given that all religions evolve and develop in tandem with highly particularized and changing sociohistorical circumstances, these characteristics should not be a surprise. They befit Catholicism's long history and its theological and institutional self-understanding as a tradition that emphasizes the interaction between faith and reason. Further, as the Catholic theologian David Tracy (1987: 95–96) has pointed out, Catholicism is a pluralistic tradition whose many intersecting continuities and discontinuities are replete with ambiguities. This pluralism allows for more thoughtful and contextualized interpretations of church doctrines and traditions than some might assume.

Catholics' Understanding of What Is Core to Their Catholic Identity

Amid the plurality of strands that constitute Catholicism, it is important to identify what contemporary Catholics view as personally important to them as Catholics and what they also consider less central. Our research shows that the doctrinal selectivity of contemporary Catholics is, in fact, much more constrained by, and attuned to, the Catholic tradition than the cafeteria metaphor suggests. The Church's foundational theological beliefs and the sacraments are at the heart of what American Catholics see as core to their Catholic identity. As indicated by our 2011 survey, almost three-quarters (73 percent) of the respondents said that "belief in Jesus's resurrection from the dead" is very important to them personally, and close to two-thirds said that church teachings about Mary as the mother of God (64 percent) and the sacraments such as the Eucharist (63 percent) are also very important. Additionally, almost half (46 percent) said that having a regular daily prayer life is very important, and over a third see devotional activities such as participation in Eucharistic adoration or praying the rosary (36 percent) as very important to them as Catholics. Helping the poor is almost as core to Catholics' identity as their belief in Jesus's resurrection, with 67 percent rating this dimension of Catholicism as very important (see Figure 3.1).

In contrast with the emphasis Catholics give to belief in the resurrection, Mary, the sacraments, and helping the poor, our respondents have less regard for the Vatican's teaching authority. Fewer than 1 in 3 (30 percent) said that the Vatican's teaching authority is very important to them, and in similar manner, they also tended to de-emphasize the personal importance to them of the Church's moral teachings. Although the Vatican and the U.S.

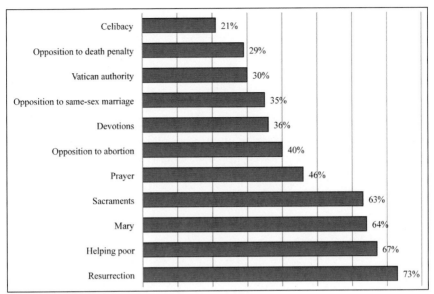

Figure 3.1 Catholics' Differentiation of the Aspects of Catholicism that are Personally Very Important to Them

Conference of Catholic Bishops have been actively involved over several decades in articulating the Church's opposition to abortion, fewer than half of American Catholics, 40 percent, said that the Church's teachings opposing abortion are very important to them personally. And even fewer said that the Church's opposition to same-sex marriage (35 percent), and the death penalty (29 percent) are very important to them. Additionally, Catholics see the current structure of the Church, despite its centuries-old tradition, as relatively unimportant to their identity as Catholics. Most strikingly, only 1 in 5 Catholics (21 percent) said that a celibate male clergy is very important to them as Catholics (see Figure 3.1), and almost half (46 percent) said that it is not important at all. The proportion currently affirming the importance of a celibate clergy is down significantly from our survey conducted in 2005; then, 29 percent said that a celibate clergy is personally very important to them as Catholics (D'Antonio et al. 2007: 24).

What Is Entailed in Being a "Good Catholic"?

We get further insight into what Catholics see as core to Catholicism when we look at their opinions of what is entailed in being a "good Catholic." In keeping with the strong trend established by past surveys, the vast majority of Catholics articulate a view of what it means to be a good Catholic that is largely independent of the church hierarchy's teachings. Large majorities said that a person can be a good Catholic without going to church every Sunday (78 percent), without obeying the church hierarchy's teaching on birth control (78 percent), without their marriage being approved by the Church (72 percent), and without obeying the church hierarchy's teaching on divorce and remarriage (69 percent). Catholics are comparatively less likely to agree that one can be a good Catholic without obeying church teaching on abortion, though still well over a majority (60 percent) express this view. These percentages are consistent with the findings from the 2005 survey, thus demonstrating a well-settled consensus among American Catholics regarding the definition of a good Catholic (see Figure 3.2).

What are the obligations of "good Catholics" to the poor and to the parish? Compared to previous surveys, there is a significant increase in the percentage of Catholics who say that one can be a good Catholic without donating time or money to help the poor. In 2005, 44 percent of Catholics said that a person could be a good Catholic without donating time or money to help the poor, but currently this figure climbed to a substantial 60 percent (see Figure 3.2). This shift may be evidence of a loosening of Catholics' felt obligations to the poor, a shift that may result, in part, from the Catholic

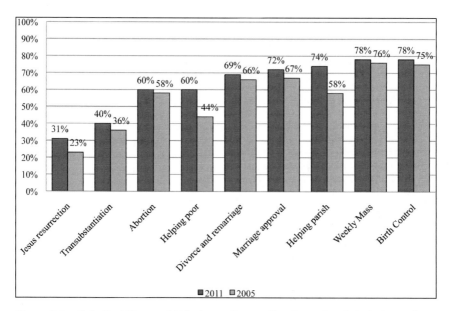

Figure 3.2 Catholics' Views of Whether a Person Can Be a Good Catholic Without Adhering to Church Teachings on . . . , 2011 and 2005

bishops' apparent reduced public attentiveness to issues of poverty and socioeconomic deprivation compared, for example to the high point of their activism on economic inequality as exemplified by their well-received pastoral letter in the 1980s, *Economic Justice for All*.

The decline in concern for the poor may also reflect other forces. It may be due to the fact that Catholics, like many Americans, have experienced economic losses as a result of the continuing post-2008 recession and are dealing with it, in part, by giving less attention to the poor as they themselves struggle to make ends meet and, or importantly, increasingly helping relatives and neighbors negatively impacted by the economic downturn (see, e.g., National Conference on Citizenship 2010). The declining percentage may also be due to what researchers call a mode effect. The more impersonal context in which our respondents completed the questionnaire in the 2011 survey, completing it electronically via the Internet (as members of a representative sample) rather than being personally interviewed via telephone, may have enhanced respondents' honesty. Research indicates that telephone respondents are significantly more likely than respondents using computer modes to give extremely positive answers to questions (Ye, Fulton, and Tourangeau 2011). Thus, in our 2011 survey, in the absence of the socially desirable pressure to acknowledge to a telephone interviewer that caring for the poor is necessary to being a good Catholic, our survey respondents may have found it easier to disavow Catholics' obligations to the poor.

We found a parallel decline in Catholics' felt obligations to the parish. Whereas 58 percent of Catholics in 2005 said that a person could be a good Catholic without donating time or money to help the parish, 74 percent currently express this view (see Figure 3.2). This increase may too be driven by the recession and/or survey mode effects. It may also be abetted by lingering concerns among some Catholics that money donated to the parish is being used to help defray diocesan legal costs associated with the sex abuse crisis, a concern that is kept alive by new and ongoing high-profile diocesan cases of abuse and institutional cover-up (e.g., in Kansas City and Philadelphia).

In keeping with the centrality of theological beliefs to Catholics' identity, Catholics are more likely to regard core theological tenets such as belief in the resurrection as important to being a good Catholic. The proportion seeing them as less central, however, has increased significantly since the 2005 survey. For example, whereas less than a quarter of Catholics in 2005 (23 percent) said that a person can be a good Catholic without believing that Jesus physically rose from the dead, almost one third said this in 2011 (31 percent). On the other hand, the percentage of Catholics who said that a person can be a good Catholic without believing that in the Mass the bread and wine really become the body and blood of Jesus has remained constant (see Figure 3.2).

Attachment to Catholicism

Although American Catholics are highly independent of the church hierarchy in defining what is entailed in being Catholic, at the same time, they also indicate that Catholicism and the Church are integral to their identity. Over three-quarters (77 percent) of American Catholics say that the Catholic Church is important in their lives, with over a third of these (37 percent) seeing it as among the most important parts of their lives and an additional 40 percent regarding it as quite important, similar to other important aspects of their lives. Far fewer, one-fifth, see the Church as "not terribly important" to them, and only 4 percent as not at all important. Although close to 1 in 10 American adults (9 percent) are former Catholics (Pew Forum 2009a: 1, 9), many Catholics nonetheless maintain a strong allegiance to their Catholic identity. Eighty-eight percent of the Catholics we surveyed said that it is unlikely that they would ever leave the Catholic Church, with 56 percent of these indicating that they would never leave. Further evidence of the personal hold of Catholicism is seen in the very large majorities who say that "being a Catholic is a very important part of who I am" (75 percent), "I cannot imagine being anything but Catholic" (68 percent), and that it is important to them that the younger generations of their family grow up as Catholics (75 percent). Catholics' responses to these statements are not predictive of how many will, in fact, leave or stay. But they do suggest that, for the most part, Catholics are strongly attached to Catholicism even as they may simultaneously question certain aspects of its structure (e.g., celibacy) and teachings (e.g., ban on contraception).

Personally Meaningful Strands within Catholicism

One reason why many Catholics continue to remain loyal to Catholicism while disagreeing with some of its teachings and practices is that there are many aspects of Catholicism that they find particularly meaningful. In response to a question that we asked for the first time in the 2011 survey, very large majorities indicated that the Mass (84 percent) and the grace of the other sacraments (80 percent) are personally meaningful to them. Equally high proportions find personal meaning in various aspects of the Church's tradition, such as the fact that the Church is universal (85 percent) and that it is part of an unbroken tradition back to the apostles (80 percent). Fewer, though still close to three-quarters (71 percent), say that the Church's tradition of the papacy matters to them.

These findings point to the diverse mix of strands within Catholicism and to the nuanced ways in which individuals assess its various aspects and position themselves vis-à-vis its varied strands. It is evident, for example, that Catholics can disagree with the pope and with Vatican teaching on various issues and, at the same time, personally value the historical and symbolic significance of the papacy. Similarly, they can disagree with the Church's teaching and yet also respect the Church's moral stance on any given issue. For example, although 6 in 10 Catholics, as noted earlier, think that a person can be a good Catholic without helping the poor and without obeying the Church's teaching on abortion, very large majorities nonetheless also say that it is personally meaningful to them that the Church shows active concern for the poor (88 percent) and that it is willing to stand up for the right to life of the unborn (72 percent; see Figure 3.3).

Our findings also shed light on an institutional dynamic within Catholicism that both reflects and maintains Catholic pluralism. Close to 9 in 10 Catholics (86 percent) find personal meaning in the fact that they can disagree with aspects of the Church's teaching and still remain loyal to the Church (see Figure 3.3). An ethos that combines communally inclusive dissent and loyalty, therefore, is a unifying thread among Catholics and,

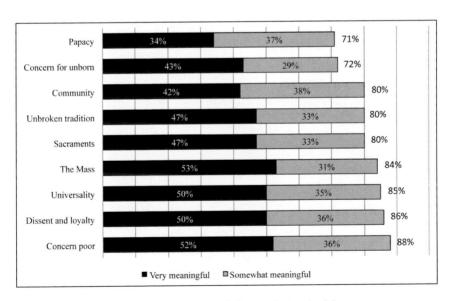

Figure 3.3 Aspects of Catholicism that Catholics Find Meaningful

along with the centrality of the sacraments and core theological beliefs and traditions (e.g., apostolic tradition, the papacy), likely bolsters Catholics' sense of (universal) community; 80 percent of Catholics say, for example, that they find meaning in the shared community they sense with other Catholics. In sum, pointing to the multidimensional layering of the diverse aspects of Catholicism that maintain Catholics' attachment to the Church, large majorities identify several aspects of Catholicism as personally meaningful to them. For a majority of Catholics, the aspects that are *very* meaningful include the Mass (53 percent), the Church's concern for the poor (52 percent), the fact that the Church is universal (50 percent), and that Catholics can selectively disagree with, but remain loyal to, the Church (50 percent; see Figure 3.3).

Ethnic Variation and Convergence in the Construal of Catholic Identity

As we discuss in other chapters, Hispanics are changing the face of American Catholicism. Demographically, they are younger, less educated, and concentrated in the West and South. In terms of Catholic identity, they tend to be more devout, more theologically conservative, and more deferential toward the institutional church and the Catholic tradition. As is evident in Figure 3.4, a greater proportion of Hispanic than non-Hispanic Catholics endorse various aspects of Catholicism as being personally very important to them. For example, 80 percent of Hispanics compared to 70 percent of non-Hispanics say that belief in the resurrection is very important, and 71 percent of Hispanics compared to 61 percent of non-Hispanics say that Mary as the Mother of God is an aspect of Catholicism that is very important to them. In parallel manner, fewer Hispanic than other Catholics say that one can be a good Catholic without fulfilling various obligations such as attending weekly Mass, without believing in certain core theological principles such the resurrection and transubstantiation, or without obeying church teaching on issues including contraception and abortion (see Figure 3.5).

Notwithstanding the ethnic gap in levels of devoutness and deference there is, at the same time, a convergence between Hispanic and non-Hispanic Catholics regarding their identification of the aspects of Catholicism that are particularly salient to them as Catholics. For both groups, belief in the resurrection, Mary, the sacraments, and helping the poor are the most frequently affirmed aspects. Reflecting the greater centrality and visibility of Mary in Hispanic devotional and communal practices, more Hispanics see

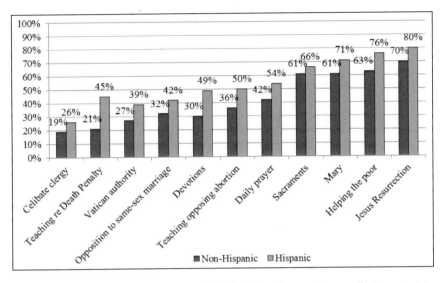

Figure 3.4 Ethnic Variation: Aspects of Catholicism that are Personally Important to Them (percentage responding "very important")

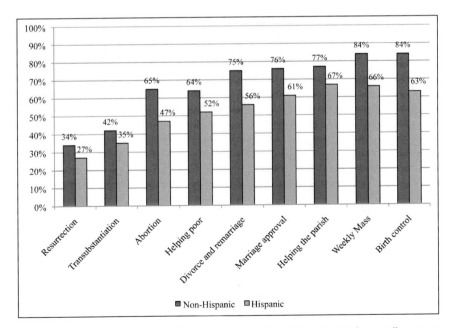

Figure 3.5 Ethnic Variation: A Person Can be a Good Catholic Without Adhering to Church Teaching On...

Mary rather than the sacraments as personally very important, whereas non-Hispanics equally affirm these two theological beliefs (see Figure 3.4).

There is also ethnic convergence regarding issues of church structure and hierarchical authority. Compared to other aspects of Catholicism, celibacy is seen as important by the fewest numbers within both ethnic groups. Hispanic Catholics moreover, similar to other Catholics, de-emphasize the Vatican's teaching authority. In fact, for Hispanics, the Vatican's teaching authority is the second least important aspect of Catholicism (after celibacy; see Figure 3.4). Similarly, among the various aspects of Catholicism that are personally meaningful to Catholics, the papacy is endorsed the least by both Hispanic and non-Hispanic Catholics, and both groups most frequently endorse the Mass and the Church's active concern for the poor as personally "very meaningful." On many varied aspects of Catholicism, there are, as we have documented, large absolute percentage differences between Hispanic and non-Hispanic Catholics. Closely similar percentages of Hispanic (46 percent) and non-Hispanic (51 percent) Catholics, however, endorse the personal meaningfulness to them of Catholics' ability to disagree with the Church's teaching while maintaining loyalty to the Church. That this view is expressed by an equal proportion of Hispanic and non-Hispanic Catholics underscores the pervasive hold of the Catholic ethos of inclusive dissent and loyalty. This finding suggests that the growing presence of Hispanic Catholics is unlikely to alter American Catholicism's rich blend of theological substance, doctrinal differentiation, and institutional loyalty.

Trends in Catholic Commitment and in the Catholicism of Highly Committed Catholics

There is much consistency over the past 25 years in American Catholics' views of what it means to be Catholic. There is also a good deal of stability in their levels of commitment to the Church. In 2011, as in past surveys, we assessed our respondents' commitment by combining their responses to three separate questions:

1. "How important is the Catholic Church to you personally?" The five response options ranged from "The most important part of my life" to "Not very important at all."
2. "Aside from weddings and funerals, how often do you go to Mass?" The five response options ranged from "At least once a week" to "Seldom or never."

3. "On a scale from 1 to 7, with 1 indicating you would never leave the Church, and 7 indicating you might leave the Church, where would you place yourself?"

We categorized highly committed Catholics as those who said that the Church is the most important or among the most important parts of their life, who attend church once a week or more often, and who place themselves at either 1 or 2 on the 7-point scale measuring their sense of whether they would ever leave the Church.

Using these high-threshold criteria, 19 percent of our respondents are highly committed Catholics, an additional two-thirds (66 percent) are moderately committed, and 14 percent have low levels of commitment. Clearly, for Catholics—as befits a church that emphasizes the individual's intertwined obligations to church, family, work, and community life—moderate religious commitment is the norm. The percentage of Catholics who are highly committed to the Church has significantly declined—from 27 to 19 percent—in the 25 years since we first began tracking American Catholics' levels of commitment. Nonetheless, there is a relative stability in the commitment patterns over time. In 2005, for example, 21 percent of the respondents were classified as highly committed Catholics, and this figure was 23 percent in both the 1993 and 1999 surveys. Further, the percentage of Catholics with a low level of commitment has not increased over the past 25 years; in fact it has slightly declined over time (see Figure 3.6). The relative stability in Catholic commitment is all the more noteworthy given that since the late 1990s, there has been almost a 3-fold increase (from 7 percent

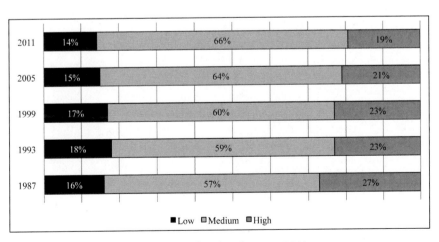

Figure 3.6 Trends in Commitment to the Church, 1987–2011

to 20 percent) in the proportion of Americans who do not identify with a religious denomination (Pew Forum 2012). Despite this societal trend, and despite the fluidity within the Catholic population due, among other factors, to people leaving the Church, the aging of current cohorts, and the influx of new immigrants, Catholic commitment overall remains steadfast and moderate.

In sum, while significant numbers of Catholics may leave the Church (Pew Forum 2009a), aggregate levels of commitment to the Church show much stability over time. The snapshot of current Catholics that our surveys captured at any one point in time—in 1987, 1993, 1999, 2005, and 2011—suggests that despite Catholic fluidity, the level of commitment of those who are Catholic at a given time is not dramatically changing. Yet, we certainly live in a changing Church and in a changing society where religion is losing some of its everyday salience.

The Demography of Highly Committed Catholics

There is not a great deal of demographic variation in patterns of Catholic commitment. Currently, Catholic men (18 percent), for example, are as highly committed as women (21 percent), and similar proportions of Hispanics (19 percent) and non-Hispanics (19 percent) are highly committed. The most notable variation is due to generation. In keeping with our earlier discussion of the rich Catholic culture embodied by the pre–Vatican II generation of Catholics (see chapter 1), older Catholics are far more likely than younger-age Catholics to be highly committed to the Church. Twice as many pre–Vatican II (41 percent) than Vatican II (20 percent) and younger Catholic generations (16 percent) are classified as highly committed.

Additionally, while educational attainment does not impact Catholic commitment, Catholic education does. By as many as 8 to 9 percentage points, respondents who attended a Catholic elementary or high school or a Catholic college are more likely than others to be highly committed Catholics. Notwithstanding the concern expressed by some Catholic college leaders that a Catholic education may fail to instill a strong sense of Catholic identity (e.g., Cernera and Morgan 2002), our data suggest that it does at least contribute to enhancing Catholics' commitment to the Church. Marital status also matters. Reflecting the long historical pattern in American society that the traditional family structure is an engine driving religious involvement, married Catholics (23 percent) are more likely than never-married (16 percent) and co-habiting Catholics (8 percent) to be highly committed to the Church. In view of the fact that more Americans today are not getting married and more are living alone (e.g., Cohn et al. 2011; Klinenberg 2012), these demographic shifts may have a dampening effect, over time, on overall levels of church participation and commitment.

The Catholicism of Highly Committed Catholics

As one would expect, highly committed Catholics are far more likely than their less committed peers to affirm the personal importance and meaningful-ness of the sacraments and theological beliefs (e.g., the resurrection, Mary as the Mother of God), the Church's apostolic tradition, and its sociomoral teachings. By the same token, by a margin of at least two to one, they are more likely than other Catholics to endorse the Vatican's teaching author-ity and its prohibition of abortion, birth control, and same-sex marriage. The clear differences between highly committed and other Catholics should not be taken to mean that highly committed Catholics march in lock-step

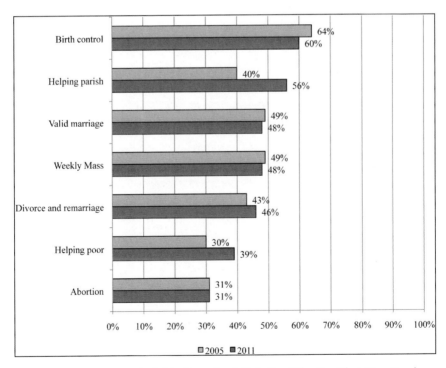

Figure 3.7 Percentage of Highly Committed Catholics Who Say That One Can be a Good Catholic Without Adhering to Church Teaching on Specific Issues, 2005 and 2011

with the Vatican, however. Rather, as is true of Catholics as a whole, many highly committed Catholics construe a Catholic identity that allows for a fair amount of individual discernment regarding the practice of Catholicism. For example, 60 percent say that one can be a good Catholic without obeying church teaching on artificial contraception, and close to a majority say that a person can be a good Catholic without going to weekly Mass (48 percent), without their marriage being approved by the Church (48 percent), and without obeying the Church's teaching on divorce and remarriage (46 percent; see Figure 3.7).

Two-thirds of highly committed Catholics (65 percent) say that the papacy is an aspect of Catholicism that is personally meaningful to them. At the same time, however, a similar proportion (62 percent) finds it personally meaningful that Catholics can disagree with church teachings and remain loyal to the Church. Indeed, just over a half (57 percent) of highly committed Catholics say that the teaching authority claimed by the Vatican is very important to them personally. In view of the structural challenges confronting the Church as a result of the shortage of priests, those exploring the possibilities for institutional change will likely find some support among highly committed Catholics. Although a celibate male clergy has long been part of Church tradition, only 40 percent of highly committed Catholics regard this aspect of Catholicism as very important.

Change since 2005

The profile of the Catholicism of highly committed Catholics today is substantially in line with the patterns documented in earlier studies. In particular, the greater identification of the personal importance of theological beliefs such as the resurrection (98 percent), the sacraments (96 percent), and Mary (93 percent), over, for example, a celibate clergy (40 percent), is consistent with the opinions expressed by highly committed Catholics interviewed in 2005. Notwithstanding this consistency, there are some significant dips in the level of support for certain aspects of Catholicism. Reflecting the larger cultural momentum in favor of same-sex marriage, fewer of today's highly committed Catholics (59 percent) compared to those in 2005 (72 percent) see church teachings that oppose same-sex marriage as very important. Similarly, fewer highly committed Catholics today (57 percent) than in 2005 (71 percent) see the Vatican's teaching authority as very important. (We discuss Catholics' views of moral authority in chapter 4.) There has also been a decline in the proportion of highly committed Catholics who regard devotions (from 79 percent in 2005 to 70 percent today) and the Church's concern for the poor (93 percent, 86 percent) as very important. On the other hand, equal numbers of highly committed Catholics today (75 percent) as in 2005 (76 percent) said that the Church's opposition to abortion is very important to them personally.

Further, there is remarkable consistency across several dimensions in how highly committed Catholics construe what it means to be a good Catholic. As is evident from Figure 3.7, there is little or no change since 2005 in the numbers of highly committed Catholics who said that one can be a good Catholic without going to Mass every Sunday (49 percent, 48 percent), without obeying church teachings on birth control (64 percent, 60 percent), divorce and remarriage (43 percent, 46 percent), and abortion (31 percent, 31percent), and without having one's marriage approved by the Church (49 percent, 48 percent).

Amid this consistency, there is a shift in highly committed Catholics' understanding of a good Catholic's obligations to the parish. Whereas 40 percent of highly committed Catholics in 2005 said that a person could be a good Catholic without donating time or money to help the parish, this proportion has increased to 56 percent within the past 6 years. Alongside this, there has also been an increase (from 30 percent to 39 percent) in the proportion of highly committed Catholics who said that one can be a good Catholic without donating time or money to help the poor (see Figure 3.7). This declining concern for the poor may, again, reflect perhaps individuals' greater attentiveness to their own family's economic well-being during recessionary times, notwithstanding the urgency of caring for the poor whose numbers have increased as a result of the recession. Or, it may reflect an emerging indifference among Catholics to the Church's social justice teaching just as they have long disregarded its teachings on sexual morality, and/ or, it may reflect a creeping indifference toward the poor.

Catholic Commitment Amid Religious and Spiritual Ferment

More Americans today (20 percent) have no religious affiliation than was true 20 years ago when approximately 7 percent expressed no religious preference. The increase in religious disaffiliation is accompanied by the perception that denominational boundaries may matter less than heretofore in demarcating morality and religious truth. Americans in general, and Protestants especially, have long voiced the opinion that an individual's everyday moral practices are more important than whether or not the person attends church (Ammerman 1997). This view appears to have become more pervasive over the last few decades. An overwhelming majority of Catholics,

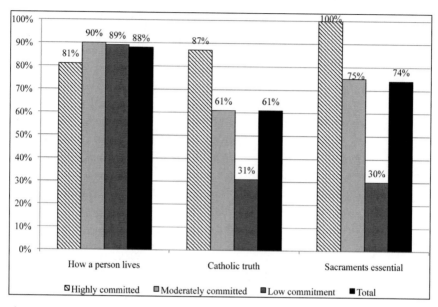

Figure 3.8 Catholics' Views of the Boundaries of Catholicism

88 percent, agree that how a person lives is more important than whether he or she is Catholic (with 56 percent of these strongly agreeing). Moderately committed Catholics (90 percent), similar to low-commitment Catholics (89 percent), are more likely than the highly committed (81 percent) to affirm this view, though as Figure 3.8 shows, it is normative across all types of Catholics.

Nevertheless, despite this openness, Catholics still believe in an institutionally bounded religious truth. Six in 10 (61 percent), agree that Catholicism contains a greater share of truth than other religions do, with 25 percent strongly agreeing with this statement. Not surprisingly, highly committed Catholics are more likely to affirm this stance, with 87 percent of them compared to 62 percent of moderately committed Catholics, agreeing that Catholicism contains a greater share of truth than other religions do (see Figure 3.8). These trends are consistent with the findings from previous Catholic surveys (e.g., D'Antonio et al. 2001: 44).

The continuing significance of an institutionalized Catholic spirituality is reinforced by the finding that 40 percent of our respondents "strongly agree" and an additional 34 percent "somewhat agree" that the sacraments of the Church are essential to their relationship with God. Although still high, the proportion of Catholics, 74 percent, who in 2011 said that the sacraments are essential to their relationship with God is significantly

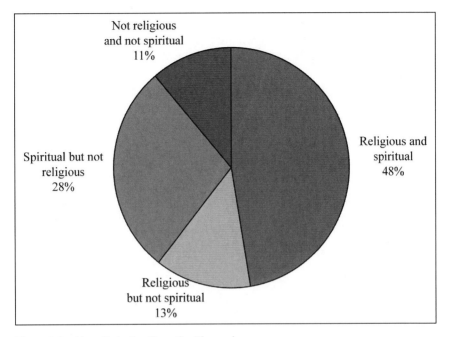

Figure 3.9 How Catholics Describe Themselves

lower than the 81 percent who said so in 2005. Nevertheless, among highly committed Catholics, a full 100 percent (in 2011) see the sacraments as essential to their personal relationship with God, and among the moderately committed, 85 percent do so. By contrast, only 30 percent of Catholics with low levels of commitment see the sacraments as essential to their relationship with God (see Figure 3.8).

Expansion of Spiritual Vocabularies and Resources

Another force challenging the hold of institutional religion on individual identity and commitment is the increased prominence of nonchurch-based spiritual sites (e.g., alternative or integrative health clinics) and resources (e.g., yoga, Reiki) and an everyday vocabulary that distinguishes spirituality from (institutionalized) religion (e.g., Bender 2010; Roof 1999). Catholics are not immune to this spiritual ferment. A plurality of Catholics in our 2011 survey (48 percent) said they are religious and spiritual, 13 percent said they are religious but not spiritual, 28 percent said they are spiritual but not religious, and 11 percent said they are neither religious nor spiritual (see Figure 3.9). These findings are consistent, by and large, with other surveys. In the 2008 General Social Survey (GSS), using a representative sample of Americans, not just Catholics, 20 percent of Catholics said they were spiritual but not religious, and in a national survey conducted in 2009 of (predominantly Catholic) participants who are members of intentional Eucharistic communities (IECs), 24 percent described themselves as spiritual but not religious (Dillon 2009).

While recognizing the increasing cultural pervasiveness of a vocabulary of spirituality, it is important also to keep in mind that spirituality is invoked in varied ways and with varied meanings by different people (e.g., Dillon and Wink 2007). For some, spirituality tends to be unrelated to or exclusive of church, as described, for example, by the following three participants in the IEC study:

"Letting go . . . through yoga meditation."

"I would say that my spiritual life is different from my religion, so my spiritual experiences have not been within my Catholic religion."

"A feeling of awe or wonderment at the amazing beauty of the natural world or the grace and kindness of God's creatures, human and otherwise."

For others, spirituality tends to include Christian theology and church participation. One IEC participant commented, "Because my spirituality is supported by and manifested in religious practice, my spiritual experiences have generally had religious associations, as well." Another said, "My spirituality experiences seem to be the result of living in accordance with Christian principles and having the example of others living in a similar way." And for others, the distinction between religious and spiritual experiences is at best blurry and arbitrary rather than well defined, as suggested by the following quote from another IEC participant: "I have had two powerful spiritual experiences—one in which I felt an overwhelming recognition of the absolute existence of Christ, both as man and God; the other an awareness of Divine energy and presence for which I yearned. Both experiences were emotional and overwhelming."

Catholics' Metaphysical Beliefs

In our 2011 survey, large numbers of Catholics indicated belief in diverse spiritual sources and metaphysical realities. Forty-two percent believe that there is spiritual energy located in physical things such as mountains, trees, or crystals; over one-third (37 percent) believes in reincarnation, and just less than a third (32 percent) believes in yoga, not just as exercise, but also as a spiritual practice (see Figure 3.10). Perhaps not surprisingly, highly committed Catholics, whose spiritual lives are more connected to

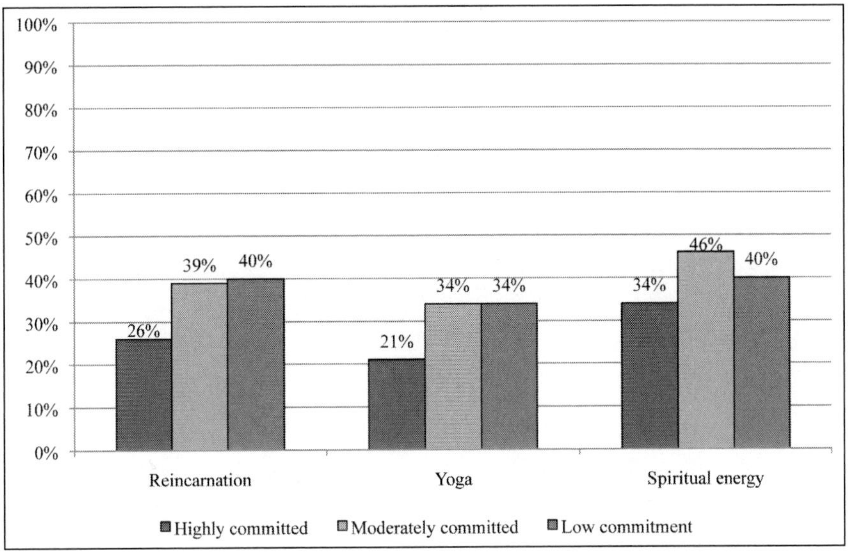

Figure 3.10   Catholics' Non-Church Spiritual Beliefs Differentiated by Church Commitment

and circumscribed by the institutional Church (e.g., weekly Mass attendance), are less likely than less committed Catholics to believe in spiritual
energy, reincarnation, and yoga. Nevertheless, pointing to the way in
which individuals today increasingly blend traditional forms of church
participation with nonchurch spirituality, between one-fifth and one-third
of highly committed Catholics express belief in diverse spiritual sources
(see Figure 3.10).

The more striking variation in spiritual beliefs comes from ethnicity. Hispanic Catholics are significantly more likely than non-Hispanic Catholics to
believe in reincarnation (53 percent, 29 percent), the presence of spiritual
energy in physical things (52 percent, 38 percent), and in yoga as a spiritual
practice (42 percent, 27 percent). Moreover, among Hispanic Catholics,
the highly committed are as likely as their least committed peers to believe
in reincarnation (43 percent, 47 percent) and spiritual energy (46 percent,
52 percent), though they are significantly less likely to believe in yoga as a
spiritual practice (33 percent, 46 percent).

Hispanics' comparatively greater tendency to affirm these spiritual
beliefs may be a reflection of a long tradition of spiritual syncretism in Latino countries and communities, and a greater willingness to look beyond
official church liturgy (e.g., the Mass) to religious festivals, feasts, and
devotion to saints for spiritual nourishment (e.g., Matovina 2012: 22–25).

This more expansive view of spirituality is not always welcomed by church officials who caution against the veneration of idols as well as rituals and beliefs that might encourage believers to stray from church-bound liturgy including the Mass. Nonetheless, during his visit to Mexico in March 2012, Pope Benedict urged Mexicans to pray to their much revered Our Lady of Guadalupe, the patron saint of the Americas, whose origins date to 16th century Aztec culture (Donadio 2012a). And during his visit to Cuba (on the same trip), Pope Benedict invoked, and visited the shrine of, the popular Cuban saint, the Virgin of El Cobre, who is also worshipped by adherents to Santeria, a religion blending Catholic and African-derived elements (Archibold and Burnett 2012).

By contrast, when Pope Benedict visited Brazil in May 2007, he made a point of denouncing the incorporation into Catholicism of pre-Columbus religious traditions that are of special sentiment to Indians in Brazil, Mexico, Peru, and Ecuador. He stated: "The utopia of going back to breathe life into the pre-Columbus religions, separating them from Christ and from the universal church, would not be a step forward; indeed it would be a step back" (quoted in Fisher and Rohter 2007: A10). Nevertheless, the canonization of the Mohawk Indian woman, Kateri Tekakwitha, in October 2012, the Church's first American Indian saint, is likely to generate interest among American Catholics as a whole in the blending of Indian traditions (e.g., prayers to the Great Spirit, drums, Sage smoke for purification) into Catholic liturgies and shrines (see Otterman 2012).

The cultural prominence of a spirituality that is independent of denominational traditions or that blends church and nonchurch beliefs and practices, and the opportunities for participating in diverse forms of spiritual expression (e.g., yoga, Reiki; cf. Bender 2010) are likely to expand in the future. These cultural forces will continue to challenge, though not necessarily displace, the dominance of institutionalized religion for Catholics and non-Catholics alike. As our findings show, although Catholics are embracing new spiritual resources, they also remain strongly wedded to the Church's institutional tradition; recall that 60 percent describe themselves as either religious and spiritual or as religious but not spiritual, and 74 percent say that the sacraments of the Church are essential to their relationship with God. Hispanics (52 percent) are more likely than non-Hispanics (34 percent) to strongly agree that the Church's sacraments are essential to their relationship with God. Yet, as we also document, Hispanic Catholics, including those who are highly committed to the Church, readily blend participation in the Church with a mix of nonchurch-based spiritual beliefs.

Conclusion

Consistent with previous surveys, American Catholics today continue to stress the personal importance to them of theological tenets such as belief in the resurrection, Mary as the Mother of God, and the Mass, as well as of the Church's social justice emphasis on helping the poor. By contrast, they regard the Vatican's teaching authority, the celibacy requirement for priests, and church teachings on contraception, same-sex marriage, and abortion as less important. They continue to take a highly differentiated view of Catholic obligations, and give individuals much leeway in determining what is entailed in being a good Catholic. Catholics' independence from the church hierarchy, however, is coupled with a strong attachment to the Church and Catholicism. There are many varied aspects of Catholicism that are meaningful to Catholics, and many Catholics value the Church's moral stance on an issue, such as, for example, the right to life of the unborn, even if they do not fully agree with the church hierarchy's teaching on the issue. Pointing to the inclusive pluralism that embeds the culture of Catholicism, close to 9 in 10 Catholics say that it is personally meaningful to them that they can selectively disagree with Vatican teaching but remain loyal to the Church. Although Hispanic and non-Hispanic Catholics differ in the extent to which they embrace different aspects of Catholicism, both groups converge in their evaluations of the theological beliefs that are most important to them, and for both groups, celibacy and the Vatican's teaching authority are the least important aspects of Catholicism.

Despite the fact that the proportion of Americans expressing no religious affiliation has almost tripled since the late 1990s (e.g., Hout and Fischer 2002; Pew Forum 2012), the trends in Catholics' commitment to the Church are relatively stable, with 1 in 5 Catholics highly committed. Highly committed Catholics tend to be older, married, and Catholic educated. They differ from other Catholics in terms of the personal importance they attach to various aspects of the Catholic tradition, and they are comparatively more deferential toward Vatican authority and church teachings. Yet, they also articulate views that disagree with official church teachings, they see a lot of latitude in what is entailed in being a good Catholic, and they are also open to structural changes in the Church. In sum, the attitudes of today's highly committed Catholics are mostly similar to those of highly committed Catholics surveyed approximately 10 years ago (2005). Change is apparent, however, along a number of dimensions. There has been a pronounced decline in the percentages of highly committed Catholics who affirm the personal importance to them of devotions, the Vatican's teaching authority, Church teaching opposing same-sex marriage, and in the proportions of those who affirm the Church's and Catholics' obligations to the parish and to the poor. Our findings also suggest that while Catholics are embracing, and most likely will continue to embrace, new spiritual vocabularies and resources, it is also likely that they will blend these resources into their Catholic identity and continue to maintain a meaningful foothold in the Church and to value and participate in its sacraments.

CHAPTER FOUR

~

American Catholics
and Church Authority

We're pastors and teachers, not just one set of teachers in the Catholic community, but *the* teachers.

—Archbishop (now Cardinal) Dolan of New York, November 2010

The church can tell me where to go and what to do, and I will obey. But no one can tell me what to think.

—Sister Ruth, New York, circa 1973

The question is, "Can you be Catholic and have a questioning mind?" That's what we're asking. . . . I think one of our deepest hopes is . . . if we can make any headways in helping to create a safe and respectful environment where church leaders along with rank-and-file members can raise questions openly and search for truth freely, with very complex and swiftly changing issues in our day, that would be our hope. But the climate is not there. And this mandate coming from the Congregation for the Doctrine of the Faith putting us [the Leadership Conference of Women Religious (LCWR)] in a position of being under the control of certain bishops, that is not a dialogue. If anything, it appears to be shutting down dialogue.

—Sister Pat Farrell, July 2012[1]

The opening quotes capture one of the most conflicted issues in the Catholic Church. The issue is the reach of the church hierarchy's authority, and the

69

pushback against it from non-ordained Catholics who insist on their right to think for themselves and who long for dialogue with, rather than unilateral pronouncements from, the bishops. Not all lay Catholics feel this intrusion or experience it as a tension with their own sense of Catholic identity, and some would respond that if Catholics cannot accept the bishops as the sole authentic teachers of Catholicism, then they should leave the Church. For many Catholics, however, the latter two quotes capture the sentiments felt and spoken at thousands of family dinners and gatherings and voiced between friends grappling in particular with difficult decisions most likely relating to some aspect of sociosexual morality.

The issue of moral authority in the Catholic Church has long been a source of debate and is fraught with ambiguity even in theological circles. Scholars look to the First Vatican Council (Vatican I) held in 1869–1870 as the event that formalized the preeminent teaching authority of the Pope because it instituted the doctrine of papal infallibility. Vatican I sought to bolster papal power in the context of political upheaval in Europe, the loss of the Papal States in Italy, and the advance of democracy and its formal separation of church and state, all of which dealt a serious blow to the long-established supremacy of the papacy in Europe. As Gene Burns (1992: 30–32) elaborates, in the wake of its political losses to liberalism, the Vatican sought to more sharply differentiate and consolidate its authority over Catholic faith and morals.

Vatican I's formalization of papal infallibility also institutionalized long established Catholic assumptions. The claim of papal infallibility has been present in the Church since the 11th century when Pope Gregory VII (1073–1085) formulated principles asserting the divine source, supremacy, and universality of papal authority and the irrevocability of papal pronouncements (Laurentin 1973: 101–102). These initiatives were critical to the subsequent enduring character of the Church and especially to the idea of the privileged authority of the pope (Congar 1967: 179, 181). Despite the theological rationale that the pope's authority was legitimated by his line of succession back to the first pope, Peter, a minority of bishops in attendance at Vatican I initially contested both the theological legitimacy and the political wisdom of the assertion of infallibility. Brian Tierney (1971), a historian of Medieval Europe, argues that the institutionalization of infallibility was driven by sociopolitical forces rather than reflecting the legitimation of a tradition present from the beginning of Christianity. He states that although "[all] the standard Catholic discussions of infallibility emphasize continuity rather than change in the church's teaching on this matter . . . it is very hard for a historian to see the emergence of the doctrine of papal infallibility as the slow unfolding of a truth that the church has always held" (862–863). Nevertheless, despite its questioning, the idea if not the dogma of infallibility has a long presence in Church tradition.

Vatican II: Redrawing the Boundaries of Church Authority

Papal authority and the authority of the church hierarchy as a whole are also rendered ambiguous by the Church's theological emphasis on the blending of faith and reason, and a stress on episcopal collegiality rather than unilateral papal authority in church governance—the latter formalized in Canon Law (see Sullivan 1991: 59). The Church's communal, dialogical, and collaborative emphases were strongly present in the bishops' deliberations at the Second Vatican Council (Vatican II: 1962–1965) and were extended to encompass the laity. Pope John XXIII convened Vatican II in an effort, as he stated, to "distinguish the signs of the times" for a Church that is not a "lifeless spectator in the face of [societal] events . . . [but which] . . . has seen . . . the emergence . . . of a laity which has become ever more conscious of its responsibilities within the bosom of the Church, and, in a special way, its duty to collaborate with the hierarchy" (John XXIII 1961, in Abbott 1966: 704–705).

Vatican II reaffirmed the core hierarchical structure of the Church. But it also emphasized a collegial and communal understanding of the Church. Thus, "Though they differ from one another in essence and not only in degree, the common priesthood of the faithful and the ministerial or hierarchical priesthood are nonetheless interrelated. Each of them in its own special way is a participant in the one priesthood of Christ . . . there is but one People of God," whose catholicity and diversity contribute to the good of the whole Church (*Lumen Gentium*, Dogmatic Constitution on the Church #10, #13; Abbott 1966: 27, 31).

Vatican II also affirmed the importance of lay expertise in guiding the Church and the necessity of ongoing dialogue as a way to resolve disagreements:

> "Let there be no false opposition between professional and social activities on the one part, and religious life on the other. . . . Let the layman not imagine that his pastors are always such experts, that to every problem which arises, however complex, they can readily give him a concrete solution, or even that such is their mission. . . . Often enough, the Christian view of things will itself suggest some specific solution in certain circumstances. Yet, it happens rather frequently, and legitimately so, that with equal sincerity some of the faithful

will disagree with others on a given matter . . . it is necessary for people to remember that no one is allowed . . . to appropriate the Church's authority for his opinion. They should always try to enlighten one another through honest discussion, preserving mutual charity and caring above all for the common good." (*Gaudium et Spes*, Pastoral Constitution on the Church in the Modern World #43; Abbott 1966: 243–244)

The Council also called for greater awareness and use of new knowledge and understandings from the arts and sciences in interpreting "the deposit of faith." It stated, for example, "In pastoral care, appropriate use must be made not only of theological principles, but also of the findings of the secular sciences, especially of psychology and sociology. Thus the faithful can be brought to live the faith in a more thorough and mature way . . . let it be recognized that all the faithful, clerical and lay, possess a lawful freedom of inquiry and of thought, and the freedom to express their minds humbly and courageously about those matters in which they enjoy competence" (Ibid. #62; Abbott 1966: 269–270).

Therefore, the exercise of papal and hierarchical authority in the Church has to be balanced with the Church's emphasis on reason and dialogue among the whole Church community, the one People of God. Specifically, following Vatican II, hierarchical authority has to be balanced with recognition of the laity's rightful role in the Church—the laity "are in their own way made sharers in the priestly, prophetic, and kingly functions of Christ. They carry out their own part in the mission of the whole Christian people with respect to the Church and the world" (*Lumen Gentium*, Dogmatic Constitution on the Church, # 31; Abbott 1966: 57). This recognition requires church officials' respect for the expertise the laity gain from living in the world, in their occupations and civic life, and "in the ordinary circumstances of family and social life, from which the very web of their existence is woven" (ibid. 58).

The Impact of *Humanae Vitae* on Catholics' Views of Moral Authority

Today, the Vatican's teaching authority is an aspect of Catholicism that, as we noted in chapter 3, is less important to Catholics' construal of their identity as Catholics than are the Church's core theological beliefs and its emphasis on helping the poor. Fewer than 1 in 3 (30 percent) say that the Vatican's teaching authority is very important to them as Catholics, 46 percent say it is somewhat important, and 20 percent say that it is not important at all. In recent Church history, Pope Paul VI's 1968 encyclical *Humanae Vitae*, which reaffirmed the Vatican's opposition to all forms of artificial contraception (as well as to abortion), is widely seen as the event that marked a serious and enduring public rupture in the legitimacy of the Vatican's authority. As is well documented (D'Antonio et al. 2007; Greeley 1972; Tentler 2004; see also chapter 1), contrary to the expectations broadly shared by American Catholic laity, priests, and theologians that Paul VI would acknowledge the morality of the use of the birth control pill and other means of contraception for married couples, he instead declared that such means were "intrinsically wrong" and contrary to the "fundamental elements of the human and Christian vision of marriage" (Paul VI 1968: 13, 12).

Paul VI's declaration was seen as all the more grievous given that Vatican II had affirmed, among its many other tenets, the importance of personal conscience in Catholic morality and, as we noted above, the importance of Church openness to lay expertise on matters in which the laity are experienced and competent. Declaring that the human person has a right to religious freedom, Vatican II stated with regard to conscience, "In all his activity a man is bound to follow his conscience faithfully in order that he may come to God, for whom he was created. It follows that he is not to be forced to act in a manner contrary to his conscience. Nor, on the other hand, is he to be restrained from acting in accordance with his conscience, especially in matters religious" (*Dignitatis Humanae*, Declaration on Religious Freedom #3; Abbott 1966: 681). In the wake of *Humanae Vitae*, many argued that the laity rather than church officials were the more competent arbiters of the morality of contraception decisions. The Vatican, however, took a contrary view. It used the encyclical not only to reaffirm its opposition to artificial contraception, but also to reaffirm its privileged teaching authority, stating: "No one of the faithful will want to deny that the Magisterium of the Church is competent to interpret also the natural moral law. It is, in fact, indisputable, as our predecessors have on numerous occasions declared, that Jesus Christ, when communicating to Peter and to the Apostles his divine authority, and sending them to teach his commandments to all nations, constitutes them guardians and authentic interpreters of the whole moral law, that is to say, not only of the law of the Gospel, but also of the natural law" (Paul VI 1968: 6-7).

Catholics prior to Vatican II had ignored various aspects of the Church's teaching, including its ban on birth control. Leslie Tentler notes that, if judged by their behavior, "Many Catholic couples in the 1930s effectively rejected *Casti Connubii* [the encyclical on Christian marriage issued by Pope Pius XI in 1930 that elaborated on the sinfulness of artificial contraception]. . . . But they did not publicly dissent from the encyclical, and even in private were apt to couch their objections in narrowly pragmatic terms" (2004: 230). The public conflict in the Church stimulated by *Humanae Vitae*, however, ushered in a new way of thinking among American Catholics that, beyond contraception per se, redefined how Catholics construe church authority and its limits (Seidler and Meyer 1989: 104–106). In the immediate aftermath of *Humanae Vitae*, large numbers of American Catholics stopped attending Sunday Mass, believing that they could not in good conscience use contraception and participate in Mass and Communion. In 1968, 65 percent of American Catholics reported weekly Mass attendance, but by 1973, this figure had declined to 55 percent (Greeley 1985: 53–55). Mass attendance rates stabilized in the late 1970s until the early 1980s at around 52 percent (Hout and Greeley 1987: 332). They further declined such that by 1987, when we conducted our first survey, 44 percent attended weekly Mass (D'Antonio et al. 1989).

The Emergence of a Catholicism Defined by Catholics on Their Own Terms

The behavior of American Catholics in the post-encyclical period marked a new dawn in American Catholicism. Three conjoint patterns emerged: (1) Catholics went to Mass, though at a lower rate than prior to the encyclical; (2) the numbers going to monthly confession continued to decline (e.g., from 37 percent in 1963 to 17 percent by 1974 [Greeley 1977: 132]); and (3) Catholics continued to use contraception. Taken together, these trends signaled that disagreement with Vatican teaching on contraception was not something that many Catholics felt should curtail their participation in the Church (Hout and Greeley 1987: 332, 340). Andrew Greeley (1977: 149) summarizes the post–*Humanae Vitae* context, saying: "The encyclical was ignored in practice by both the clergy and the laity in the United States. Almost four-fifths of both groups agreed that birth control was not sinful. . . . Most bishops in the United States . . . signaled to their clergy that it was all right to leave birth control decisions to the Catholic married couples themselves. This was a necessary decision under the circumstances, but it could scarcely help the credibility of the bishops." Nor could it help the credibility of the Vatican.

In any event, the new Catholic reality was the presumption that a good Catholic could attend Mass and receive communion *and*, contrary to Vatican teaching, use contraception. The Church's on-the-ground acceptance of artificial contraception is recalled in the recent remarks of the *New York Times* columnist Frank Bruni (2012): "When my mother dutifully mentioned her I.U.D. during confession back in the 1970s, the parish priest told her that she really needn't apologize or bring it up again. Which was a good thing, since she had no intention of doing away with it. Four kids were joy and aggravation enough." The response to *Humanae Vitae* thus marks the watershed in Catholics' appropriation of their own individual discernment in deliberating over questions of Catholic faith and morality and the simultaneous rupture in the credible authority of the church hierarchy. Henceforth, individual Catholics rather than the church hierarchy would determine the terms of what is entailed in being a good Catholic. And no set of issues more forcefully demonstrates this lay independence than questions of sexual morality.

Catholic Conscience and Moral Decision-Making

Individual freedom, as we have noted in chapter 1, is a foundational strand in American culture and has strongly influenced the character and vitality of religion in the United States. Although far more pronounced in American Protestantism, this cultural influence also penetrates American Catholicism, especially its post–Vatican II incarnation. The Church's own affirmation at Vatican II of the principles of lay expertise and freedom of conscience further bolstered the individual discernment of Catholics. Given the institutional and theological legitimacy of Vatican II, Catholics' exercise of conscience— even though its practical interpretations frequently contravene specific pronouncements of the church hierarchy—can nonetheless be seen as in accord with Catholic teaching (on conscience) rather than as evidence simply of the declining authority of the church hierarchy. Rather, the moral independence of Catholics demonstrates, in part, the discerning exercise of personal conscience that is in continuity with, and fully recognized as authentic to, the Catholic tradition.

When Catholics are asked questions about "who should have the final say about what is right and wrong" on various moral issues, a minority express acknowledgment that such decisions should be made jointly by individual Catholics and church leaders. Close to one-third of Catholics say that decisions about a Catholic getting married without an annulment (32 percent), and having sexual relations outside of marriage (30 percent) should be made jointly by individuals and church leaders. Although fewer say that decisions about abortion (28 percent), same-sex relations (26 percent), and contraception (23 percent) should be made jointly by individuals and church leaders, nonetheless, about a quarter do so (see Figure 4.1). In all decisions other than marriage annulment, a majority of Catholics say that individuals alone should be the final moral arbiters, and notably, on contraception, two-thirds of Catholics affirm that this decision should reside with the individual alone. By contrast, seeing church leaders alone as the locus of moral authority is a minority view, though one in five Catholics continues to see the bishops as the final arbiter of individuals' decisions regarding divorce and remarriage, and abortion (see Figure 4.1).

Hispanic Catholics are less likely than non-Hispanic Catholics to endorse the view that individual Catholics should be the final arbiters of decisions regarding contraception (60 percent compared to 69 percent), abortion (47 percent compared to 54 percent), and divorce and remarriage without an annulment (38 percent compared to 51 percent). Similar proportions of Hispanic and non-Hispanic Catholics, however, say that the individual should have the final say about the morality of decisions regarding same-sex sexual activity (57 percent and 56 percent, respectively) and nonmarital sexual activity (54 percent and 52 percent, respectively). Despite some differences between Hispanic and non-Hispanic Catholics, the overall pattern of sociomoral liberalism in the views of Hispanic Catholics—that fact that approximately 5 in 10 (47 percent) to 6 in 10 (60 percent) affirm that it should be individual Catholics rather than church leaders alone who should decide regarding various sociosexual issue—fits with a more general pattern of moral liberalism found to be characteristic of Latino Catholics compared to Latino Protestants (e.g., Bartowski et al. 2012; Ellison et al. 2011).

Catholics who are highly committed to the Church[2] are significantly more likely than less committed Catholics to say that the bishops alone

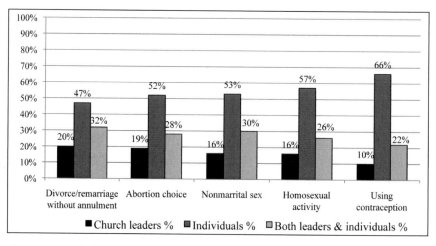

Figure 4.1 Catholics' Views of Moral Authority with Respect to Catholics' Decision Making

should be the arbiters of right and wrong, but they too vary their opinions depending on the question at issue. Less than half express this view with regard to abortion (45 percent), and even fewer, just over a third, say that the bishops alone should be the locus of moral authority when it comes to decisions about divorce/remarriage (39 percent), same-sex relations (36 percent), and nonmarital sexual relations (36 percent). Only a quarter (25 percent) take this view regarding contraception.

In sum, Catholics as a whole tend to rely foremost on their own individual authority in moral decision-making. A minority of respondents acknowledges a role for the bishops, but it is a view that sees the bishops as co-counselors rather than unilateral authority figures. Further, Catholics nuance their views of moral authority depending on the question at issue. They tend to more strongly emphasize the singular authority of individuals on the more private personal issues of contraception, abortion, and sexual relations. The comparatively greater recognition that Catholics give to the moral authority of church leaders on the question of divorce and remarriage may stem from the ritualized, public, and ceremonial status of marriage (cf. Durkheim 1912), and the place of church officials in solemnizing marriages as well as annulments (and remarriages).

Change over Time in Catholics' Views of Moral Authority

Catholics' views of moral authority have, overall, remained relatively consistent over the past 25 years. However, the survey data also point to clear patterns of both stability and change in Catholics' assertion of the primacy of individual moral authority in decision-making (see Figure 4.2). Underscoring that Catholics have long made up their own minds about the morality of contraception, attitudes toward contraception decision-making show the least amount of change (+ 4 percent) over time; 62 percent of Catholics in 1987 and 66 percent in 2011 say that individual Catholics should decide for themselves about using contraception rather than deciding jointly with, or relying solely on, church leaders. Similarly, there has been little change in Catholics' views with respect to abortion decisions; only 7 percent more Catholics today (52 percent) compared to 45 percent in 1987 say that individuals themselves should make the final decision regarding abortion. This relatively stable trend reflects and is a part of the long-term stability in the attitudes of Americans as a whole toward abortion since it was legalized in 1973.

We do see a significant amount of change, however, with respect to other moral decisions. There has been a substantial increase in the proportion of Catholics who say that the individual should have the final say about what is

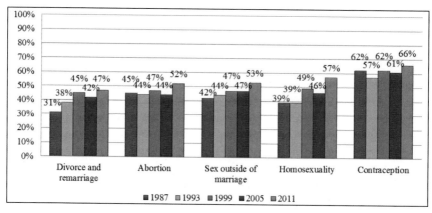

Figure 4.2 Trends in Catholics' Views of Moral Authority, 1987–2011
(Percentage saying final moral authority is individuals)

morally right or wrong concerning sexual relations outside of marriage (+ 11 percent), and even more substantially, regarding decisions about divorce/remarriage (+16 percent), and same-sex relations (+18 percent; see Figure 4.2). Taken as a whole, this increase in the assertion of the moral authority of the individual Catholic over and above that of church officials is evidence of the declining influence and narrowing scope of the hierarchy's relevance in the private lives and decisions of individual Catholics. Taken on its own, this pattern of decline in the church hierarchy's authority fits with what sociologists would regard as evidence of secularization. The dominant thesis in the sociology of religion, secularization tends to be equated with the declining influence of institutional religious authority in individual lives and in public culture (e.g., Chaves 1994).

In the context of Catholicism, however, the application of this definition of secularization is somewhat problematic. The changed understanding of Catholic identity pushed forward by the institutional church itself at Vatican II means that the assertion of individual authority over hierarchical authority has to be seen, at least in part, as evidence that Catholics take seriously the church-mandated obligation to exercise conscience and to blend faith and reason in their everyday lives. In this framing, Catholics are being deferential to the authority of the (pluralistic) Catholic tradition while questioning the unilateral authority of the Vatican. Catholics' views of the preeminence of individual authority in moral decision-making are also at one with the on-the-ground redefinition of the terms of Catholicism first made visible with American Catholics' response to *Humanae Vitae*. That marked a watershed whereby Catholics uncoupled their church participation and commitment to Catholicism from adherence to Vatican teaching on sexual morality.

Same-Sex Relations

In addition to the significance of Vatican II in reframing Catholics' understanding and exercise of conscience, the increasing tendency of Catholics today to disregard the authority of the bishops can also be understood in terms of the larger cultural and institutional contexts surrounding the specific moral decisions at issue. The remarkably large increase in the numbers who view the individual as the final moral arbiter of same-sex decisions reflects the rapidly shifting cultural momentum in the United States in favor of gay/lesbian rights, including same-sex marriage. Even within the relatively short interval between 2005 and 2011, we saw a significant 11 percent increase in the proportion of Catholics who assert the moral primacy of the individual in decisions about same-sex relations. Beyond our survey, Catholics are more likely than other religiously affiliated Americans to express support for same-sex marriage. In a nationwide poll conducted in March 2011, for example, 45 percent of Latino Catholics and 41 percent of white Catholics compared to 36 percent of white mainline Protestants, 23 percent of black Protestants, and 16 percent of white evangelicals indicated support for same-sex marriage (Jones and Cox 2011: 6). Further, and not coincidentally, most of the states that have legalized same-sex marriage are in the politically liberal Northeast—including Massachusetts, New Hampshire, Vermont, Connecticut, New York—and along with Maryland, are also those that have been the cradle of American Catholicism.

The Vatican continues to emphasize its teaching that "homosexuality is an objectively disordered condition," and some organizations such as the Boy Scouts of America continue to uphold their prohibition excluding openly gay boys from membership and openly gay men from leadership positions in their organization. In general, however, in the post–Stonewall era, being gay has increasingly come to be acknowledged as a normal identity. This new understanding was facilitated by the removal in 1974 of "homosexuality" as a mental disorder (DSM II), and its subsequent elimination in 1986 as a sexual dysfunction (DSM III), from the revised official classifications of mental health diagnoses by the American Psychiatric Association in its Diagnostic and Statistical Manual (DSM). The normalization of gay and lesbian sexuality is nudged along by the coming-out of prominent television stars (e.g., Ellen DeGeneres, Rosie O'Donnell, Anderson Cooper) and politicians (e.g., ex-Congressman Barney Frank), as well as by expressions of public support from political leaders (e.g., President Obama, New York Mayor Michael Bloomberg) and prominent business executives (e.g., Lloyd Blankfein, the CEO of Goldman Sachs who supports "Out on the Street"). The elimination in 2011 of the U.S. military's "Don't ask, don't tell" policy that required gay service men and women to remain closeted, is also a significant milestone.

The acceptance of gays and lesbians is also furthered by the activism of several gay rights organizations, including in the Catholic Church, Dignity. Dignity is a 40-year-old national organization of gay and lesbian Catholics with chapters in many cities across the United States. Through a weekly Mass liturgy, social events, and community outreach activities, its participants affirm the coherence of being gay *and* Catholic (e.g., Dillon 1999: 115–163). Equally important, the lived experience of Catholics and non-Catholics alike increasingly encompasses close family members, friends, and colleagues who are gay and who provide first-hand evidence that gays and non-gays are really very much alike in terms of how they think, what they value, and how they live their lives. Many Catholics give serious weight to church teachings on human equality, social justice, and respect for minority rights, and this, too, undoubtedly contributes to their increased acceptance of same-sex relations. At the same time, Catholics have mixed views regarding the bishops' activism against same-sex relationships and the drive toward sexual equality. In our 2011 survey, a slim majority (52 percent) expressed agreement with the bishops' opposition to same-sex marriage, and just less than a majority (48 percent) disagreed with the Church's efforts against it.

The gap between Catholics' views of same-sex relations and those of the church hierarchy is underlined by remarks made by David Avila, then a policy advisor to the U.S. bishops. Writing in October 2011 in *The Pilot*, the official weekly newspaper of the Boston Archdiocese, he stated: "The scientific evidence of how same-sex attraction most likely may be created provides a credible basis for a spiritual explanation that indicts the devil." *The Pilot* subsequently apologized for the column and for its failure to recognize its "theological error." Although Avila was not writing on behalf of the bishops, the fact that such views are held by an advisor to the bishops gives pause to the expectation that the bishops are in the process of developing a more complex understanding of same-sex attraction. Rather, the church hierarchy's continued subscription to the view that same-sex relations are morally wrong places church leaders at odds with the views of large majorities of American Catholics (64 percent) and Americans as a whole (58 percent) who say that homosexuality should be accepted by society (Pew Forum 2011). The changing views of Catholics regarding same-sex issues and identity are also further evidence of how Catholics' lived experiences pose a challenge to the church hierarchy's exercise of a top-down unilateral authority.

Divorce and Annulment

Even though all of the moral decision-issues under study here pertain in some way or other to sexual behavior, the issue of divorce and remarriage without an annulment also taps into a specific, Church-defined institutional context. Lay Catholics have long been uncertain how to understand the Church's position on annulments and how the process works. Reflecting both an increase in the prevalence of divorce in American society and post–Vatican II efforts to make the Church more relevant in modern life, it is only within the last 30 years or so that large numbers of American Catholics have petitioned to have their marriage annulled. Before 1970, approximately 400 annulments were granted annually by Catholic Church tribunals in the United States, whereas between 1980 and 2000, this figure increased to over 50,000 per annum (Wilde 2001). The number of American annulments granted peaked in 1991 (at 64,000) and has in fact declined since then, with only 35,000 granted in 2007 (Allen 2012). This decline apparently is not due to a tightening in the annulment process but to the fact that fewer American Catholics are seeking annulments (Allen 2012). The negative publicity surrounding annulments (e.g., Kennedy 1998), and perhaps too, individual Catholics' own reservations more generally with the Catholic Church's teachings on marriage, divorce, and remarriage, may account for the decline in annulment petitions. These factors may also be contributing to the increase in the proportion of Catholics in our survey data who emphasize that individuals rather than church leaders should have the final say in decisions about divorce and remarriage. These factors may also be contributing to the increase in the numbers of Catholics who are choosing to marry outside the Church (see chapter 6).

Marital Status and Moral Authority
Regarding Divorce and Remarriage, and Nonmarital Sex

Marital status is an important demographic and social variable, differentiating individuals on a number of other important variables and lived experiences. There is no difference, however, between married and unmarried Catholics in their views of the source of moral authority concerning divorce and remarriage. Even the subset of unmarried Catholics who are themselves divorced or separated is no more likely than married Catholics to say that individuals are the final arbiters of right and wrong in this area. By contrast, unmarried Catholics are much more likely than their married counterparts to say that individuals should have final say as to whether nonmarital sex is right or wrong. Six in 10 unmarried Catholics (including two-thirds of those who are living with a partner) say that individuals are the proper source of moral authority when it comes to the question of nonmarital sex, as compared with fewer than half of married Catholics (47 percent) who say this. Among both groups, fewer than 1 in 5 say that church leaders have the sole authority in determining the morality of nonmarital sex. Pre–Vatican II Catholics (37 percent) are less likely than their successor generations (well over half overall, and close to two-thirds among post–Vatican II women) to assert the primacy of individual authority regarding nonmarital sex decisions.

Mass Attendance, Region, and Views of Moral Authority

Perhaps not surprisingly, Catholics who attend Mass most frequently are also those most likely to put their trust in church leadership on questions about right and wrong. Even among those who report attending Mass at least once a week, however, fewer than half say they look solely to church leadership for guidance regarding such decisions. And, again, underscoring the settled moral status of contraception for Catholics, a plurality of weekly Mass attenders (44 percent) says that Catholic individuals should have the final say in making decisions about using contraception. Among the minority of Catholics (21 percent) who say that you cannot be a good Catholic without obeying the church hierarchy's teaching on birth control, close to half (49 percent) attend Mass weekly or more often.

Region also matters in differentiating Catholic opinion. Catholics who reside in the Northeast are consistently more likely than those from other regions of the country to rely on their own individual judgments—rather than those of church leaders—on questions of right and wrong about abortion and about same-sex and nonmarital sexual relations. In fact, on all five decision-issues covered by our survey—a Catholic using contraception, favoring choice on abortion, engaging in same-sex sexual relations, engaging in nonmarital sexual relations, and a divorced Catholic marrying without an annulment—upwards of half of Catholics living in the Northeast said that individuals themselves are the best arbiters of right and wrong.

As our current and long-term trend data demonstrate, Catholics are confident in their own ability to make judgments about personal decisions in the arena of sexual morality, issues on which many of them disagree with the Vatican. This is a consistent, long-term, and escalating trend. It is reflective of changes in the institutional Church's and in Catholics' own understanding of Catholicism, and it is intertwined with larger cultural changes and specific institutional dynamics and doctrines within the Church. Catholic attitudes, overall, are fairly predictable, and the thrust of change observed is in line with previously established patterns of weakened adherence to the authority of the church hierarchy. Whether regarding the primacy of individual moral authority or, as we discussed in the previous chapter, what is considered personally important and meaningful to them as Catholics and what it means to be a good Catholic, Catholic opinion leans heavily toward personal independence in assessing the terms of Catholicism. Although any stable trajectory or trend can, in principle, shift direction at any future point in time, we have not seen this occur in Catholic attitudes over the past 40 years.

Impact of Sex Abuse Scandal on Bishops' Moral Authority

One set of events that may further accelerate Catholics' independence from the Vatican and church leaders is the ongoing impact of the problem of priest sex abuse and its cover-up by church officials—what Pope Benedict has conceded is a "sin that exists inside the church" (Donadio 2010a: 4). The sexual abuse of boys and girls by priests, both in the United States and in many other countries (e.g., Ireland, Belgium, Germany, Mexico, Canada, and Nigeria), continues to generate media headlines. To help gain a better understanding of Catholics' experiences with and reactions to this issue, our 2011 survey included several new questions on the topic. Among our respondents, 7 percent of individuals said that they personally know someone who was abused by a priest, and 12 percent said that they personally know a priest who has been accused of abuse.

Not surprisingly, given that most of the abuse cases stem from earlier decades, older Catholics are more likely than the youngest Catholics to know someone who has direct personal experience with the abuse. One in 10 of those in the pre–Vatican II generation say they know someone who was abused by a priest, as do 9 percent of those in the Vatican II generation and 7 percent of those in the post–Vatican II generation. Among millennial Catholics, by contrast, only 3 percent say that they know someone who was abused by a priest. Similarly, nearly 1 in 5 of the pre–Vatican II generation say they personally know a priest who has been implicated in the scandal, as do 16 percent of those in the Vatican II generation. By contrast, fewer than 1 in 10 millennial Catholics say they personally know a priest who has been accused of abuse.

There is little connection between frequency of Mass attendance and knowing someone who has been abused by a priest, with roughly comparable numbers of regular and infrequent Mass-goers saying that they know someone who was abused. Among those who attend Mass weekly, however, more say they know a priest who has been implicated than among those who attend Mass yearly or less often. This finding is a reflection perhaps that more frequent Mass-goers know more priests than those who attend Mass less often.

Bishops' Handling of the Sex Abuse Issue

Catholics vary in their views of how the bishops have handled accusations of sexual abuse by priests. Over a third (38 percent) say that the Catholic bishops as a whole have done a fair job in handling the accusations. On the other hand, fewer than a third (31 percent) say they have done a poor job, and at the opposite end of the spectrum, fewer still say that the bishops have done a good (24 percent) or excellent (5 percent) job handling the issue. Evaluations of the bishops' handling of the situation are more positive among those who attend church regularly than among those with lower levels of attendance. However, even among those who offer the most favorable ratings of the bishops' handling of the issue, the balance of opinion leans negative. Among those Catholics who attend Mass weekly, 61 percent give the bishops a fair or poor rating, compared with 37 percent who give them a good or excellent rating. Reinforcing the wisdom in the adage that all politics—and all religion—is local, Catholics' assessments of the job their own local bishop has done responding to the sex abuse issue are somewhat more positive than their assessments of the bishops overall. Here again, however, the balance of opinion leans negative, with a majority of Catholics, 57 percent, giving their own local bishop a fair or poor rating for his response to allegations, and 41 percent giving their bishop a good or an excellent rating. Weekly Mass-goers stand out from other Catholics for their relatively positive assessments of their local bishop's handling of the issue. More than half of Catholics who attend Mass weekly give their bishop excellent or good marks for his handling of the situation, whereas half or more of those who attend Mass less often give their local bishop fair or poor ratings.

Impact of the Sex Abuse Scandal on the Bishops' Political and Pastoral Legitimacy

The attenuation of the bishops' authority that has been the post–*Humanae Vitae* reality has been exacerbated by the sex abuse scandal. Most Catholics say that the scandal has had a significant impact on the political credibility of church leaders. More than 8 in 10 say that the issue of the sexual abuse of young people by priests has hurt the credibility of church leaders who speak out on social or political issues either a great deal (47 percent) or somewhat (38 percent). Further, and extending into the core spiritual territory of Catholicism, three-quarters say that the sexual abuse issue has hurt the ability of priests to meet the spiritual and pastoral needs of their parishioners a great deal (39 percent) or somewhat (39 percent; see Table 4.1). These views are prevalent across all generations, with a majority in each saying that the sex abuse issue has had negative consequences both for church leaders' political credibility and for priests' ability to meet the spiritual and pastoral needs of their flock. Similarly, though weekly Mass-going Catholics are less likely than those who seldom or never attend Mass to say that the scandal has had a negative impact on church leaders' political credibility and on priests' pastoral role, large majorities at all levels of Mass attendance say that the scandal has had significant ramifications in these regards. Compared with Hispanics, non-Hispanic Catholics are more likely to say that church leaders' political credibility has been harmed, but there is little difference in the views of non-Hispanics and Hispanics as to the impact of the scandal on the ability of priests to meet the spiritual and pastoral needs of their parishioners (see Table 4.1).

Table 4.1 Impact of Sexual Abuse by Priests on Church Leaders' Political Credibility and Priests' Ability to Meet Spiritual and Pastoral Needs of Parishioners (in percentages)

	Church Leaders' Political Credibility Has Been Hurt...		Ability of Priests to Meet Spiritual and Pastoral Needs of Parishioners Has Been Hurt...	
	Great Deal/ Somewhat %	Only a Little/ Not At All %	Great Deal/ Somewhat %	Only a Little/ Not At All %
Total	85	15	78	22
Pre–Vatican II	89	11	79	21
Vatican II	89	11	83	17
Post–Vatican II	86	14	78	22
Millennial	74	26	71	29
Men	85	15	80	20
Women	85	15	77	23
Attend Mass weekly	82	18	72	28
Monthly	82	18	74	26
Yearly	86	14	81	19
Seldom/never	91	9	86	14
Non-Hispanic	88	12	79	21
Hispanic	78	22	77	23
Northeast	88	12	82	18
Midwest	88	12	77	23
South	80	20	74	26
West	83	17	79	21

Despite enduring concerns about the sexual abuse issue, and notwithstanding Catholics' moral independence from the bishops, most Catholics give both the U.S. bishops as a whole and their own local bishop positive ratings overall. Seven in 10 Catholics (71 percent) say they are very or somewhat satisfied with the leadership of the bishops of the United States, compared with 29 percent who are only a little or not at all satisfied. And similarly, 74 percent say they are very or somewhat satisfied with the leadership of their local bishop, compared with 26 percent who are only a little or not at all satisfied. Though most Catholics are generally satisfied with church leadership, there is a clear link between views of the bishops' handling of the sex abuse issue and Catholics' overall assessment of bishops' leadership. Among those who think the bishops have done an excellent or good job handling accusations of sexual abuse by priests, nearly 9 in 10 are satisfied with the overall leadership of the bishops, compared with a 64 percent level of overall satisfaction among those who think the bishops have done a fair or poor job handling accusations of abuse. Similarly, many more of those who say their local bishop has done an excellent or good job handling the abuse issue give their local bishop positive ratings overall (91 percent), compared with those who give their local bishop fair or poor marks for his handling of allegations of abuse (60 percent). Further, as documented in chapter 7, a majority of Catholics support the bishops' political interventions on specific issues, such as immigration reform (74 percent), opposition to health care legislation (52 percent), and opposition to same-sex marriage (52 percent).

Conclusion

In sum, as we have documented in this chapter, Catholics strongly subscribe to the principles of religious freedom and conscience and have long made up their own minds about where they stand regarding the morality of contraception, abortion, same-sex and nonmarital sexual morality, and issues of marriage and divorce. Catholics are open to taking account of church teachings and the views of church leaders, but the majority reserve for themselves the responsibility to be the final moral arbiter of right and wrong. Despite lingering concerns among Catholics about the sex abuse scandals, the bishops' handling of the issue, and the scandal's impact on pastoral and spiritual life, many Catholics express a positive view of church leadership in general. Many too welcome the bishops' political activism on issues such as immigration, whereas some have reservations when it comes to church leaders' activism on sexual issues (e.g., same-sex marriage), which is a domain of activity that for many decades Catholics considered a matter of private morality, notwithstanding the bishops' recent reinsertion of their views on contraception, for example, into the public domain (Goodstein 2012b).

Prior to Vatican II, Lenski's path-breaking study of the religious factor and how it impacted American society spotlighted the inherent tension of, and the implications posed for Catholics by, the seemingly contradictory values of personal autonomy and obedience. It is ironic that in the first quarter of the 21st century, this same tension continues to be a major feature of contestation between the church hierarchy and American Catholic laity and religious sisters. Although the Vatican and the bishops continue to insist on their singular teaching authority, derived from Jesus through Peter and his successors, many lay Catholics, including those in the pre–Vatican II generation, value personal autonomy and conscience as highly or higher on some teachings. As Lenski noted, individuals' value orientations, and whether they align more closely with obedience than with personal autonomy, not only have implications for church life, but for participation in society more broadly. Vatican II's emphasis on an informed, active, and engaged laity seemed to favor autonomy over obedience within the context of a Church tradition that seeks to balance commitment to faith and reason.

On teachings about sociosexual matters including the use of contraception, support for choice regarding an abortion, divorce and remarriage without an annulment, nonmarital sex, and homosexuality, American Catholics show a transition over time away from seeing the bishops as the locus of moral authority. The prevailing view among Catholics as a whole is that individuals alone and/or individuals in dialogue with church leaders should be the moral arbiters of such matters.

CHAPTER FIVE

~

Catholic Women:
Commitment and Change

Gender and the relevance of gender differences occupy an especially knotty and contested space in Catholicism. The Catholic tradition gives a highly elevated place to Mary as the Mother of God; scriptural accounts show that many women featured prominently in the life, death, and resurrection of Jesus; and women also had significant visibility in the early Church. Yet, the Church's tradition of an all-male priesthood and of an exclusively male church hierarchy substantially diminishes women's full participation in the everyday sacramental and institutional practices of the Church. This is a tension that Catholic women—and men—have long abided, though it has become more fraught in recent decades as women have achieved greater equality in legal status, the labor force, and across many institutional arenas where they had previously been marginalized, including politics, business, academia, sports, and the military. Women have also gained executive and leadership prominence within many of the institutional structures of the Church itself; increasingly, they occupy managerial positions in Vatican and diocesan offices, and in Catholic colleges, hospitals, and service organizations.

Women's Declining Commitment to the Church

For several decades, women have been able to maintain an active loyalty to Catholicism and to live with the irony presented by the twin realities of their commitment to and marginalization within the Church. The irony is that despite their deep attachment to the Catholic sacraments and tradition, their full participation in the Church's sacraments is restricted. They are excluded from ordination to the priesthood and encounter institutional obstacles to their participation in lesser roles such as deacon and altar server. Women's ironic situation is not necessarily for the ages, however. In fact, there is emerging evidence that women's long-standing loyalty to the Church can no longer be taken for granted. Our survey data gathered at intervals between 1987 and 2011 show a great deal of consistency in trends in Catholics' attitudes, and as we document in this chapter, while there are some differences between women and men, there is also much consensus across both genders in their practical understanding of Catholicism. The overall general stability in Catholic attitudes over time and the relatively narrow set of gender differences apparent in the 2011 survey belie, however, a substantial shift in our data over the past 25 years.

On three key indicators of Catholic commitment—frequency of Mass attendance, the importance of the Church in their lives, and their sense of whether they would ever leave the Church—women show significant change over time. These trends are such that they have erased what had been significant gaps between women and men. In 1987, 52 percent of women compared to only 35 percent of men attended weekly Mass. But while men's weekly Mass habits have declined only somewhat, to just 30 percent in 2011, women's have fallen dramatically. By 1993, 9 percent fewer women reported weekly Mass attendance than in 1987, down to 43 percent. This figure dropped an additional 12 percent by 2011, with the result that less than one-third of women, the same proportion as men, were currently going weekly to Mass (see Figure 5.1).

In parallel fashion, whereas 58 percent of women indicated in 1987 that the Catholic Church was among the most important parts of their life, the proportion indicating this in 1993 dropped to 49 percent and continued to fall such that in 2011, this was true of only 35 percent of women. Again, the percentage of men who indicated that the Church was among the most important parts of their life remained relatively similar across the 25 years of our surveys: 39 percent in 1987, 37 percent in 1993, and 35 percent in 2011. Indeed, the relative stability in men's ranking of the importance of the Church and the precipitous decline in women's, means that today a slightly larger proportion of men than women say that the Church is among the most important parts of their life (see Figure 5.2). Reinforcing this pattern of attenuation in women's commitment over time, we see a similar though less startling pattern of decline in looking at their responses to the statement, "I would never leave the Catholic Church." Sixty-one percent of women affirmed this view in 1987, but by 2011, this was true of 55 percent, the same proportion as men (56 percent), more of whom affirmed this view in 2011 than in 1987 (see Figure 5.3).

The fact that there is strong evidence of a dip in women's commitment to the Church over the past 25 years does not mean that this pattern of decline will necessarily continue. Trends in women's weekly Mass attendance, their views of the importance of the Church in their life, and their sense of whether or not they are likely to leave may level out at where they are currently (2011 data). It is also the case that on any one or on all three of these indicators, the graph line could ascend based on the responses to future surveys. Notwithstanding this caution about the future direction of these trends, our survey data present clear evidence that Catholic women today are not as committed to the Church as Catholic women in 1987 were. Moreover, given the many intrusions by the church hierarchy especially on women's independence in the interval since we gathered our data (April 2011)—e.g., the bishops' opposition to contraception insurance, and the Vatican's reprimands of the LCWR, and of feminist theologians (e.g., Goodstein 2012a)—it would not be a surprise if more women were to reduce their commitment to the Church.

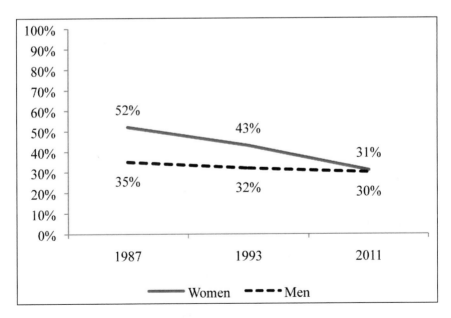

Figure 5.1 Trends in Catholics' Weekly Mass Attendance Differentiated by Gender, 1987–2011

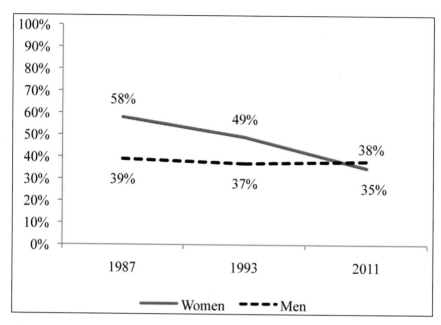

Figure 5.2 Trends in Catholics' Views of the Importance of the Church in Their Lives, Differentiated by Gender, 1987–2011

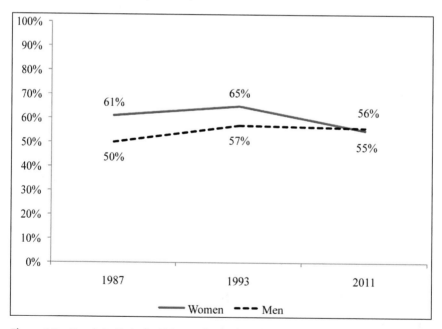

Figure 5.3 Trends in Catholics' Views of Whether They Might Leave the Church, Differentiated by Gender, 1987–2011

Social and Cultural Forces Driving Change in Women's Commitment to the Church

What is driving the 25-year trend of decline in women's commitment tracked by our data? Many social scientists look to changes in the larger society for clues to explain shifts in individuals' participation in specific activities and domains of life. Putnam (2000: 194–203) suggests that the post-1970s' decline in Americans' church-going and communal activities is partly explained by women's increased labor force participation, thus leaving women with less time to devote to church and other voluntary activities. It is true that employment rates among women grew sharply in the 1970s and 1980s (Smith 2008: 6). Given the work and family time bind that women in particular face compared to men (e.g., Hochschild and Machung 1990), women's increased employment could have an understandable impact on their ability to commit time and effort to church and community activities. Yet, the timing of the labor force increase does not coincide with the timing of decline in Catholic women's commitment to the Church. By 1987, the year of our first survey, women were already accustomed to juggling the demands of work and family life and were, at the same time, highly committed to Catholicism. Indeed, women's employment slowed in the 1990s and has decreased since 2000 (Smith 2008: 6), thus, if anything, giving women more time for church. Yet, as we have documented, far fewer Catholic women today show the same level of commitment to Catholicism as did Catholic women in the 1980s.

Our survey data do indicate, however, that family contextual factors impact at least one dimension of Church commitment, Mass attendance, and do so in gendered ways. Given women's greater share of family care roles (e.g., England 2005) and the gender disparities that characterize health (e.g., Moen and Chermack 2005), it is not surprising that more women than men say that family responsibilities (47 percent, 37 percent) and health issues (28 percent, 18 percent) are important reasons why they don't go to church more often. Understandably, the two younger cohorts of women (approximately 47 percent of them) are more likely to cite family responsibilities, whereas the oldest women—30 percent of them—are the most likely to cite health reasons. It is also apparent that family considerations play a role in men's Mass attendance habits. Lending support to the "feminization of religion" thesis, which has assumed that, historically, church participation is more women's than men's domain (e.g., Douglas 1977), more men (30 percent) than women (20 percent) say that they go to church in order to please someone close to them like a spouse or a parent. Men (29 percent) are also more likely than women (22 percent) to say they don't go more often because the Mass is boring. We can thus infer from these responses that women's drop in Mass attendance and in church commitment as a whole is likely also to eventuate in a decline in men's commitment to the Church.

Spiritual Ferment

Putnam (2000: 216–246) also identifies the rapid diffusion and rising popularity of television from the 1950s onward as having a dampening impact on individuals' church habits as well as on their tendencies to socialize informally with others and to engage in community activities. The nature and scope of communications media have changed dramatically in recent decades and even within the past five years. The rise of the Internet and of digitally sophisticated yet easy-to-use mobile social media are greatly impacting the conduct of everyday life. While it is not apparent how this sea-change in communication habits might, in and of itself, have an emergent negative impact on Catholic women's commitment to the Church, it may play an indirect role.

The accessibility and more immediate diffusion of information via new media may contribute to stimulating women's interest in, and opening up their knowledge about, other religious and spiritual avenues and groups. We know from several other research studies that women are more interested than men in exploring new spiritual opportunities (Roof 1999; McGuire 2008; Dillon and Wink 2007). Indeed, we found in our 2011 survey that, among non-Hispanic Catholics, women were significantly more likely than men to believe in spiritual energy (44 percent, 31 percent) and in yoga as a spiritual practice (31 percent, 23 percent). Partaking in such practices may contribute to dampening women's commitment to the Church. Further, women are less likely than men to strongly agree that Catholicism contains a greater share of truth than other religions do (21 percent, 29 percent). This view may lead some women to pursue a diverse range of spiritual and religious options that may or may not include participation in various aspects of the Catholic tradition.

Women's Greater Disaffection with the Church's Teaching on Sexual Issues

It is also apparent that many Catholics who reduce their church involvement cite dissatisfaction with the Church's teachings on sexual morality as a motivating factor. In general, irrespective of denomination, people who leave the Church tend to do so gradually, and their exit tends to result from a mix of practical (e.g., geographical mobility) and changing life-course circumstances (e.g., children leaving home) rather than theological reasons (e.g.,

Dillon and Wink 2007). The Pew Forum (2009a: 23–24) similarly finds that most Catholics who leave the Church say that they gradually drifted away (63 percent). However, among those who leave, a majority (58 percent) cite as an important reason for leaving the fact that they stopped believing in church teachings (Pew Forum 2009a: 24). More specifically, 41 percent cite church teachings on abortion or homosexuality, 33 percent birth control, and 28 percent church teachings on divorce and remarriage.[1]

The salience of sexual issues in motivating Catholics to leave the Church may be especially pronounced for women, and it may also contribute to dampening the commitment to the Church of those women who stay. For example, in our 2011 survey, women were significantly more likely than men to show independence from the Vatican's teaching authority when it comes to personal moral decision-making. As we document in chapter 4, a majority of women and men emphasize that individual Catholics rather than church leaders should be the final arbiters in such decisions. Women, however, are more likely than men to say that individual Catholics taking church teachings into account, rather than church leaders, should have the final say in deciding whether to practice artificial birth control (70 percent, 63 percent) or to engage in same-sex sexual activity (61 percent, 53 percent). Additionally, women are less likely than men to say that the Church's opposition to same-sex marriage (28 percent, 37 percent) is personally very important to them. Young, non-Latina women, in particular, distance themselves from the hierarchy on this issue: only 15 percent of millennial non-Hispanic women say that the Church's opposition to same-sex marriage is personally very important to them. Relatedly, women (26 percent), too, are more likely than men (19 percent) to strongly disagree with the bishops' opposition to same-sex marriage. Again, this is especially true of young, millennial non-Latina women, only 14 percent of whom agree with the bishops' position. Indeed, only 14 percent of this group of young Catholics say that the teaching authority claimed by the Vatican is very important to them.

Women's relatively greater affirmation of individual moral authority and their questioning of the Vatican's stance on sexual issues (e.g., same-sex relations) may be a reflection of the fact that, as feminist sociologists (e.g., Smith 1990) would point out, they are the ones who have to grapple more immediately in their everyday and every night lived experiences with the practical consequences of the Church's sexual prohibitions. Hence, they are more skeptical of church leaders' knowledge of and insights about these intimate sexual matters and, at the same time, are more understanding of, and empathetic toward, individuals' resolution of decisions encompassing sexual behavior (e.g., contraception, same-sex relations).

That women have over time become more independent of the Vatican's teaching authority is underscored by the absence of a gender differential on abortion. In the late 1980s, for example, while there was a strong consensus among women and men about what was entailed in being a good Catholic, women (41 percent) were significantly less likely than men (54 percent) to say that one can be a good Catholic without obeying church teaching on abortion (D'Antonio et al. 1989: 66). By contrast, today, a similar majority of women (60 percent) and men (59 percent) express this view, with women having changed their attitude significantly more than men (by a 24, as compared to a 12, percentage point increase). Much of this shift in women's understanding that one can be a good Catholic without obeying church teaching on abortion had occurred by the mid-1990s (e.g., D'Antonio et al. 1996: 108) and continued through the current survey.

Generational Change

We also infer from our data that generational change is a significant force driving the decline in women's commitment. The passing of the highly committed pre–Vatican II generation (see chapter 1), and especially of its women who for decades have been the source of so much of the Church's vitality, marks not solely a generational displacement but a displacement, too, of the culture of commitment that had sustained the Church. For example, when we asked our respondents about the personal meaningfulness of Catholicism, there was, as on other questions (e.g., being a good Catholic, personal importance of aspects of Catholicism), a great deal of consensus in the views expressed by women and men. Nonetheless, for women as a whole, the most frequently identified aspect of Catholicism that they considered *very meaningful* was the fact that Catholics can disagree with certain aspects of church teaching and still remain loyal to the Church. Not all women share that view with equal fervor. There is a generational split with older-age women, those born before 1960 (65 percent), significantly more likely than their younger peers, those born after 1960 (47 percent), to emphasize loyalty amid dissent.

That there is a generational split among women on the issue of loyalty and dissent presages the larger, significant shift in women's commitment to the Church that is evident in our trend data over time. The emergent generational divide among Catholic women suggests that younger women—and millennial non-Hispanic women in particular—are not likely to stay within the fold of a Church whose sexual teachings and church practices are so out of step with their lived experiences. Unlike their grandmothers and mothers, Catholic women born after Vatican II seem less willing to give the institutional church the benefit of the doubt and to stay loyal to the Church and Catholicism while hoping for change.

Institutional Challenges

Women's place in the Church is receiving renewed scrutiny today not only because it raises important questions about the Church's commitment to women's independence and equality, but also because the Church is facing a number of institutional challenges that converge to place it at a critical juncture. One challenge is the continuing impact of the sex abuse scandal and its fallout for the credibility and pastoral effectiveness of priests. In our survey, as we noted in chapter 4, almost half the sample (47 percent) said that sex abuse by priests has hurt a great deal the credibility of church leaders who speak out on social or political issues, and over a third (39 percent) said that it has hurt a great deal the ability of priests to meet the spiritual and pastoral needs of their parishioners. There is a strong consensus among women and men in their views of the impact of the sex abuse crisis. But, hinting at women's pent-up frustration with the Church, they are, at a statistical trend level, more likely than men (50 percent compared to 44 percent) to say that it has hurt the ability of priests to speak out on social or political issues.

The Shortage of Priests

The second challenge strikes at the heart of Catholicism and its sacramental, institutional, and communal life: the shortage of priests. Although long predicted and not unexpected (Schoenherr and Young 1993), the aging of current cohorts of priests coupled with the post–Vatican II generational decline in newly ordained priests and the growth in the absolute number of Catholics in the United States are converging trends that are now reaching close to a crisis point. As chapter 2 documents, whereas there were 1,600 parishioners for every priest in the mid-1980s, today there are 3,600 parishioners for every priest. The number of priests has declined by 25 percent, and while the shortfall has been compensated to some extent by an increase in the number of permanent deacons and lay ecclesial ministers serving in parishes, the shortage is evident in many parishes. In some dioceses, recent initiatives that included parish reconfigurations and church closures were driven, in part, by other demographic factors (such as the changing geographical location of Catholics). Current diocesan deliberations aimed at parish administrative reorganization, however, explicitly acknowledge that currently in many dioceses there are simply not enough priests available to execute the traditional parish-centered pastoral and administrative duties of the priest. In many parishes, one visible manifestation of the priest shortage is a reduction in the frequency of Mass. It further appears that unless some creative structural and theological modifications are formally incorporated into the Church's understanding of the priesthood, the availability of the Mass and the Eucharist will undoubtedly continue to decline.

This scenario has implications for the enactment and maintenance of the Church's core theological and sacramental tradition, and for Catholics' individual and communal identity as Catholics. The Mass is the institutional—and the theological and communal mechanism—that is core to Catholicism. As affirmed in the *Catechism of the Catholic Church* and in numerous papal statements, "The Eucharist is the source and summit of the Christian life" (#1341). In our 2011 survey, when we inquired about the reasons why people go to Mass, the stronghold of the liturgy and the Eucharist on the Catholic imagination loomed large. Very large majorities of women and men said that they go because they enjoy taking part in the service (87 percent women, 83 percent men) and because they feel a need to receive the sacrament of Holy Communion (women 82 percent, men 79 percent). Well over half, and again, similar proportions of women (60 percent) and men (58 percent), said that they go because they enjoy being with other persons in their church.

Without the Eucharist as a core habitual practice, Catholics' participation in and connection to the Church and the Catholic tradition would thus become severely attenuated. The Mass, and especially the consecration of the Eucharist, which is the one sacramental performative act that requires an ordained priest, is the communal coming-together of Catholics in worship, an act that in and of itself is important to the maintenance of Catholicism. The Eucharist is also the ritual practice that fully enacts the essential theology predicated on Christ's life and death. As the *Catechism* (#1341) elaborates, the command of Jesus to "Do this in memory of me" is not simply commanding a cognitive remembrance of Christ's action at the Last Supper. Rather, "the command of Jesus to repeat his actions and words until he comes does not only ask us to remember Jesus and what he did . . . it is also a memorial of Christ, of his life, of his death, of his Resurrection, and of his intercession in the presence of the Father." Thus, in the absence of the ritualized performance of the Consecration of the Eucharist, Catholic life and the Catholic tradition would lose its vital source and summit.

The scenario we have outlined points to the threat of an institutional crisis in and for the Church. We do not use the word lightly. Following the social theorist Jurgen Habermas (1975), we use the word "crisis" to denote the existence of a *systemic* impediment to the maintenance of an institution's core mission and identity. One can conclude that Catholics and the Church face a crisis insofar as the shortage of priests—and the attendant decline in the availability of the Mass and the Consecration of the Eucharist—presents a systemic institutional impediment to maintaining the mass loyalty of Catholics to the Church. The Eucharist is at the core of Catholicism and central to the Church's theological, institutional, and communal identity. Without it, it is hard to imagine Catholicism.

Parish Restructuring and Women's Roles in the Church

Catholics' views of what might be acceptable alternative options in response to the priest shortage and the attendant pressing sacramental and pastoral needs of the Church, provide timely input into how new parish reconfigurations might be made effective, as well as providing further insight into what Catholics value about Catholicism. Very large majorities of men and women, Hispanics and non-Hispanics, are open to the possibility of sharing a priest with other parishes, sharing lay staff with other parishes, merging parishes into one, and bringing in a priest from another country to lead the parish. Fewer, however, though still a large majority of two-thirds, see reducing the number of Saturday vigil and Sunday Masses, or having a Communion service instead of Mass as acceptable options. The least acceptable options to Catholics are not having a priest available to administer Last Rites or to visit the sick, and closing the parish (see Figure 5.4). In sum, in thinking about

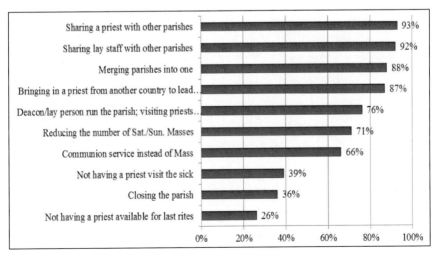

Figure 5.4 Catholics' Views of Acceptable Options in Response to the Priest Shortage

the role of priest and what changing arrangements a priest shortage might entail, Catholics differentiate between the administrative and the sacramental roles of the priest, and while open to a reduced number of Masses and a reduced liturgy (e.g., a Communion service), they draw a line when confronted with the absence of a priest at life's end and parish closure, circumstances that speak to the core theology of individual forgiveness, redemption and afterlife, and the communal center of Catholicism.

Beyond the priest shortage per se, there is strong support among Catholics for women's roles in the Church. Very large percentages of men and women indicate support for women as readers at Mass, religious education directors, parish administrators, youth ministers, altar servers, and Eucharistic ministers. A substantial three-quarters support women in the role of deacon, and 62 percent support women as priests (see Figure 5.5). The group most likely to support women priests is women born since 1960. Not coincidentally, these are the cohorts of women who have had the opportunity to participate more intimately in the Church's sacramental life as altar servers and to witness their same-gender peers availing of the opportunity. In our survey, 17 percent of millennial and 9 percent of Generation X women reported having been altar servers, a privilege denied their mothers and grandmothers.

Hispanics and non-Hispanics express relatively similar levels of support for women's roles (see Figure 5.6). And although comparatively fewer Hispanics support women as Eucharistic ministers, altar servers, parish admin-

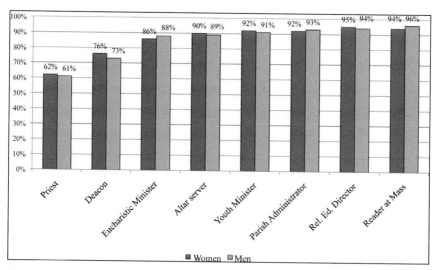

Figure 5.5 Catholics' Support of Roles for Women in the Church, Differentiated by Gender

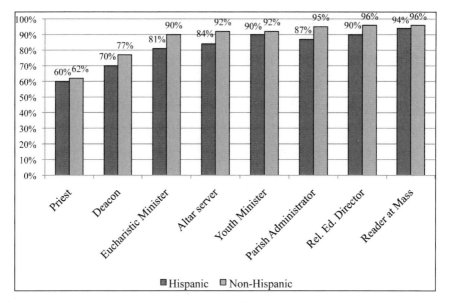

Figure 5.6 Hispanic and Non-Hispanic Catholics' Support of Roles for Women in the Church

istrators, and deacons, equal percentages of Hispanics and non-Hispanics support women in the role of priests. Hispanic Catholics' greater tendency to favor women as priests rather than in secondary roles (such as deacons, etc.) may reflect the alleged "matriarchal core" that is said to characterize Latino communities whereby women are presented as having important leadership roles in their communities' communal religious activities. Although several scholars of Latino/a Catholicism repeat Diaz-Stevens' (1994) emphasis on the "matriarchal core" in Latino Catholicism, Carroll (2007: 129–138) is highly critical of the empirical basis for such claims. In any case, in our survey, whether or not it derives from a more general respect for women's leadership authority, Hispanic Catholics are as likely as non-Hispanic Catholics to favor the idea of women priests.

Complexity of Women's Ordination

Women's ordination is a complex theological subject on which not only the Vatican but Catholic theologians have much to say. As outlined in Vatican teaching, one of the three main reasons used by the Vatican to explain the Church's opposition to the ordination of women is that even if the Pope wanted to ordain women he does not have the authority to do so because

Christ called only men and not women to be his disciples and thus to ordain women would be to go against the intentions and actions of Jesus. A second reason is that only a man can mimic the iconic male figure of Jesus during the Consecration of the Eucharist; and the third reason is that a male-only priesthood has been the Church's constant tradition (see, for example, John Paul II 1994; Congregation for the Doctrine of the Faith 1977, 1995). Many Catholic theologians argue that these theological reasons are open to dispute and, in any case, can be reinterpreted in light of the contemporary era to provide a strong theological rationale in support of women's ordination (e.g., Dillon 1999). The charge in favor of women priests has also been joined by Catholic priests in Ireland, Austria, and Australia, among other countries, who see women's ordination as a legitimate pastoral response to the pressing need for church revitalization (e.g., Goodstein 2011).

Despite, or because of, the institutional and cultural ferment in favor of ordaining women priests, the Vatican recently reaffirmed its unambiguous opposition. Pope Benedict XVI used his sermon at Mass on Holy Thursday (April 5, 2012), the day on which the Church commemorates Christ's institution of the priesthood at the Last Supper, to reassert that it is part of the Church's divine constitution that women cannot be priests. He also condemned acts of disobedience by priests and others who speak in favor of women's ordination (Donadio 2012b). The Vatican's firmness on ordination may reflect its belief that it is necessary to insist that the question is settled in order to maintain respect for Catholic tradition and the authority of church teaching. Yet, by not allowing dialogue about the doctrinal possibility of women priests, especially in light of the priest shortage and the centrality of the Eucharist and of gender equality to Catholics' lived experiences, the Vatican may in fact be further undermining its credibility among broad swaths of Catholics.

Notwithstanding the theological and cultural reasons in favor of women's ordination, there are also cultural factors that can inhibit doctrinal and institutional change. As a transnational universal Church, the Church exists in many countries in which the understanding of gender equality and of women's roles is much different to its construal in the West. In such contexts, it would be culturally difficult for the Church to impose women priests even if it were bolstered by a strong theological rationale. It is also likely that some national churches would reject the theological principle of women Catholic priests even if their ordination were to be confined to Western societies. Thus, one might anticipate the emergence of new tensions, if not a schism, in the universal Church somewhat akin to what has occurred in the Anglican Church over the ordination of gay bishops.

Moreover, even in Western societies such as the United States, there are deep-seated cultural expectations of what a priest should look like. For many, the iconic male priest is not an image that is easy to reimagine, tamper with, or shelve. In our survey, we found that when presented with a set of possible scenarios, Catholic women and men were more disposed to married men than to either single or married women as priests. Over one-third strongly agreed that it would be a good thing if priests who have married were allowed to return to active ministry, and if married men were allowed to be ordained as priests. By contrast, just a quarter strongly agreed that it would be a good thing if married women and if celibate women were allowed to be ordained as priests (see Figure 5.7). Notwithstanding the "matriarchal core" alleged to characterize Latino communities, Hispanic Catholics, too, were more likely to endorse the married men ordination scenarios than either of the two women priest scenarios; and fewer Hispanic than non-Hispanic Catholics expressed strong agreement with any of these respective scenarios (see Figure 5.8). Clearly, Catholicism's long tradition of male priests, and of celibate male priests in particular, is imprinted in the Catholic imagination. When intertwined with deep-seated stereotypical assumptions about women (and about celibate women in particular), these strands of cultural resistance present hurdles in moving the Church forward on women's ordination, notwithstanding the urgent practical need for more priests.

We also know, however, from other major changes in society and in the Church, that it frequently takes institutional change to effect a broader change in attitudes in the public-at-large. This has been the case following some key Supreme Court decisions where the implementation of new social arrangements (e.g., regarding racial integration, women in sports)

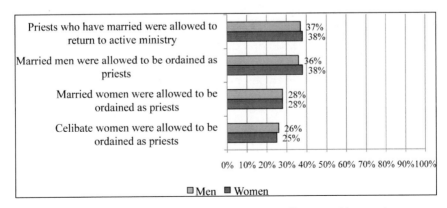

Figure 5.7 Catholics' Views of Ordination Scenarios, Differentiated by Gender (percentage that "strongly agree")

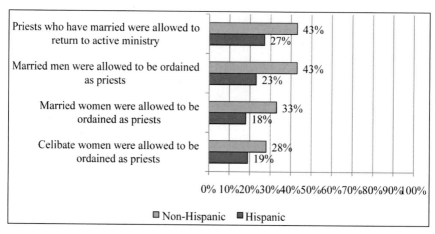

Figure 5.8 Hispanic and Non-Hispanic Catholics' Views of Ordination Scenarios (percentage that "strongly agree")

works to bring about a normalization of things previously deemed morally or normatively unacceptable. In the case of the Church, research by Ruth Wallace (1992) shows that despite initial resistance in priestless parishes to the idea of lay women parish administrators, the laity came to strongly embrace the change. Women parish administrators do most of the things that a pastor would do other than consecrate the Eucharist, and for all intents and purposes they are or become the "pastor." Once the parishioners experience women in these new roles and grow accustomed to the changed nature of the parish, they are overwhelmingly accepting and enthusiastic about having women as parish leaders. Wallace's findings thus suggest that change is sometimes a less onerous process on the ground than augured by the many factors hindering it. This may be especially true when a larger value or a larger good is being served. In the case of Catholics, their strong attachment to the Mass and to the Church's sacramental and communal life may go a long way toward alleviating any reservations they might have about the idea of women priests.

Conclusion

Looking at our surveys over time, it has become quite evident that women's long-standing loyalty to the Church and commitment to Catholicism can no longer be taken for granted. On key indicators of commitment—weekly Mass attendance, attitudes about the importance of the Church in their lives, and whether they might ever leave the Church—Catholic women show a steep trajectory of decline over the past 25 years. This decline is such that women's levels of commitment to the Church are now on a par with men's, whereas in 1987, women's commitment far exceeded men's. Many conjoint factors would appear to be driving this decline. Among these are issues of cultural and generational change, spiritual ferment, advances in women's equality in other institutional spheres, women's comparatively greater disaffection with Vatican authority and the Church's teachings on sexuality, as well as the lingering fallout from the sex abuse crisis. In the current context of an acute shortage of priests and the practical threat this poses to the core sacramental practices, theological unity, and communal identity of Catholics, women's continuing exclusion from ordination seems anathema to many observers. Given that Catholics lay great store in the Mass and in the Church's sacramental and communal tradition, it is not surprising that there is strong support among Catholic men and women alike for women's roles in the Church, with 6 out of 10 supporting the idea of women as priests.

CHAPTER SIX

~

Generational Changes in Catholic Practice

The 25 years of American Catholicism documented by these five surveys paint a portrait of great change as well as remarkable consistency over time. So far, our data suggest that the landscape of Catholic identity remains strong and consistent, even as generational replacement and increased cultural diversity changes the face of Catholics in the United States. The gender differences discussed in the last chapter portend that even greater change may be on the horizon.

In this chapter, we examine how the demographic changes described earlier in this book have implications for the way Catholics practice their faith, too. Moving away from the ethnic Catholic neighborhoods and into areas that had little or no Catholic presence, living and working among people of many different faiths, sending children to public schools, attending Mass in ever-larger parishes in the suburbs—all these changes impacted the way Catholics live their faith. Some of these changes we can even document in our survey data.

Marriage

For example, the likelihood that a Catholic will marry another Catholic is related to how numerous other Catholics of marriageable age are in the community. With Catholics now dispersed from the old ethnic neighborhoods, growing up and working with those of many different faiths as well as those with no particular faith, the pool of available spouses now includes many

107

non-Catholics. And Catholics who marry non-Catholics are less likely to marry in the Church in a sacramental marriage.[1] The number of marriages celebrated in the Church has declined by more than half since we began this series of surveys—from 341,622 in 1987 to 165,400 in 2011—while the U.S. Catholic population has increased by about 12 million. To put it another way, this is a shift from 6.4 Church-sanctioned marriages per 1,000 U.S. Catholics in 1972 to 2.5 per 1,000 Catholics in 2011.

It's not that Catholics are less likely to be married. In our survey, 54 percent of adult Catholics said they are married (see Figure 6.1), which is slightly higher than the 51 percent of the U.S. adult population that is married (Cohn et al. 2011).

Instead, many Catholics are choosing to marry outside of the Church, in a nonsacramental or civil marriage ceremony. Two-thirds of the married Catholics in this survey said that their current marriage is approved by the Church as a valid marriage. Hispanics were only slightly less likely than non-Hispanics to be married (51 percent compared to 56 percent), and married Hispanics were just as likely as married non-Hispanics to say their current marriage is a sacramental marriage.

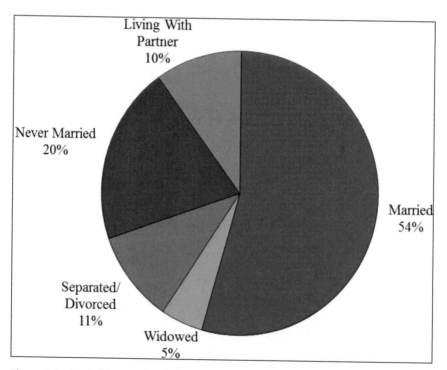

Figure 6.1 Marital Status of Catholics

It is differences among the generations that most clearly show how demographics impact practice. Most pre–Vatican II Catholics are either married (47 percent) or widowed (39 percent). And nearly all of them (95 percent) say that their marriage is a sacramental marriage. In comparison, about two-thirds of Vatican II or post–Vatican II Catholics are married or widowed, and about two-thirds of each generation say that their marriage is a valid Church marriage. Among millennial Catholics, however, just over a quarter are married (28 percent) and only half of those are sacramental marriages. Although many more of this generation will marry in time (after all, the oldest in this generation were 31 years old at the time of the survey), it is likely that the proportion married in a sacramental marriage will remain about half.

In fact, most lay Catholics agree that you can be a good Catholic without your marriage being approved by the Church. This proportion has increased from just over half (53 percent in 1987) to almost 3 in 4 (72 percent in 2011). Pre–Vatican II Catholics are significantly less likely than younger Catholics to agree with this statement. Hispanics are less likely than non-Hispanics to agree.

Parish Registration and Mass Attendance

Demographic changes are also having an impact on Catholic practices related to parish life. In fact, some would argue that parish life is less important to Catholics today than it was in 1987, pointing out that Catholics are less likely now to register in a parish or to attend Mass every Sunday.

Parish registration, which according to our surveys was steady at about two-thirds of Catholics in 1999 and 2005, declined 10 percentage points between 2005 and 2011. (See Table 6.1) This decline in the percentage of Catholics who are registered in a parish is, however, in part a function of the demographic changes described in chapter 2. We find that 64 percent of

Table 6.1 Trends in Mass Attendance and Parish Registration, 1987 to 2011
(Aside from weddings and funerals, how often do you attend Mass?, percentage responding)

	1987 %	1993 %	1999 %	2005 %	2011 %
At least once a week	44	42	37	34	31
Two or three times a month	13	15	19	16	13
About once a month	17	18	15	14	9
Less than monthly	26	25	29	36	47
Registered in a parish (yes)	—	—	69	68	58

non-Hispanic Catholics, compared to 46 percent of Hispanic Catholics, were registered in a parish in 2011. Parish registration among non-Hispanic Catholics is unchanged (within the margin of error) compared to what we found with our English-only surveys in 1999 and 2005, but Hispanic Catholics are less likely to be registered. This is a pattern that is likely to persist, at least until Hispanic immigrants become more fully assimilated into American culture, because parish registration is a practice that the Catholic Church in the United States adopted from the dominant Protestant culture and is not a typical Catholic practice in other parts of the world.

We do see a gradual decrease in the percentage who say that they attend Mass at least weekly, from 44 percent in 1987 to 31 percent in 2011, but little change in the percentage who attend less than weekly (but more than monthly). Catholics who attend Mass monthly or less than monthly increased from 43 percent in 1987 to 56 percent in 2011.

Some of the change in Mass attendance comes from generational replacement, as the pre–Vatican II Catholics age out and are replaced by Vatican II, post–Vatican II, and millennial Catholics, who are less regular than the oldest generation in their Mass attendance. The most striking change in practice occurs between the pre–Vatican II Catholics and those who came after them, as shown in Figure 6.2. Pre–Vatican II Catholics are more than twice as likely as younger Catholics to attend Mass at least weekly. And Hispanic Catholics (who tend to be younger, on average, than non-Hispanic Catholics) attend Mass at the same rates as non-Hispanic Catholics.

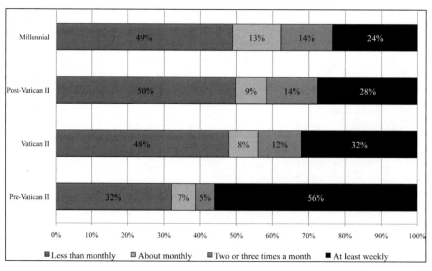

Figure 6.2 Aside from Weddings and Funerals, About How Often Do You Attend Mass?

Previous studies have shown that some of the reasons for the different patterns of attendance among the generations have to do with age-specific behaviors and dispositions that social scientists call "life-cycle effects." For example, older people tend to increase their practice of religion more as they age, in part because they have more free time at their disposal as their family and work obligations decrease. They also spend more time than younger people do in thinking about the end of life. Similarly, teens tend to decrease their practice of religion as they break away from their family and institutional ties in the process of becoming adults. They often return to religious practice as they marry and start families (Dillon and Wink 2007). Although our generation-specific data do not lend themselves to an examination of life-cycle effects,[2] we observe that the differences in religious practice across these generational cohorts reflect some of the life-cycle effects that we would expect to find in panel data.

Nevertheless, much of the difference in Mass attendance between pre–Vatican II Catholics and those who came after them is evidence of the lingering effect of the generational culture of pre–Vatican II Catholics. These Catholics grew up in a time when going to Mass weekly was a core part of Catholic identity and an entrenched behavioral norm. In fact this generation was taught, in no uncertain terms, that missing Mass was a mortal sin that must be confessed to a priest and atoned for before one could again approach the Communion rail. Although the teaching has not changed, the emphasis since Vatican II has been more one of encouraging the faithful to gather together for Sunday Eucharist and less on fear of eternal punishment for missing an obligation. We can observe some of this difference in the different reasons people give for why they attend Mass as well as why they miss Mass.

We asked people in the 2011 survey to tell us the important reasons why they go to church, providing them a list of six reasons. (See Table 6.2) The top three reasons that most Catholics said were important to them included "I enjoy taking part in the service and experiencing the liturgy" (85 percent), "I feel a need to receive the sacrament of Holy Communion" (81 percent), and "I enjoy being with other persons in our church" (59 percent). There is no difference between Hispanics and non-Hispanics in the proportion that agreed "I feel a need to receive the sacrament of Holy Communion" is an important reason; Hispanics were slightly less likely than non-Hispanics to say that the other two are important reasons for them to go to church.

The differences among the generations in the importance of these reasons may reflect some of the life-cycle effects alluded to above. For example, nearly all of the oldest two generations say that spiritual fulfillment—

needing to receive the sacrament and experiencing the liturgy—are important reasons why they go to church, compared to about 3 in 4 of the younger generations who feel the same. On the other hand, very few pre–Vatican II Catholics are concerned with pleasing or satisfying someone close to them, which is an important reason for about 4 in 10 Millennials. Pre–Vatican II Catholics are more likely than other generations to be widowed, and they probably no longer have a parent reminding them of their obligation, unlike millennial Catholics who are more likely to be married or to be living with their family of origin.

More importantly, half or more in all four generations cite being with others they enjoy as an important reason why they go to church. In fact, about two in three of the oldest as well as the youngest generation say this is an important reason why they go.

We also find that Hispanics are similar to non-Hispanics of each generation in their expressions of the important reasons for attending Mass, with just a few exceptions. Hispanic Catholics of the Vatican II generation are a little more likely than non-Hispanics of the same generation to say that they attend out of obligation ("The Church requires that I attend") and a little less likely to say they attend because they enjoy taking part in the service or they enjoy being with others persons in church. Likewise, post–Vatican II Hispanics are more likely than non-Hispanics of the same generation to agree that an important reason they attend is out of habit or because the church requires that they attend. They are less likely than non-Hispanics to say that they enjoy taking part in the service or they enjoy being with others in church.

Table 6.2   Reasons People Go to Church (percentage responding "important reason")

	Pre–Vatican II %	Vatican II %	Post–Vatican II %	Millennial %
I enjoy taking part in the service and experiencing the liturgy	95	92	81	75
I feel a need to receive the sacrament of Holy Communion	94	82	77	77
I enjoy being with other persons in our church	69	60	51	63
The church requires that I attend	41	34	39	34
I want to please or satisfy someone close to me, like a spouse or parent	11	21	24	38
Mainly, it's a habit	16	23	34	48

The reasons people gave for not attending more often also reflect some of the same life-cycle effects. Younger Catholics are more likely than older Catholics to cite family responsibilities, conflict with the Mass schedule (such as Sunday morning soccer games or work schedules), or "I'm too busy" as important reasons for not attending church more often. More than a third of millennial Catholics say that important reasons why they don't attend more often are because "It's boring" or because they have a conflict with the Mass schedule, compared to only about 1 in 10 pre–Vatican II Catholics who feel that way (see Table 6.3).

The most common reason cited for not attending church more often—given by 4 in 10 across the generations—is that "I am just not a religious person." In fact, half of those who told us they seldom or never attend Mass cited this as an important reason why they don't attend. Post–Vatican II and millennial Catholics, who are most likely to have jobs and families, are more likely to cite family responsibilities than not being religious as an important reason why they don't attend more often. Hispanics are more likely than non-Hispanics to cite family responsibilities, health reasons, or conflict with the Mass schedule as an important reason why they don't attend church more often.

The Relationship between Knowledge and Belief in the Eucharist

The Catholic Church teaches that in the consecration of the Eucharist, the bread and wine really become the body and blood of Jesus Christ. *The Catechism of the Catholic Church* says, "In the most blessed sacrament of the

Table 6.3   Reasons People Don't Attend Church More Often (percentage responding "important reason")

	Pre–Vatican II %	Vatican II %	Post–Vatican II %	Millennial %
I am just not a religious person	43	41	38	40
Family responsibilities	31	29	53	48
Health reasons	27	16	23	29
Sermons are poor	25	24	24	29
It's not a mortal sin to miss Mass	20	31	32	29
I'm too busy	18	21	34	38
It's boring	12	24	23	36
Conflict with the Mass schedule	8	13	30	37

Eucharist 'the body and blood, together with the soul and divinity, of our Lord Jesus Christ and, therefore, *the whole Christ is truly, really, and substantially* contained'" (#1374, italics in original, 1995: 383). This is a key doctrine of the faith and a teaching that sets Catholics apart from most other Christians.

However, for many Catholics there is a gap between their knowledge of the Church's teaching regarding the real presence and what their beliefs are. Interestingly enough, many Catholics believe what their church teaches even when they do not know that their church teaches it. Perhaps this is just a classic case of source amnesia—people believe many things that they have learned even though they are unable to recall the source of that belief. It turns out, though, that what people believe is at least as important to their practice of the faith as what they know.

To explore the implications of this gap, we asked both a knowledge question and a belief question in our 2011 survey. We found that half of adult Catholics (50 percent) knew the Church's teaching regarding the real presence and half did not. We also found that close to two-thirds of adult Catholics (63 percent) believed that "at the consecration during a Catholic Mass, the bread and wine really become the body and blood of Jesus Christ." Therefore, more Catholics believed the statement about the real presence of Christ in the Eucharist than understood its source as a doctrinal teaching of the Church. But how are these two items related? Is it important to know what the Church teaches regarding the real presence, or is believing that Christ is present in the Eucharist sufficient for one to be a "good enough" Catholic? After all, 4 in 10 Catholics in our survey agreed with the statement, "A person can be a good Catholic without believing that in the Mass, the bread and wine really become the body and blood of Jesus."

These two questions on belief in and knowledge of the real presence can be used to place Catholics into four distinct types. (See Figure 6.3) The first are the **knowledgeable believers** who know what the Church teaches regarding the Eucharist and also express a belief in this teaching. Not quite half of adult Catholics in this study (46 percent) are knowledgeable believers.

The opposite of this type, and the second largest group in size (33 percent of respondents), are the **unknowing unbelievers**. They do not know what the Church teaches regarding the Eucharist nor do they believe in this teaching. Among all those Catholics who do not know what the Church teaches regarding the real presence, two-thirds are in this type.

A third type, **unknowing believers**, actually believe in the real presence but do not know what the Church teaches about this. Instead, they believe wrongly that the Church teaches that the bread and wine are only symbols of the body and blood of Jesus Christ. This group constitutes 17 percent of all

Catholics, but they make up a third of the Catholics who do not know what the Church teaches regarding this doctrine.

A final type, only 4 percent of respondents, is the **knowledgeable doubters**. These Catholics are aware of what the Church teaches but say they do not believe it. Among all Catholics who know what the Church teaches about the real presence, fewer than 1 in 10 (9 percent) say that they do not believe the doctrine.

Using a statistical technique called logistic regression, we can describe some of the characteristics that are typical among Catholics of each type. For example, the typical knowledgeable believer is a white, Vatican II or post–Vatican II Catholic (born between 1941 and 1978) from the South or the Midwest, who has not gone to college and votes Independent. This type tends to be moderately (but not highly) committed to the Church, attends Mass weekly, prays daily, and says they will never leave the Church.

The typical unknowing unbeliever, a third of adult Catholics, is more likely to be a white, Vatican II or post–Vatican II Catholic who lives in the Northeast and votes Democrat or Independent (but not Republican). This type seldom or never attends Mass, seldom or never prays, and says they might consider leaving the Church (although they still identify themselves as Catholic).

The third largest type, the unknowing believer (17 percent of adult Catholics) is a little more challenging to classify, as they are not concentrated in a particular generation. The typical unknowing believer is Hispanic and

		Knowledge: Which of the following statements best describes the Catholic teaching about the bread and wine used for Communion?	
		1) The bread and wine really become the body and blood of Jesus Christ. (50%)	2) The bread and wine are only symbols of the body and blood of Jesus Christ. (50%)
Belief: Do you believe that at the Consecration during a Catholic Mass, the bread and wine really become the body and blood of Jesus Christ?	1) Yes, does happen (63%)	I. Knowledgeable Believers: (46%) Among those that know, 91% believe	II. Unknowing Believers: (17%) Among those that do not know, 33% believe
	2) No, does not happen (37%)	III. Knowledgeable Doubters: (4%) Among those that know, 9% do not believe	IV: Unknowing Unbelievers: (33%) Among those that do not know, 65% do not believe

Figure 6.3 Four District Types of Catholics

lives in the Midwest or West. This type is more likely to be a Democrat or an Independent than a Republican and typically has not attended college. They are committed to the Church, although they attend Mass irregularly.

The fourth type is the knowledgeable doubter. This type is only 4 percent of adult self-identified Catholics. The typical member of this group is a millennial Catholic (born in 1979 or later) who is white, college educated, and living in the Northeast or the West. They are irregular Mass attendees but pray daily. They are more likely to have a moderate to high commitment to the Church, although they say they might consider leaving.

Despite the variation among these four types in terms of their characteristics and even their religious practice, their motivations for attending Mass are surprisingly consistent. We asked these Catholics to tell us, among a half-dozen different motivations, which is a very important reason for them to attend church. Across all four types, at least three in four said that an important reason for them is they enjoy experiencing the liturgy. The experience is apparently rewarding and meaningful even if they do not share the same intellectual understanding of it.

Similarly, more than half to about two-thirds said that an important reason for attending is that they enjoy being with others in church. Again, the experience of being with others is an important motivation for all four types.

Finally, all four types also agreed that feeling the need to receive the sacrament of Communion is an important reason why they attend. Although a majority within each type agreed that this is an important reason, the believers were even more likely than the unbelievers to say that this is an important reason for them to attend Mass. Believing in the real presence adds meaning to their experience of the sacrament, whether or not they understand that this is also what the Church teaches.

Participation at Mass and in Parish Life

Before Vatican II, when the Mass was said in Latin by a priest standing with his back to the congregation, there was little for lay Catholics to do but pray silently, follow along in their missal (if they had one), and sit, stand, kneel, and sing at the appropriate times. After Vatican II, the Mass suddenly became a much livelier place for lay Catholics. The priest faced the congregation and spoke in English (or the vernacular of the particular country where the Mass was being celebrated) with the congregation responding in the same language, either in song or in prayer. The liturgical roles for lay people also expanded, so that in addition to ushering people to their seats and singing or leading song, lay Catholics could be trained for service as lectors (readers), altar servers (assisting the priest at Mass), and extraordinary ministers of Communion (assisting in the distribution of Communion). (See Table 6.4)

Some lay Catholics are taking advantage of these opportunities to more actively participate in the Mass. Among Catholics who say they attend Mass at least monthly, one in three has served as a lector, one in four as a greeter or usher, one in five as an altar server or as a music minister, and one in six as an extraordinary minister of Communion (Eucharistic minister).

The role of usher or greeter, which predated Vatican II, shows little variation across generations. Vatican II generation Catholics, who no longer have children to monitor (like the younger generations have) and are more mobile than many of the pre–Vatican II generation, are a little more likely than the other generations to serve as ushers or greeters at Mass. Pre–Vatican II Catholics are more likely than the younger generations to have participated in music ministry, perhaps singing in a choir or playing an instrument. This role (music minster) also predated Vatican II. Many pre–Vatican II Catholics have fond memories of choral hymns in Latin or Gregorian chant performed by a choir.

The ministry of lector, which is a new role for lay people, is being adopted more by the younger generations. Just 1 in 10 regularly attending pre–Vatican II Catholics has ever served as a lector, compared to a third of post–Vatican II or millennial Catholics who are attending Mass at least monthly. Among post–Vatican II Catholics, Hispanics are more likely than non-Hispanics to have served as a lector.

The role of extraordinary minister of Communion (or Eucharistic minister, as it is often called) is also new since Vatican II but is less common among those of any generation. No more than a fifth of regular Mass attenders of any generation has served as an extraordinary minister of Communion.

In fact, Catholics appear to be somewhat reluctant to become involved in parish life outside of Mass. As we saw in chapter 2, 2 in 3 Catholics

Table 6.4   Participation In Liturgical Ministries among Regular Mass Attenders (percentage serving within each generation)

	Pre–Vatican II %	Vatican II %	Post–Vatican II %	Millennial %
Lector	10	28	34	35
Usher/greeter	19	30	20	23
Altar server	12	24	17	27
Music ministry	30	17	16	20
Eucharistic minister	17	20	13	13

agree that most Catholics don't want to take on leadership roles in their parish. We found evidence of that reluctance in another question on the survey. We asked lay Catholics if they have ever served as a member of a parish committee, and just 17 percent said that they have. Even among those who attend Mass at least monthly, only 3 in 10 have served on a parish committee. Pre–Vatican II and Vatican II Catholics are twice as likely as younger Catholics (43 and 39 percent, respectively, compared to 19 and 24 percent of younger Catholics) to have served on a parish committee. Post–Vatican II Hispanics are a little more likely than non-Hispanics of that generation to have served on a parish committee (16 percent compared to 9 percent).

Religious Practice beyond the Parish

One behavior that we are exploring for the first time in this survey is Catholics' participation in other religious or faith-sharing groups, apart from or in addition to their participation in Mass. These groups are relatively new, and there is little in the sociological literature about them (see Lee and D'Antonio 2000).

We asked about participation in four specific types of religious groups: (1) RENEW, which is a spiritual renewal, small-group faith-sharing process that began in the Archdiocese of Newark in 1976 and has spread around the world; (2) an intentional Eucharistic community, which is a small faith community, rooted in the Catholic tradition, that gathers outside the parish setting to celebrate Eucharist on a regular basis; (3) some other type of small Christian community (or faith-sharing group); or (4) a Hispanic/Latino religious community. Each of these groups involves typically a relatively small number (less than 100) of regular participants who come together for faith-sharing and community-building activities. Some, like RENEW, are organized within a parish and others, like intentional Eucharistic communities, more often operate independently from a parish.

Although these religious groups have been operating for 40 years or more, they are still relatively uncommon experiences for most Catholics. Only about 15 percent of Catholics report they have ever been a member of a small Christian community, 9 percent have been a member of a Hispanic/Latino religious community, 7 percent have participated in RENEW, and just 4 percent have participated in an intentional Eucharistic community. In general, pre–Vatican II Catholics are more likely than post–Vatican II or millennial Catholics to have participated in RENEW or in another small Christian community (or faith-sharing group). On the other hand, millennial Catholics are more likely than pre–Vatican II Catholics to have participated in a Hispanic/Latino religious community.

Not surprisingly, Hispanics are more likely than non-Hispanics to have participated in a Hispanic/Latino religious community (25 percent compared to 2 percent, respectively), but Hispanics are also a little more likely than non-Hispanics to report participating in a small Christian community (21 percent compared to 12 percent). This is an emerging trend that bears watching as it could have important implications for the shape of parish life in the future.

We combined those who said they have participated in any of these four types of small faith communities and compared them to those who have never participated in any of them to look for characteristics that distinguish Catholics who participate in these extraparochial groups from those who do not. One in five Catholics has participated in at least one of these small faith communities. We found that there are some interesting differences between those who participated in these groups and those who do not.

Catholics in these small faith communities look very much like those who are not. Women and men belong in equal proportion, all generations and all political parties are represented, as are all races and ethnicities—in fact, half of those participating in one of these small faith communities are Hispanic. They are no more likely than other Catholics to have attended Catholic schools, although there is an association for non-Hispanics between small faith communities and attendance at a Catholic college. On the other hand, they are more likely than other Catholics to have been married in the Church and to have a Catholic spouse. They are also more likely than other Catholics to score high on our commitment index (39 percent, compared to 14 percent among those who do not belong to one of these groups).

In general, participation in these small faith communities is associated with stronger Catholic identity and practice. For example, members of these groups are more likely than other Catholics in general to say that each of these is "very" important to them as a Catholic: belief in the resurrection (92 percent), the sacraments (86 percent), teachings about Mary as the Mother of God (81 percent), helping the poor (80 percent), regular daily prayer life (70 percent), opposition to abortion (64 percent), participating in devotions (60 percent), church involvement in social justice (57 percent), opposition to same-sex marriage (54 percent), the teaching authority of the Vatican (52 percent), and opposition to the death penalty (51 percent).

In addition, Catholics who participate in these small faith communities are more likely than those who do not to agree strongly that the sacraments of the Church are essential to their relationship with God (65 percent), that being a Catholic is a very important part of who they are (64 percent), that it is important to them that younger generations of their family grow up as Catholics (57 percent), and that they cannot imagine being anything but Catholic (55 percent). They are more likely than other Catholics who do not participate in these faith groups to say that the Church's emphasis on the sacraments is very meaningful to them personally (67 percent) and that the Church is the most important or among the most important parts of their life (65 percent). Other aspects of the Church they find very meaningful include the fact that the Church is part of an unbroken tradition going back to the apostles (70 percent), that it is universal (68 percent), and the sense of having a shared community with other Catholics (65 percent).

In terms of Catholic practice, participation in small faith communities is associated with higher levels of Mass attendance (57 percent attend Mass at least weekly), more frequent prayer (71 percent pray at least daily), and active participation in parish life. Members of these small faith communities are more likely than other Catholics to be registered in a parish (78 percent) and to have served as a member of a parish committee (48 percent) or as a reader at Mass (42 percent), an extraordinary minister of Communion (28 percent), an usher (34 percent), an altar server (30 percent), or in music ministry (30 percent). They are more likely than those who do not participate in such groups to *disagree* that you can be a good Catholic without donating time or money to help the poor (53 percent), without donating time or money to help the parish (39 percent), or without one's marriage being approved by the Church (42 percent).

Catholics who participate in small faith communities also tend to be more supportive of the bishops than those who do not participate in these groups. For example, they are more likely to agree that the bishops should have the final say in deciding the moral authority of things such as a divorced Catholic remarrying without an annulment (32 percent), birth control (18 percent), free choice regarding abortion (30 percent), homosexual activity (27 percent), or sexual relations outside of marriage (25 percent). They are more likely to *disagree* that church leaders are out of touch with the laity (51 percent). They are more likely to express satisfaction with the leadership of the bishops in general (81 percent) and with their local bishop (83 percent), and they are more likely to say they try to follow the bishops' guidance and instructions on political and public policy matters (15 percent) or at least take into consideration what the bishops have to say on such matters (67 percent).

Participation in these small faith communities is *not* associated with particular attitudes about parish life or leadership, reasons for attending or not attending Mass regularly, attitudes about women's roles in the church, support for the bishops' positions on government policy, or attitudes about their handling of the sex abuse crisis. Some have speculated that participation in a small faith community might reduce a person's attachment to the parish, but that does not appear to be the case.

Conclusion

While Catholic identity and core beliefs have remained relatively consistent across the 25 years documented by these surveys, the way Catholics practice their faith has changed in some important ways. Many of these changes are related, at least in part, to the dramatic demographic changes that have characterized the Catholic experience in the United States in this quarter century. For example, Catholics are less likely now than they were 25 years ago to be married in the Church or to be married to another Catholic. Some of this change is related to greater openness and acceptance among Catholics toward people of other faiths, but much of the change is simply due to the fact that Catholics no longer live in the ethnic Catholic neighborhoods or attend the Catholic schools that isolated earlier generations. Catholics live in the same pluralistic culture as other Americans, and this experience is changing the way they practice their faith.

Catholics are also less likely to be registered in a parish than they were 25 years ago, but again this is related to demographics. The increased number of Hispanic Catholics explains the difference in parish registration, as non-Hispanic Catholics are still registered at the same rate as before. Hispanic Catholics, many of whom have immigrated to the United States from other countries that do not share the expectation that one should register in a parish, are less likely to register in a parish. Weekly Mass attendance has also declined as the pre–Vatican II generation, who grew up with a very strong cultural expectation of weekly attendance, is gradually being replaced with Catholics who hold that attending Mass at least monthly is good enough.

While Catholics' appreciation for the Eucharist remains central to their belief, fully half do not know what it is that the Church teaches about the Eucharist—that the body and blood of Jesus Christ is really present in the bread and wine that make up the sacrifice of the Mass. Nevertheless, 2 in 3 believe that this is true, whether they know that this is what the Church teaches or not. Only a very small percentage of mostly younger Catholics know this teaching and reject it as a belief.

Although opportunities for more active participation in the liturgical life of the parish have broadened since Vatican II, most Catholics still limit their participation to attendance at Mass. Among Catholics who attend Mass at least monthly, only a third or fewer participate in any of the liturgical roles such as lector, usher, or music minister. This may gradually change, though, as Catholic parishes grow ever larger and the numbers of priests available to staff them continue to decline. Perhaps the next survey will shed more light on this.

As for extra-parochial participation in small faith group experiences, our data indicate that non-Hispanics of the pre–Vatican II and Vatican II generations tend to participate in Small Christian Communities and RENEW groups, while Hispanics of the post–Vatican II and millennial generations are more likely to participate in the Hispanic small groups. Participation in these groups is associated with strong Catholic identity, regular participation in parish life, and support for the hierarchy of the Church. This suggests that, while the composition of the small groups is changing, their impact on Catholic identity and participation in parish life is not.

The next chapter examines Catholics' voting behavior and political participation. We explore how Catholic identification with a political party has changed over time and look at the ways that Catholic identity affects political participation.

CHAPTER SEVEN

~

Religion and Party Politics

"There is no Catholic vote—and it's important!" said E.J. Dionne explaining how the Catholic vote has turned into a swing vote in national elections. He contends that

> [it's] very hard for Republicans to get less than 40 percent of the Catholic vote, and it's hard for Democrats to get less than 40 percent. But in any given election you will have 15 to 20 percent of the Catholic vote that is in play. One of the most interesting things about the Catholic vote is that Catholics almost always vote for the winner. That's because they are diverse philosophically, but also diverse ethnically and racially. [Besides] you do have this real difference between those Catholics who lay the heaviest stress on the church's social justice tradition and those who lay the heaviest stress on abortion and gay marriage and stem cell research. (Dionne 2012: 1)

Mitt Romney, the 2012 Republican candidate for president selected Representative Paul Ryan (R-WI) as his running mate. Ryan, a Catholic and chair of the House Budget Committee, not only is a Catholic standard-bearer for the Church's stand on abortion and gay marriage, but also claims to be the Church's standard-bearer for his understanding of the Church's teachings on social justice (Rowe and Winters, *National Catholic Reporter* 2012: 5). The Democratic Vice President, Joe Biden, also is a Catholic, with a long history of support for the Church's social teachings. And he supports the Roe v. Wade Supreme Court decision. The Catholic vote was, indeed, contested in the 2012 election.

American Catholics are now the largest denomination in the United States, at just under 25 percent of the population. They have played an increasingly active role in local and national politics through their ability to organize their various ethnic groups into effective party organizations. A dominant Catholic vote can be traced back to FDR, the New Deal, and the urban ethnic political organizations, primarily Democratic, in control of most cities along the East Coast and west to Chicago. The Democratic Catholic vote reached its peak (near 80 percent) with the election of John F. Kennedy in 1960, the first and so far the only Catholic elected to the presidency. The assassination of President Kennedy in 1963 raised Vice President Lyndon B. Johnson to the presidency, and in 1964, he was elected in a landslide with the Catholic vote again near 80 percent. Hubert Humphrey garnered 57 percent of the Catholic vote in 1968 in his loss to Nixon; in 1976, Jimmy Carter won the presidency with 54 percent of the Catholic vote (see Table 7.1). But in 1980, it was Reagan who wooed and won 50 percent of the Catholic vote; and Reagan won 54 percent in the 1984 election (Carty 2008: 184, 187).

The Catholic population continued to grow during the next three decades, and as their levels of education, occupation, and income increased, Catholics moved to the suburbs and to the South. Party identity slowly shifted, especially during the Reagan years. In 1988, about the same percentage of Catholics (45 percent) identified with each party, with increasing evidence of Republicans having closed the gap (Leege et al. 2002: 161; see Figure 7.1). In 2004, Catholics gave George W. Bush a majority (52 percent) of their votes, thus helping to defeat Senator John Kerry, a Catholic who many Catholics and some bishops believed was not Catholic enough. Disillusion with the wars in Iraq and Afghanistan, and Bush's efforts to privatize Social Security, led to another boost for the Democrats in 2006. In 2008, Obama won the presidency with 54 percent of the Catholic

Table 7.1   The Catholic Vote for President, by Party, 1968 to 2012 (in percentages)

Party	1968 %	1972 %	1976 %	1980 %	1984 %	1988 %	1992 %	1996 %	2000 %	2004 %	2008 %	2012 %
Democratic	56	39	57	41	46	52	50	55	50	47	54	50
Republican	37	59	41	50	54	47	30	37	49	52	45	48

Note: Percentages do not always add to 100% due to votes cast for third party candidates.

Source: National Election Studies, from CARA's direct tabulations from NES data series. NES estimates are based on post-election surveys. Published by Center for Applied Research in the Apostolate (CARA), Georgetown University, cara@georgetown.edu.

vote, promising to pass a new health care bill, end the war in Iraq, and to lead the country in a new direction. The new health care bill included provision of contraceptive and gynecologic assistance to all women. That created new tensions with the Catholic bishops in 2012, leading several bishops to public condemnation of President Obama and his administration. Nevertheless, in the 2012 election, President Obama again won the Catholic vote with 50 percent of Catholics voting for the president and 48 percent for Mitt Romney. Although Romney won the white non-Hispanic Catholic vote by 59 percent to 40 percent, Obama won the Hispanic vote, 75 percent to 21 percent. It was that large margin that made the difference, especially in such swing states as Colorado, Nevada, and New Mexico.

Catholics in Congress: Changes over Time

Table 7.2 shows a growing Catholic presence in the U.S. House and Senate going back to 1960. Of the 90 Catholics in the U.S. House in 1960, 76 were Democrats and 14 were Republicans. In the Senate, the 12 Catholics were all Democrats. The dominance of Catholic Democrats in Congress persisted through the 2008 elections. Of the 256 Democrats elected to the House in 2008, 96 were Catholics. Among the 179 Republicans elected, 41 were Catholic. In the Senate 17 of the 57 Democrats were Catholic, with 9 Catholics among the 41 Republicans.

The 2008–2009 recession, with its massive job losses, the housing mortgage collapse, and the battles over the new health care bill in 2009 and 2010, led to a major turnaround in 2010. The Republicans regained control of the House with 242 Republicans, of whom 63 were Catholics (a gain of 22); among the 193 Democrats, 69 were Catholic (a loss of 27 seats).[1] In the Senate, where change is slower, the 2010 elections found the Democrats in

Table 7.2 Catholic Members of the U.S. Senate and House of Representatives, by Party, 1960 to 2012 (actual numbers)

	1960	1970	1980	1984	1988	1992	1996	2000	2004	2008	2010	2012
Catholic Senators												
Democrats	12	10	10	9	13	13	12	14	14	17	15	17
Republicans	0	3	4	9	6	8	9	11	11	9	9	9
Catholic Representatives												
Democrats	76	72	82	88	82	75	75	76	72	96	69	73
Republicans	14	24	24	38	49	35	52	50	49	41	63	61

control with 51 seats, including 15 Catholics, and the Republicans with 47 seats, 9 of whom were Catholic. Two Independents caucus with the Democrats. The 2012 elections included small losses by the Republicans (9 House seats and 2 Senate seats). The Republican majority (233) now includes 61 Catholics, while the Democrats include 73 Catholics. The results over the past several elections suggest that election outcomes may be explained by the influence of local concerns and the degree of fit of one's religion with party ideology. Increasingly, as Dionne noted, one party gives moral weight to sexual issues like abortion, same-sex marriage, stem-cell research, and a strong religious fundamentalism. The other party focuses more moral weight on the issues of social justice and respect for science.

In this setting, the Catholic vote still counts, as both parties strive to attract Catholics with their increasingly distinctive ideologies and Catholic candidates.

Our 2011 survey provides an opportunity to glimpse the degree to which American Catholics reflect the ideologies of the two parties and how these leanings correlate with their core religious beliefs, religious practices, and attitudes toward many of the hot-button political issues in contemporary American society. We begin with a review of how Catholics' party identity has changed over time.

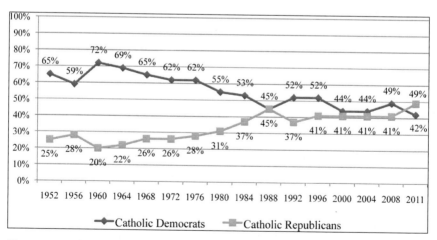

Figure 7.1 White, Non-Latino American Catholics, by Party Identification, 1952–2011

Source: Leege et al. (2002: 161). If Hispanic/Latino Catholics were added, the Democratic figures would be higher. See also Bliss Institute, Akron University, Fourth National Survey on Religion (2004). For 2008 and 2011 figures, please see "Trends in Party Identification by Religion," the Pew Forum on Religion and Public Life (2011).

American Catholics and Party Affiliation: A Demographic Profile of Change over Time

Figure 7.1 presents a 60-year review of white, non-Latino American Catholics by party affiliation. Democratic dominance among white Catholics has been declining since 1960. If blacks and Latinos were added, the Democratic figures would be higher (see Table 7.3). In recent elections, white Catholics have been about split between the two parties, with Democrats depending more and more on blacks, Latinos, Native Americans, Arabs, and Asian Americans to maintain a party advantage. As the 2012 election year gathered steam, African Americans (about 2 percent Catholic), who currently constitute about 13 percent of the U.S. population, were more than 90 percent Democratic. Latinos constitute 16 percent of the U.S. population. They account for 32 percent of the U.S. Catholic population, and in our 2011 survey, 73 percent said they were Democrats and 23 percent Republicans. Other national polls showed Latinos giving the Democratic Party a 3 to 1 lead.

In 2011, our fifth survey, respondents identified themselves as strong, not strong, or leaning toward the Republican or Democratic Party. We examined the data first by placing the strong and not strong Democrats or Republicans into their respective parties. Those leaning toward one or the other party were labeled Independents and were grouped with self-identified Independents. The result from this arrangement was Republicans (22 percent), Democrats (36 percent), and Independents (41 percent). We then added those Independents leaning toward one or the other party to that party, and the results were Republicans (40 percent), a gain of 18 percent from the Independent leaners; Democrats (57 percent), a gain of 21 percent from the Independent leaners. In this second run, the percentage of Independents who claimed no party identity was reduced to 3 percent. We then compared the leaners separately as either Democrats or Republicans on beliefs, attitudes, and practices, and in almost all items the differences between the leaners and their parties were not significant. For our analysis of the survey data, we used the party figures that were most inclusive: 57 percent Democrats, 40 percent Republicans, and 3 percent Independent. Since Independents were only 3 percent of the survey sample, we did not include these Independents in the analysis.

Several patterns are clear from Table 7.3. Democrats are in the majority by ratios of almost 3 to 2 in overall party affiliation and with women and men. They are also a majority among all four generations. With the millennial generation, however, the Democratic Party lead is only 10 percentage points. Moreover, the Democratic advantage disappears when we look only

Table 7.3   Demographic Profile of American Catholics, by Party Identification (in percentages)

	Republicans %	Democrats %
Gender		
Male	40	56
Female	40	57
Is your marriage approved by the Church? (percent responding "yes")	69	67
Is your spouse Catholic (percent responding "yes")	77	78
Party Affiliation (within each generation)		
Pre–Vatican II	38	62
Vatican II	40	57
Post–Vatican II	40	57
Millennials	45	55
Ethnicity (within part percentages)		
Hispanics	12	40
Non-Hispanic	88	60
Ethnicity (within each ethnic group)		
Hispanics	23	73
Non-Hispanic, white	49	49
All others (5% of total N)	41	59
Education		
Less than high school	9	17
High school	26	38
Some college	30	24
BA or more	36	22
Catholic School Education		
Primary school	44	33
High school	22	17
College	10	7
Income		
$100,000 or more	29	18
Less than $25,000	17	28
$25,000–$49,000	21	37
$50,000–$99,999	33	27

at white, non-Hispanic Catholics; in this situation, the parties are tied at 49 percent. With the white, non-Hispanic women, 52 percent are Democrats and 48 percent Republicans. The reverse is true of the men, with 48 percent Democrats and 52 percent Republicans. Hispanic Catholics are a growing part of the Catholic population and, as noted earlier, our survey found them favoring the Democrats by 73 percent to 23 percent. Democrats also enjoy a 6 to 4 advantage among the other ethnic groups (blacks, Native Americans, Asians, and other) who constitute 5 percent of the Catholic total.

Catholic Republicans are much less ethnically diverse in our survey, with 88 percent of party members being non-Hispanic whites. There are significant differences in levels of formal education between the parties. Only 10 percent of the Republican Catholics have less than a high school education, while 2 out of 3 have some college, with more than 1 in 3 having a bachelor's degree or more. In contrast, more than half of the Democrats have a high school education or less, with only 1 in 5 having a bachelor's degree or more. The educational differences are reflected also in income levels: less than 1 in 5 (17 percent) Republicans reported annual incomes under $25,000 (the current poverty level), while among Democrats almost 3 in 10 (28 percent) reported that income level. At the top income level, 3 in 10 Republicans reported incomes of $100,000 or more, true of only 18 percent of Democrats. Republicans also reported more Catholic school education, although the numbers were not significantly different. As we will see in chapter 8, much of the difference between Democrats and Republicans in education and income is a function of the new waves of immigrants from Latin America in the past 40 years.

Catholic Identity and Religiousness among Democrats and Republicans

Reports in the media based on national surveys, especially when focused on election matters, indicate that the more religious the American, the more likely is he or she to be a Republican. The Gallup report of April 25, 2012, explained its findings this way:

> For the purpose of this analysis, an American's relative degree of religiousness is based on responses to two questions, asking about the importance of religion in one's life and about church attendance, yielding three groups: Very religious—Religion is an important part of daily life and church/synagogue/mosque attendance occurs at least every week or almost every week. This group makes up 41 percent of registered voters interviewed April 19–23. Moderately religious—All others who do not fall into the very religious or nonreligious

groups but who gave valid responses on both religion questions. This group makes up 27 percent of registered voters. Nonreligious—Religion is not an important part of daily life and respondents seldom or never attend church/synagogue/mosque. This group makes up 32 percent of registered voters.

On May 2, 2012, Gallup released the following follow-up statement: "As a general rule in today's political world, the more religious the American, the more likely he or she is to be a Republican and vote for Republican candidates." Gallup went on to state that "[t]his rule of thumb is evident among white Catholic voters."

Our survey provides an opportunity to measure the degree of religiousness of American Catholics, and also among white Catholics only. In discussing political affiliation differences among our Catholic respondents, we first used two questions that are similar to those used by Gallup to measure religiousness, and then we expanded on the number of questions that we believe provide a more in-depth measure of a Catholic's degree of religiousness—the nature of his or her Catholic commitment. Here we look for similarities and differences in Catholic identity and commitment among Democrats and Republicans.

We found only minor differences (within the margin of error) between Catholic Republicans and Democrats on Mass attendance rates, either among those who go to Mass every week, or those who seldom or never attend Mass (see Table 7.4). Nor did the exclusion of Hispanics make any difference. We found the same pattern in our 2005 survey, the first time we asked people for their political party affiliation (D'Antonio et al. 2007).

Our second measure of religiousness involved essentially the same question as the Gallup poll used, namely, determining how important the Church is in one's life. Our question was "How important is the Catholic Church to you personally?" We found no significant differences between white/

Table 7.4 Mass Attendance of Catholic Democrats and Republicans

Mass Attendance	All Catholics*		White Non-Hispanic Catholics**	
	Republicans %	Democrats %	Republicans %	Democrats %
At least weekly	34	29	31	28
Two to three times a month	13	12	12	9
Once a month	8	9	9	8
A few times a year	23	26	25	26
Seldom or never	21	24	23	29

*Percentages include Catholics of all races/ethnicities
**Percentages include only white, non-Hispanic Catholics

non-Hispanic Republicans and Democrats, with 40 percent of Republicans and 35 percent of Democrats saying it is the most important or among the most important influences on their lives. At the other end of the spectrum, 3 percent of the Republicans and 4 percent of the Democrats say it is not very or not at all important. There were no differences either when only non-Hispanic white Catholics are compared.

In chapter 3, we examined how Catholics sort out and distinguish the aspects of Catholicism that are very important to their identity as Catholics. Our review of those aspects in Table 7.5 showed again that there is agreement across party lines regarding their relative importance for all Catholics, as well as for white, non-Hispanic Catholics. A majority of both parties see the Resurrection, the Sacraments, and the Church's teachings about Mary as the church teachings most important to them as Catholics. However, Catholic Democrats are significantly more supportive than Catholic Republicans of the core aspect of helping the poor.

In addition, an equal proportion of Catholic Democrats and Republicans said that a daily prayer life and devotional activities such as the rosary are similarly important to between a third and a half of them, with and without

Table 7.5 Percentages of Democrats and Republicans Who Say These Aspects of Catholicism Are Very Important to Them Personally

	All Catholics		White Non-Hispanic Catholics	
	Republicans %	Democrats %	Republicans %	Democrats %
Belief in Jesus's resurrection	76	71	75	65
The sacraments (e.g., Eucharist, etc.)	65	61	64	59
Church teachings about Mary Mother of God	64	63	61	59
Helping the poor	61	72	58	68
Having a regular daily prayer life	50	44	46	38
Participating in devotions (praying the rosary)	36	35	32	27
Teaching Authority claimed by the Vatican	33	28	29	23
A celibate male clergy	23	19	21	16
Social justice activities	28	37	25	30
Church teachings opposing same-sex marriage	40	31	39	26
Church teachings opposing the death penalty	22	33	17	24
Church teachings opposing abortion	48	35	45	27

controlling for the Hispanic vote. An interesting finding is that regardless of the importance to them personally, the addition of the Hispanics in the count added from 1 to 5 percentage points to the totals, in rating the importance of the particular aspect to their Catholic identity. In no cases did it change the direction of the importance.

Only a minority of either party said the teaching authority claimed by the Vatican is very important to them. An even smaller minority said a male celibate clergy is very important to them, and almost half said it is not important at all.

Again, only a minority of Democrats and Republicans said social justice activities[2] and opposing the death penalty are very important to them. On the other two issues, opposing same-sex marriage and opposing abortion, Republicans are significantly more likely than are the Democrats to say these aspects are very important to them, thus maintaining the pattern that the Republicans are more in line with the bishops' teachings on these aspects of human sexuality than are the Democrats. The Democrats identify more strongly than Republicans with the bishops' teachings centering on helping the poor and social justice activities and, also, to some degree, opposition to the death penalty. The Hispanic vote tends to increase support for the bishops' position by 5 to 9 percentage points, but the overall pattern does not change. Thus, we find that Catholic Democrats and Republicans reflect the positions taken

Table 7.6   Percentages of Republicans and Democrats Who Say "You Can Be a Good Catholic" without . . .

	All Catholics		White Non-Hispanic Catholics	
	Republicans %	Democrats %	Republicans %	Democrats %
Going to Mass every Sunday	76	80	80	89
Obeying the Church's teaching on birth control	76	80	79	92
Obeying the Church's teaching on divorce/remarriage	67	73	68	83
Obeying the Church's teaching on abortion	53	65	56	73
Marriage being approved by the Church	68	75	70	82
Donating time/money to help the poor	62	59	65	65
Donating time/money to help the parish	72	76	73	83
Believing in the Real Presence in the Eucharist	36	42	36	47
Believing in Jesus's resurrection	27	35	26	42

by the political parties with which they identify, although their support or opposition does not appear to be as polarized as we find in the votes in Congress.

Another important measure of Catholic identity is the way Catholics think about who is a "good Catholic." As shown earlier in chapters 1 and 3, Catholic opinions about who is a good Catholic reflect a very personal reliance on conscience rather than on the Church's doctrine. We find this same pattern when we compared Democrats and Republicans, both including and withholding the growing Hispanic vote (Table 7.6). Half or more of Republicans and Democrats agree that one can be a good Catholic without obeying the Church's teachings on birth control, divorce and remarriage, abortion, and having one's marriage approved by the church. Again, Hispanic votes tend to reduce the size of the responses for Democrats and for Republicans, but do not change the overall pattern.

These opinions involve matters of personal behavior, and as we have seen in similar type questions, the laity—regardless of party affiliation or whether the vote involves white, non-Hispanic Catholics or includes Hispanics—tends to affirm the right of conscience to decide. Still, even in this setting, Republicans are significantly less likely than are the Democrats to affirm the right of conscience regarding the question of abortion.

There are two aspects of Catholicism about which only a minority of Democrats and Republicans said one can be a good Catholic: Catholic Republicans (27 percent) and Democrats (35 percent) said you can be a good Catholic without believing in Jesus's resurrection, and 36 percent and 42 percent respectively that you can be a good Catholic and not believe in the Real Presence of Christ in the Eucharist. These responses are consistent with their identifying Jesus's resurrection and the sacraments as two of their most important core beliefs.

Table 7.7: Percentages of Republicans and Democrats Saying the Locus of Moral Authority Should Rest with Church Leaders Alone

| | All Catholics | | Non-Hispanic | |
	Republicans %	Democrats %	Republicans %	Democrats %
Divorce and remarriage without an annulment	25	17	24	12
Use of contraception	15	7	14	7
Choice regarding abortion	27	14	28	15
Active homosexuality	22	12	22	13
Nonmarital sex	23	12	22	14

Our findings about where Catholics believe the locus of moral authority should rest on the series of hot-button issues relating to human sexuality have consistently found the laity looking to themselves and their individual consciences rather than to the Church's leaders alone. Over time, the percentages supporting church leaders alone have continued to decline, and more Catholics have suggested that there should be some kind of dialogue between the Church's leaders and the laity to arrive at meaningful decisions. Until such an occurrence should take place, Catholics rely more and more on their own conscience in these matters. Republicans and Democrats are alike in seeing either the individual and her or his conscience, or both (laity and church leaders) in dialogue as the proper locus of moral authority. Again, it is interesting that the Hispanic vote mirrors the non-Hispanic vote very closely.

In sum, a review of all items that dealt with attitudes, beliefs, and practices that focused on commitment to and importance of being a Catholic, importance of personal autonomy and conscience, being active in parish life as reader at Mass or as choir member, experience with RENEW and other small Christian communities revealed Democrats and Republicans to be very much alike in their experience and expression of being Catholic. Differences between them were most notable when questions involved issues that had become politicized. We turn now to take a closer look at these issues.

Catholic Attitudes on Moral Issues Involving Partisan Political Positions

We asked three questions that dealt with partisan political issues that the bishops had been actively involved in during the period since our 2005 survey (see Table 7.7). The bishops opposed the health care bill (Affordable Care Act) because they asserted that it could or would in some way provide financial support for abortions. Two of 3 (68 percent) Catholic Republicans in our survey support the bishops' position; only 4 in 10 (42 percent) Democratic Catholics support the bishops. Similar voting results were found with regard to the bishops' opposition to same-sex marriage. On the third issue, the bishops' support for immigration reform, large majorities of both parties (Republicans 69 percent, Democrats 78 percent) support the bishops. When we remove the Hispanic vote from the totals, we find Republican and Democratic support equal at 68 and 70 percent, respectively.

Larger party differences *are* found in the responses to the five issues derived from *The Challenge of Peace Pastoral* (1983) and the pastoral letter *Economic Justice for All* (1986) that reflect the Church's social teachings in these two major areas (see the second part of Table 7.8). While both parties strongly support the idea of more funds for health care for poor children, the Democrats are significantly more supportive by a margin of 21 and 24 percentage points respectively. On funding for the military, which the bishops opposed, Republicans are significantly more supportive of funding the military (63 percent to 48 percent), reflecting their party position, that is, more funding. On stricter enforcement of the death penalty, a majority of both parties continue to oppose the bishops' plea to end the death penalty.[3] However, Catholic leaders in several states have taken action to abolish the death penalty, as occurred this year in Connecticut. Large majorities of both parties (Republicans 75 percent and Democrats 85 percent) agree with the bishops in their efforts to reduce spending on nuclear weapons. Finally, 7 in 10 Republicans favor further cutbacks in welfare programs, a position taken by only 4 in 10 (42 percent) Democrats.

The key moral issues cited above are part of our national budgets. Perhaps surprisingly, it is the Republican Party that has taken the lead in reframing these moral issues in 2012. Representative Paul Ryan (R-WI), chair of the House Budget Committee, and the Republican Party's vice-presidential candidate, declared that his Catholic faith helped shape the Republican Budget plan for fiscal year 2013 by stressing local control and concern for the poor. Ryan's vision of the common good is that it is best sought at the local level. He also believes that priority must now be given to lowering the federal debt

Table 7.8: Percentages of Republicans and Democrats Who Support the Position Taken by the Catholic Bishops on the Following Issues:

	All Catholics		White/Non-Hispanic	
	Republicans %	Democrats %	Republicans %	Democrats %
Bishops' opposition to health care reform bill	68	42	68	36
Bishops' support for immigration reform	69	78	68	70
Bishops' opposition to same-sex marriage	63	44	64	38
Attitudes toward Church teachings, by party affiliation (percentage agreeing strongly or somewhat)				
More government funds for health care for poor children	68	89	63	87
More government funds for the military	63	48	60	52
Stiffer enforcement of the death penalty	68	58	68	56
Reduced spending on nuclear weapons	75	85	74	89
Further cutbacks in welfare programs	70	42	73	45

and shrinking the federal government, which will require big cuts in federal programs, but excluding the military.

After examining Ryan's budget, Bishop Stephen E. Blaire of Stockton, California, speaking for the Catholic bishops' Committee on Domestic Justice and Human Development, called a proposed cut in benefits for children of immigrants "unjust and wrong." He acknowledged, "Congress faces a difficult task to balance needs and resources and allocate burdens and sacrifices. Just solutions, however, must require shared sacrifice by all, including raising adequate revenues, eliminating unnecessary military and other spending, and fairly addressing the long-term costs of health insurance and retirement programs. The House passed budget resolution fails to meet these moral criteria" (*National Catholic Reporter*, May 11–24, 2012, NATION, 5). Ryan has defended his budget as reflecting the Catholic teachings on the principle of subsidiarity as best he understands it, adding that "a preferential option for the poor does not mean a preferential option for big government" (Ibid.).

There are at least two visions of what the Catholic faith embraces regarding the moral responsibility of government to "provide for the general welfare." Our survey shows that Catholics reflect these two visions: the Republican vision looks more to personal charity and help for the needy through local groups; the Democratic vision sees local action as the first step, but believes that in our society, the federal government has a moral obligation to step in when local and state governments are not able to provide the services that the Catholic Church believes are the birthright of all people. Thus, Social Security, the GI Bill, Medicare, Medicaid, food stamps, and school lunch programs are examples of federal assistance to "the least of these" whom the Church has long supported. Our survey also shows the Catholic laity to be much closer to the middle than to the extremes on such questions as more government funding for health care for poor children and in not making more cutbacks on welfare programs. On the Health Care Reform Act that was passed in March of 2010 (see Table 7.8), we find 2 of 3 Republicans and 6 of 10 Democrats support their party's position. E.J. Dionne may be correct that there is no Catholic vote, but it also seems to be true that in one way or another it does matter.

Conclusion

In the course of the past 65 years, Catholics have become assimilated into the main cultural features of American society, as we have pointed out in the introduction and chapter 1. This cultural assimilation is found also in American political life. It is found especially in the slow but steady process by which the once dominant political ideology of the Democratic Party that attracted large majorities of Catholics to support Democrats as presidential candidates, and House and Senate members, has given way to a situation in which the two parties are more and more evenly matched, even as their ideologies diverge. Thus, the fact that our survey has found that Catholics lean toward the Democratic Party by a three to two ratio is cause for pause.

The survey was taken just six months after the 2010 elections where the Republicans ousted the Democrats from control of the House and reduced the majority Democrats in the Senate to just 51 to 47. While our data show that those Catholics who say they are leaning toward one or the other party seem to be supporting the Democrats more than the Republicans, there is the unknown factor of how many of either party or leaning toward either party will actually register and then cast their vote. The fact that one-third of the Catholic population is now of Hispanic background, and that they seem to favor the Democrats by more than three to one, will be examined in more detail in chapter 8 in which we report on the millennial generation, now 45 percent Hispanic.

We have provided an extensive examination of all the questions in our survey to find evidence that would support or not support the conventional wisdom that Republicans are friendlier to religion than are Democrats. This conventional wisdom is said to hold across all religious groups: we have addressed it here only as regards Catholics. Much of the wisdom seems to be based on a limited number of beliefs and practices, namely church attendance and a personal statement of the Church's importance in one's life. Our findings from those two items do not support those of Gallup. Nor did our findings using those questions in the 2005 survey fit their findings. When we examined all of our questions for signs of differences between Catholic Republicans and Democrats, we found first that the differences or similarities did not change significantly with or without the Hispanic party affiliation, despite the fact the Hispanics are overwhelmingly Democratic. Democrats and Republicans go to Mass about the same rate, sing in choirs, are readers at Mass and Eucharistic ministers, join groups like RENEW and other small Christian Communities, and say they could not imagine being anything other than Catholic.

Catholic Democrats and Republicans do differ, however, when it comes to beliefs or policies that have become politicized. They overwhelmingly assert the primacy of conscience when confronting questions about the locus of moral authority or who can be a good Catholic, but when they look at the political issues like abortion, same-sex marriage, cutting back on welfare programs, and the like, their responses to questions regarding support or opposition mirror the political party they identify with, even if only in a leaning way. They differ in our survey as they differ in the public square, in two distinct directions.

An alternative way to think about which political party is friendlier to religion is to recognize that the answer really depends on which political issues are seen as more or less religious (and moral). If it is religious to hold that the government has a moral responsibility to "reach out to the least of our members" with programs that provide health care to those who otherwise cannot afford it, or food stamps, and so on, then the evidence might be that the Democratic Party is more religious. If, on the other hand, the important moral issues have to do with abortion, same-sex marriage, and small government that believes that concern for the "least of these" is best and only to be handled on the local level, and is not a moral concern of the federal government, then the evidence might support the argument that the Republican Party is friendlier to religion.

It is interesting to note that those Catholics who say they are leaning toward one or the other party mostly responded in the same direction as the party they are leaning toward. What is most clear from our survey is that one would not be able to distinguish Democrats from Republicans at a Catholic Mass based on any of the great quantity of data that our survey provided. Perhaps we should take comfort from the fact that 85 percent of Democrats and Republicans in our fifth survey said that one of the things most meaningful to them as Catholics is that you can disagree with church teachings and still be loyal Catholics.

CHAPTER EIGHT

~

Millennial Catholics

At the beach, faith not forgotten

Isla Vista, a bustling beachside neighborhood that is home to throngs of students attending the University of California, Santa Barbara (UCSB), is not the sort of place where one might expect to meet devout young Catholics. In a friendly place with a beautiful climate and beautiful beaches, there are many things to do. Yet, on any given Sunday evening, and even on weekdays (especially during Lent), one will find many high-spirited young Millennial Catholics at Mass in Saint Mark's Catholic Church, the university parish and Catholic student ministry at UCSB. Prior to the start of Sunday evening Mass, the gathering bustles with students: some warmly greeting each other, some rehearsing as part of the music group, others checking the altar and the assigned readings, and still others in thoughtful contemplation. The tall, well-spoken, and popular pastor, Father John Love, ensures a prayerful and reverential liturgy and is adept at making insightful connections between the day's scriptural readings and the pressing issues in students' lives (homework deadlines, money constraints, unrequited love). At Holy Communion, most avail, though some decline, of the opportunity to receive both the bread and the wine. St. Mark's participants are devout; the adobe-style, white, nondescript building does not have traditional kneelers but nonetheless, most in attendance either find a kneeling cushion or, without hesitation, kneel on the cold floor, heads bowed at the most solemn times.

The St. Mark's gathering captures the changing face of the Catholic Church—a large proportion are of Latino ancestry—coming from Mexico, El Salvador, Peru, and Guatemala, among other countries—and some are first generation for whom Spanish is more natural than English. In addition to the student-oriented Sunday evening Mass, two Masses are celebrated each Sunday morning: one in English, one in Spanish. All the Masses at St. Mark's are well attended, and the church's busy week of activities includes Vespers (immediately after each weekday evening Mass), religious-themed lectures and discussions, scriptural study, and other meeting groups; Blessed Sacrament devotions are held monthly. "Fish on Friday" is a popular Friday evening supper for the community at large, and there are several community service projects each year including a lunch program for homeless people. The annual Spring spiritual retreat is a big attraction.

The students who attend St. Mark's are in the younger age band of the millennial generation. We highlight their religious engagement simply as a snapshot to show that while survey research patterns can paint a general picture that tends to highlight a certain religious indifference among Millennials, it is also true that for many, church involvement and immersion in the Catholic tradition is a meaningful part of their busy, everyday lives.

In the opening chapter, we noted the importance of generation as a variable in the understanding of 20th-century American Catholicism and discussed the distinctiveness of the pre–Vatican II generation: the generation that embodies both the pre–Vatican II Church of Pope Pius XII and the doctrinal and institutional changes of Vatican II. Today the pre–Vatican II generation has dwindled considerably, and the millennial generation is coming into increased prominence. This latter generation, born between 1980 and 1993 (and who in 2011 were in the 18–31 age group), numbers about 15 million in the general U.S. population. It is more racially and ethnically diverse than earlier cohorts. Currently, Hispanics make up 45 percent of Millennials, and within another 30 years or so, it is likely that they will become the majority among American Catholics.

A Demographic Profile of the Millennial Generation

Millennial Catholics are distinguished from previous generations by the substantial presence of Hispanics, a demographic feature that in turn gives rise to additional sociodemographic differences within this generation. Only a minority of Hispanic millennial Catholics (39 percent) have never been married, whereas among non-Hispanics almost two-thirds (62 percent) have not been married. Further, twice as many Hispanics (27 percent) as non-Hispanics (12 percent) are living with a partner. The gap between Hispanics and non-Hispanics is especially evident in the domain of education. Among Hispanic Millennials, 29 percent have not completed high school, whereas this is true of just 3 percent of non-Hispanic Millennials. At the other end of the spectrum, over a third of non-Hispanics (35 percent) but fewer than 1 in 10 of Hispanic Millennials (9 percent) has a college degree (see Table 8.1).

Sociologists have long documented a strong positive relation between levels of educational achievement and personal/household income (e.g., Hout 2005; 2012). The glaring educational gap between Hispanic and non-Hispanic millennial Catholics is reflected in differences in annual family income: half of the Hispanics (52 percent) but only 15 percent of non-Hispanics report family incomes under $25,000; and at the upper end, 7 percent of Hispanics but 47 percent of non-Hispanics report incomes of $75,000 or more. The sociological literature shows that for most of the 20th century, high school graduation rates of Latin Americans, as well as of African Americans and Native Americans, "lagged far behind" those of European ancestry, and at the turn of the 21st century, college graduation rates and income disparities also showed a widening racial/ethnic gap (Fischer and Hout 2006: 12–16). The income and education gaps between young Hispanic and non-Hispanic Catholics today exacerbate the challenges facing Hispanic Millennials in the current period of economic turmoil. The stark education and income differences between Hispanic and non-Hispanic Millennials may also shed light on their different marital patterns, and they are also likely contributing to the notable variation in each ethnic group's political party affiliations. Hispanic Catholics, including those in the millennial generation, are overwhelmingly Democratic (73 percent; 3 to 1), while a majority of non-Hispanic Catholics (55 percent) are Republican (see Table 8.1).

Millennials' Construal of and Attachment to Catholicism

We turn now to the aspects of Catholicism that millennial Catholics see as very important to them personally. Our research over the last few decades has shown that the aspects of Catholicism most likely to be affirmed by American Catholics in general are grounded in the Church's early history: Jesus's resurrection, helping the poor, Mary as the Mother of God, and the sacraments. While both Hispanic and non-Hispanic Millennials say that these beliefs are very important to them personally as Catholics, a greater

Table 8.1   A Demographic Portrait of Hispanic and Non-Hispanic Millennial Catholics (in percentages)

	Hispanic %	Non-Hispanic %
Race/ethnicity	45	55
Marital Status		
Married	31	26
Never married	39	62
Divorced, widowed, or separated	3	5
Living with partner	27	12
Gender		
Male	49	50
Female	51	50
Education		
Some high school or less	29	3
High school grad	38	23
Some college, associate degree	24	39
College graduate and higher	9	35
Catholic Education		
Grade school	17	39
High school	8	21
Catholic college/university	1	12
Income		
Less than $25,000	52	15
$25,000 to $49,999	29	25
$50,000 to $74,999	11	14
$75,000 to $99,999	5	16
$100,000 or more	2	31
Party affiliation (includes those leaning toward one or the other party)		
Republican	25	55
Democrat	71	43
Independent	4	2

percentage of Hispanic than non-Hispanic Millennials endorse the personal importance of these beliefs to them. In addition, half of the Hispanic (52 percent) but only one-third of other Millennials (33 percent) say that

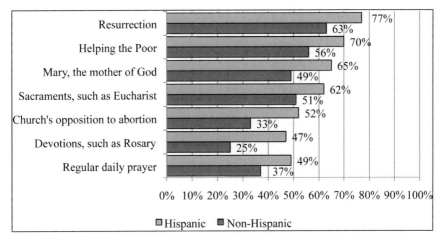

Figure 8.1 Catholic Identity of Millenials: Aspects of Catholicism that are "Very Important"

the Catholic Church's teachings opposing abortion are very important to them. Almost half (49 percent) of the Hispanics say that having an active prayer life is very important to them, while this is true of over a third (37 percent) of the other Millennials. Similarly, far more Hispanic (47 percent) than non-Hispanic (25 percent) Millennials say that devotions such as praying the rosary and adoration of the Eucharist are a very important part of their Catholic identity (see Figure 8.1).

Large majorities of both Hispanic and non-Hispanic Millennials indicate a high level of attachment to Catholicism (see Table 8.2). Thus they affirm that "being Catholic is an important part of who I am," that "the sacraments are essential to my relationship with God," that "it is important to me

Table 8.2   Millennial Catholics' Attachment to Catholicism (percentages strongly or somewhat agreeing)

	Hispanic %	Non-Hispanic %
Being Catholic is an important part of who I am	86	68
Sacraments of the Church are essential to my relationship with God	86	67
Catholicism contains a greater share of truth than do other religions	83	50
Important to me that younger generations of my family grow up Catholic	83	71
I cannot imagine being anything but Catholic	77	62
How a person lives is more important than whether he or she is Catholic	77	89

that younger generations of my family grow up Catholic," and that "I cannot imagine being anything but Catholic." In all instances, however, a larger proportion of Hispanics express these views. Hispanics are also much more likely than non-Hispanics to say Catholicism contains more truth than do other religions, while recognizing along with the non-Hispanics that "how a person lives is more important than whether he or she is Catholic." (See Table 8.2)

The phrase, "being a good Catholic," is deeply embedded in the psyche of American Catholics, and though dating from an earlier era, it is well familiar, too, to millennial Catholics. Hispanics are much less likely than other millennial Catholics to say that one can be a good Catholic without obeying the Church's teachings on divorce and remarriage (52 percent, 76 percent) and on abortion (48 percent, 64 percent), without believing in the Real Presence of Christ in the Eucharist (33 percent, 51 percent), and without belief in Jesus's resurrection (25 percent, 41 percent). Nevertheless, on matters such as going to Mass every Sunday or using artificial contraception, very large majorities of both groups see these matters in ways that are highly independent of official Church teachings. Almost 9 out of 10 non-Hispanics and two-thirds of Hispanics agree that a person can be a good Catholic without adhering to the Church's teaching on contraception (89 percent, 66 percent), or attending weekly Mass (87 percent, 68 percent).

As we found in comparing Hispanic and non-Hispanic Catholics as a whole (see chapter 3), a larger proportion of Hispanic than non-Hispanic Millennials say that the Mass, the Church's history of an unbroken tradition back to the apostles, and its concern for the poor and for the unborn are aspects of Catholicism that are personally very meaningful to them. And although it is a minority Hispanic view, Hispanics (41 percent) are more likely than other millennial Catholics (25 percent) to say that the papacy is very meaningful to them (see Table 8.3).

Table 8.3   Aspects of the Catholic Church That Are Very Meaningful to Millennial Catholics (percentages saying item is very meaningful)

	Hispanic %	Non-Hispanic %
The Mass	62	41
Church's active concern for the poor	56	42
The Church as part of an unbroken tradition	50	36
The Church is universal	52	47
The Church's willingness to stand up for the unborn	51	38
The papacy	41	25

Given that Hispanics are generally more likely than non-Hispanics to affirm the doctrinal and institutional aspects of Catholicism, it is all the more noteworthy that a similar plurality of Hispanic (42 percent) and non-Hispanic (41 percent) millennial Catholics say that the fact that Catholics can disagree with aspects of Church teaching and still remain loyal to the Church is very meaningful to them. Thus, as is true of Catholics as a whole, a significant minority of Millennials feel assured that they can disagree with Church teaching on contraception or divorce, for example, and still value the meaningful significance of the papacy and the Church's larger tradition.

When it comes to the role of the Church in society, Hispanics are significantly more likely than non-Hispanics to advocate an activist role on behalf of social justice (see Table 8.4). A total of 65 percent of Hispanic Millennials, but only 21 percent of non-Hispanic Millennials, strongly agree with the stance the U.S. bishops have taken on immigration reform. Similarly, in keeping with Hispanics' comparatively greater emphasis on the personal importance to them of the Church's concern for the poor (noted above), they are twice as likely as non-Hispanic Millennials (66 percent, 30 percent) to strongly agree that more government funds should be used to provide health care for poor children. There is less division among millennial Catholics regarding the issues of same-sex marriage and health care reform, two issues that dominated public debate at the time of our 2011 survey. Less than a third of Hispanic Millennials (29 percent) and one-quarter of non-Hispanics (24 percent) strongly agree with the bishops' opposition to same-sex marriage, and less than a fifth of Hispanics (19 percent) and non-Hispanics (15 percent) say they strongly agree with the bishops' opposition to the 2010 health care reform bill. Notwithstanding, Hispanics generally show strong support for measures that enhance socioeconomic equality, and the fact that a minority of them support the bishops' opposition to health care reform may derive, in part, from the bishops' publicly reiterated concerns that the reforms would include access to abortion. As we noted above, for a majority of Hispanic Millennials (52 percent), unlike for their non-Hispanic peers (33 percent), opposition to abortion is an aspect of the Church's teaching that is personally very important to them as Catholics.

Millennial Catholics' Views of Mass

The millennial generation, Catholic and non-Catholic alike, is less religiously active than older-age Americans (e.g., Pew Forum 2010; Smith and

Table 8.4 Attitudes toward Social Issues for Millennial Catholics (percentages strongly agreeing)

	Hispanic %	Non-Hispanic %
Stance of U.S. bishops on immigration reform	65	21
More government funds should be used to provide healthcare for poor children	66	30
Bishops' opposition to 2010 healthcare reform	19	15
Bishops' opposition to same-sex marriage	29	24

Snell 2009). Among Catholics, millennial Mass attendance rates are the lowest of all four generations of Catholics today. Whereas one-fifth (20 percent) of millennial Catholics report weekly Mass attendance, close to a third of Vatican II and post–Vatican II cohorts and over a half of pre–Vatican II Catholics do so (see chapter 6). Hispanic millennial women, however, are significantly more likely than their ethnic and same-age peers to be found at weekend Mass, with over a third of them (36 percent) reporting this activity. Despite Millennials' comparatively lower commitment to Mass-going, many of them do value the Mass; as indicated above, among Millennials, 62 percent of Hispanics and 41 percent of non-Hispanics say that the Mass is very meaningful to them, even though they also agree that a person doesn't have to go to Mass every week to be a good Catholic.

Like Catholics as a whole, Millennials enjoy the sacramental and liturgical aspects of Mass. Given the relatively greater general devoutness of Hispanic Millennials, it is interesting that when it comes to the Mass, larger proportions of non-Hispanic than Hispanic Millennials affirm that they "enjoy taking part in the liturgy" (Hispanics 59 percent, non-Hispanics 93 percent) and that they "feel the need for Communion" (non-Hispanics 85 percent, Hispanics 70 percent). Similarly, the non-Hispanic Millennials (74 percent) are more likely than the Hispanics (54 percent) to say that they enjoy being with others in church.

The two groups also differ in the reasons they give for not going to Mass more often. Far more Hispanics (64 percent) than non-Hispanics (39 percent) cite family responsibilities as an important reason for not going more often, and similarly, Hispanics (47 percent) are more likely than others (20 percent) to cite health reasons for not going to Mass more often. For non-Hispanics, the most frequently endorsed reason for not attending Mass more often is the view that "I'm just not a religious person." Further, the idea that "it is not a mortal sin" to miss or not regularly attend Mass was checked by one in five Hispanic and one in three non-Hispanic Millennials.

The Interaction of Gender and Ethnic Differences among Millennial Catholics

Thus far, we have highlighted the ethnic differences among millennial Catholics. There are also, however, some important gender differences and, more specifically, an interaction between ethnicity and gender that points to the emergence of a more finely graded portrait of the millennial generation of American Catholics that may, or may not, take on increased salience with time. A general pattern of findings in our data is that Hispanic millennial women are by and large the most devout and attuned to the Catholic tradition, and non-Hispanic millennial women are the most disengaged from and autonomous of the Church. For example, a much larger proportion of Hispanic millennial women than of any of the other three subgroups—non-Hispanic women, Hispanic men, non-Hispanic men—say that helping the poor, the sacraments, Church opposition to abortion, and devotions such as Eucharistic adoration are aspects of Catholicism that are very important to them personally, and that the Mass, the Church's emphasis on the sacraments, its willingness to stand up for the right to life of the unborn, and the papacy are aspects of Catholicism that are very meaningful to them (see Table 8.5). Further reinforcing these views, far fewer in this than in any other subgroup say that a person can be a good Catholic without obeying the Church's teaching on abortion or without going to Mass every Sunday (see Table 8.5).

Table 8.5   Gender Differences among Millennial Catholics in Their Construal of Catholicism (in percentages)

	Hispanic		Non-Hispanic	
	Women %	Men%	Women %	Men %
Good Catholic without Mass on Sunday (Agree)	62	78	88	85
Good Catholic without obeying on abortion (Agree)	43	54	68	64
Good Catholic without obeying on divorce and remarriage (Agree)	50	58	81	74
Papacy (Very meaningful)	49	37	21	30
Rights of unborn (Very meaningful)	62	44	32	42
Emphasis on Sacraments (Very meaningful)	51	44	37	39
The Mass (Very meaningful)	72	57	41	43
Devotions (Very important)	52	45	20	32
Oppose abortion (Very important)	59	45	30	37
Sacraments (Very important)	66	58	53	51
Helping the poor (Very important)	78	65	53	60

Hispanic millennial women are also by far the most likely to agree, for example, that the sacraments of the Church are essential to their relationship with God, that it is important to them that younger generations of their family grow up Catholic, that being a Catholic is a very important part of who they are, and that they can't imagine being anything but Catholic (see Table 8.6). In short, Hispanic millennial women are the most highly committed of their generation to the Church: in fact, 23 percent of them compared to 11 percent of non-Hispanic millennial Catholic women and 13 percent of millennial men, can be categorized as high commitment Catholics. Overall, they are significantly more likely than their age peers to demonstrate a high level of engagement with the various strands of Catholicism.

By contrast, non-Hispanic millennial women stand out for their apparent disengagement from and indifference toward Catholicism. Compared to their age peers irrespective of gender or ethnicity, they are the least likely to say that helping the poor, devotions, church teaching on abortion and same-sex marriage, and the Vatican's teaching authority are personally very important to them. Similarly, only a small minority of them say that the Church's unbroken tradition back to the apostles, shared community with other Catholics, the Church's willingness to stand up for the right to life of the unborn, and the papacy are aspects of Catholicism that are meaningful

Table 8.6 Gender Differences among Millennial Catholics in Attachment to Catholicism (percentages strongly agreeing)

	Men		Women	
	Non-Hispanic %	Hispanic %	Non-Hispanic %	Hispanic %
Being Catholic is important part of who I am	34	30	18	52
Sacraments of the Church essential to my relationship with God	35	53	25	48
Catholicism contains a greater share of truth	26	34	10	40
Church among the most important parts of my life	33	37	22	46
I cannot imagine being anything but Catholic	33	36	20	44
Important that younger generations of my family grow up Catholic	39	46	28	56
How a person lives is more important than whether Catholic	51	40	57	35

to them. And by the same token, they are by far the least likely to endorse views such as that being a Catholic is a very important part of who they are, that they cannot imagine being anything but Catholic, that the Church is among the most important parts of their lives, and that they want younger members of their family to grow up as Catholics. Similarly, only 1 in 4 non-Hispanic women (half as many as Hispanic women) say that the sacraments of the Church are essential to their relationship with God, and even fewer non-Hispanic millennial women, only 1 in 10, agree that Catholicism contains a greater share of truth than other religions (see Table 8.6).

Further in line with these patterns, non-Hispanic millennial women are also by far the most independent of the church hierarchy's authority. They are the most likely of all four millennial subgroups to agree that individual Catholics should be the final arbiters of moral decisions pertaining to artificial contraception, abortion, and same-sex activity (see Table 8.7). They are also the most likely among their peers to disagree with the bishops' opposition to same-sex marriage—only 14 percent of them compared to between 28 and 34 percent of others agree with the bishops on this issue; and they are also the most likely to say that a person can be a good Catholic without obeying the Church's teaching on divorce and remarriage (see Table 8.5).

There is strong support across the sample as a whole, including within the millennial generation, regarding alternative liturgical and other parish-administrative options in response to the priest shortage. Nevertheless, Hispanic male Millennials emerge as the least inclined to support women's roles in the Church. They are less likely than their age peers to express support for women in the role of altar server, Eucharistic minister, religious education director, deacon, and parish administrator. And while an equal proportion of millennial Hispanic (65 percent) and non-Hispanic (65 percent) women support women as priests, millennial men, especially non-Hispanics

Table 8.7 Gender Differences among Millennial Catholics Regarding the Church Hierarchy's Authority on Sociosexual Issues (percentages agreeing)

Individual Catholics Should Make Up Their Mind Regarding the Morality of:	Men		Women	
	Non-Hispanic %	Hispanic %	Non-Hispanic %	Hispanic %
Artificial birth control	64	63	71	57
Homosexual activity	47	55	68	54
Abortion	52	46	60	39
Divorce and remarriage	45	42	50	28
Nonmarital sex	57	52	58	52

(53 percent) more than Hispanic (58 percent), are less likely to do so. At the same time, notwithstanding their support for women in the role of priest, Hispanic millennial women are the least likely of all four subgroups to say that they strongly agree with scenarios such as allowing married men and especially married or celibate women to be ordained to the priesthood. The reticence to embrace specific change scenarios may be a reflection of this subgroup's comparatively greater attachment to the Mass, the sacraments, and to other core aspects of the larger Catholic tradition, as well as of their greater deference to the Vatican, which continues to reaffirm doctrinal opposition to women's ordination and to uphold the celibacy requirement for ordained (non-Episcopalian/Anglican) men.

Conclusion

The 2010 Census shows that one-quarter of Hispanics live in poverty. Our data show that over a quarter of Hispanic millennial Catholics have less than a high school education (28 percent), and well over a third has only a high school education (38 percent). Less than 10 percent have a college degree. In contrast, over a third of non-Hispanic Millennials (35 percent) have a college degree, and an additional 39 percent have some college education. Such educational disparities translate into disparities in income. While over a half of Hispanic millennial Catholics (52 percent) have an income of less than $25,000 a year, approximately the same proportion of non-Hispanic Millennials (55 percent) have an income that is between $25,000 and $100,000. Thus, for many Hispanic Millennials, poverty is not an abstract concept. It is, rather, a fact of their lives, and it contributes to how they conceive of themselves as Catholics, to what they value in and expect of the Church, and their support for the translation of Catholic social teaching into public policy. Among the Millennials, Hispanic women are by far the most devout and the most attached and committed to Catholicism, and non-Hispanic women are the least engaged with Catholicism and the Church. Ironically, the deep-seated Catholic commitment exemplified in the steadfast attitudes and practices of pre–Vatican II American Catholics will not be carried on by their ethnic great-granddaughters but by the new cohorts of young Hispanic women who are remaking American Catholicism as their own.

CHAPTER NINE

~

Conclusions: Continuities and Changes in American Catholicism

Much has happened in the Church and in American society since our last survey (conducted in 2005). President Barack Obama became the nation's first African American to occupy the White House, and the crisis in U.S. banking and finance that came to the fore in 2008–2009 saw the federal government make unprecedented interventions to prop up the economy. The financial crisis and the ensuing recession continue to have forceful economic consequences from Wall Street to Main Street, and many American families confront unemployment and a severe downturn in their economic resources.

In the interval since our last survey, Pope Benedict XVI (who assumed the papacy in 2005) has had time to make his imprint on the Church. Very different in personality and style to his predecessor, Pope John Paul II, Benedict has nonetheless continued the Vatican's pastoral outreach efforts and has made pilgrimages to several countries, including to the United States in 2008. A recurring theme throughout Benedict's papacy is his emphasis on the importance of a revitalized Catholic faith against the forces of secularism in everyday culture and in legislation that undermines Catholic teaching (e.g., legal abortion, same-sex marriage). The sex abuse scandal also reasserted itself into the public domain in the interval since our last survey and continues to receive wide-ranging coverage in national newspapers in the United States and elsewhere. Recent criminal cases in the United States have resulted, for example, in the unprecedented jailing of a priest in Philadelphia for "child endangerment" due to lax supervision of abusive priests.

The Persistence of Catholics' Catholicism

Notwithstanding these and other significant developments in the Church and American society, our research demonstrates many continuities in the attitudes and practices of American Catholics and how they construe the Church and their place in it. Catholics continue to be the country's single largest denomination, and composing approximately 24 percent, they continue to maintain what has been for a long time now (since the 1960s) a stable share of the U.S. population. A substantial majority continue to remain highly attached to the Church and to value the many elements of the Catholic faith and tradition.

How American Catholics construe what it means to be Catholic is remarkably resilient. It is evident from our series of surveys that Catholics today, as they have done for at least the last 25 years, define Catholicism on their own terms. This construal, however, is not as arbitrary or as random as it might appear from a superficial glance at opinion poll data. Catholics are highly independent in what they see as central and less central to Catholicism, but there is coherence in their attitudes. They identify core dimensions of Catholic theological belief (e.g., the resurrection, Mary as the Mother of God) and core aspects of the larger Catholic tradition, including the Church's concern for the poor, its universal community, apostolic succession, and the papacy as aspects that are personally important and meaningful to them as Catholics. At the same time, they draw a clear line between these aspects of the Catholic theological, sacramental, and communal tradition and the Vatican's teaching authority, specifically its strictures regarding the structure of the Church as exemplified by celibacy, women's ordination, and its sociosexual teachings. For Catholics, being Catholic is motivated largely by participation in the sacramental and communal life of the Church and the spiritual and communal nourishment this provides. These core strands in Catholicism enrich Catholics' everyday experiences at the same time as their lived experiences lead them to keep the moral authority of the church hierarchy at arm's length.

Some readers and observers may wonder why Catholics bother being Catholic or calling themselves Catholic if their Catholicism is so apparently diffuse and selectively independent of church teachings and church authority. But as we have noted, religion, and specifically Catholicism and its orthodoxy, is far more internally differentiated and encrusted by pluralistic strands than is often acknowledged. There is much ambiguity in any religious tradition. Not surprisingly, given Catholicism's long history and its transnational presence, it contains multiple strands of equally important and, what at times might appear as, contradictory strands. The Church's theological and institutional self-understanding is of a tradition that combines faith and reason, not faith alone and not reason alone. This exemplifies a "contradiction" of opposites only if one were to embrace Enlightenment-fundamentalism (cf. Habermas 2008) that sees faith as the opposite of reason.

In practice, however, faith and reason are highly compatible, and it is their compatibility that in part strengthens the centrality of interpretive nuance in Catholicism (Dillon 1999). Moreover, reflecting and extending this emphasis on balancing faith and reason, the Church obliges Catholics to engage reflexively with the Catholic tradition and to use their own individual judgment in ascertaining what it means to be Catholic and to give voice to their Catholicism in everyday life. This exhortation was at the core of Vatican II. Further, Vatican II emphasized the value of unity in and amid the diversity of Catholicism: "All men are called to belong to the new People of God. . . . In virtue of [its] catholicity each individual part of the Church contributes through its special gifts to the good of the other parts and of the whole Church. Thus through the common sharing of gifts and through the common effort to attain fullness in unity, the whole and each of the parts receive increase . . . differences [among its members] do not hinder unity but rather contribute toward it. . . . All men are called to be part of this catholic unity of the People of God, a unity which is harbinger of the universal peace it promotes" (Lumen Gentium #13; Abbott 1966: 30-32). Church leaders and commentators are free to shake their heads at what may often seem to be a lazy Catholicism. But we think it is important to point out that there is a solid sociotheological basis to how Catholics construe what it means to be Catholic.

It is also important to recognize that faith or religious activity is not a black box defined by all-or-nothingness. Just because religious identity is salient for many people, this does not mean that they suspend their intellects and wean their minds and hearts and bodies from all other influences. Many Catholics demonstrate a high level of attachment to the Church—being Catholic is an important part of who they are, and they want to stay Catholic and want their children to be Catholic. But notwithstanding this strong attachment, commitment to the Church, for most Catholics, is a moderate commitment. It is not overarching and does not subsume their other activities. This moderateness is in keeping with Catholicism's history as a public church rather than a sect. It does not require its members to withdraw from society and to rigidly separate their religious from their secular obligations; at least since Vatican II, it requires active engagement in society across its many domains (see, e.g., Casanova 1994).

Catholic moderation also fits with the Church's blending of faith and reason, and its eschewal, in particular, of biblical fundamentalism. Within

Catholicism, there is always room to maneuver; the teaching is not easily reduced to formulaic pronouncements. Indeed, if one were to try to define a Catholic orthodoxy, the closest summation of it would probably be the consistent ethic of life thesis as articulated by the late Cardinal Bernardin. Yet, as we know, it seems very difficult, thus far in history at least, for any one Catholic or for any one political party and its adherents to embody this ethic in practice. For some years now, the American Catholic laity no longer composes a single political or voting bloc (see chapter 7). There are no differences in the devoutness of Catholics who are Democratic or Republican nor in how they construe their identity as Catholics and the authority of Rome. They do, however, diverge on the ethic of life issues (e.g., abortion) as well as on other partisan policy issues (e.g., welfare spending; see chapter 7).

Faith, moreover, is a complicated thing. And what it means to be religious and/or spiritual is also complicated. What people believe and how they experience the sacred is often not coherent. This is not because religion lacks coherence or rationality. Rather, it is because the realm of faith encompasses a lot of ineffable things that defy articulation and explanation. Additionally, some specific tenets of faith may, for some participants in the tradition, simply defy belief, as shown, for example, by Catholics' views regarding transubstantiation (see chapter 6). But, because mystery inheres in faith, and certainly in Catholicism, we should not be too surprised that the mystery of faith is not always apprehended fully by all Catholics. Indeed, Pope Benedict has commented on this very issue, saying that Catholics "should not be surprised that many people have difficulty accepting Church teaching that Jesus is truly present in Eucharist. The real presence is a mystery, and a 'God who becomes flesh and sacrifices Himself for the life of the world puts human wisdom in crisis'" (Wooden 2007: 13).

In any case, even if there is unbelief in, or a misinformed understanding of, certain core aspects of the Church's theology, those Catholics can still find meaning in the Mass, for example, or in other aspects of Catholicism, and in being Catholic. Being Catholic is as much about a certain sensibility and certain habits and worldviews as it is about discrete tenets of faith. And it does a disservice to the theology and sociology of Catholicism to try to package it, or to expect it to be packaged into, some monolithic, undifferentiated, and uncomplicated thing.

Church Authority

As part of their differentiation between what they consider the more central and less central aspects of Catholicism, Catholics give short shrift to the hierarchy's claims to authority. More and more, as we have documented, Catholics see individual conscience rather than the pope and the bishops as the final arbiter of what is morally permissible for Catholics when it comes to decisions regarding contraception, choice on abortion, same-sex and nonmarital sexual activity, and divorced Catholics remarrying without an annulment. American Catholics have long made up their minds on contraception, going back to their response to *Humanae Vitae*, Pope Paul VI's 1968 encyclical reaffirming the Church's opposition to artificial contraception. Over the years, their moral independence has broadened to related sociosexual issues, including most recently, same-sex activity where Catholics are in the vanguard of American opinion favoring the legalization of same-sex marriage (see chapter 4).

The domain of sociosexual behavior is the field of activity that most clearly illuminates the relevance of lived experience in putting a check on the church hierarchy's use of authority. And, despite the surge of hierarchical intrusion on a number of broadly related issues in recent years—converging around sex and gender, and the teaching authority of the hierarchy—it is unlikely that Catholics will cower in the face of condemnation by the Vatican and the bishops. Indeed, the response to these intrusions underscores Catholics' moral and intellectual independence. It also demonstrates Catholics' solidarity with nuns and others who are on the front lines of an on-the-ground Catholicism, whether in schools, hospitals, social service and community organizations, local parishes, or on the streets ministering to the marginal in society. (e.g., National Catholic Reporter 2012; Goodstein 2012a; Kristof 2012).

Women's Declining Commitment to the Church

Amid so much continuity in American Catholics' construal of what it means to be Catholic, the steep decline in women's commitment to the Church during the 25-year span from our first to our current survey stands out all the more. Throughout this book, we have emphasized the relative stability and constancy in Catholic attitudes over the 25 years of our surveys. Catholics are relatively constant in how they construe Catholic identity, what it means to be a good Catholic, the terms of their relationship to the Church and church authority, and in maintaining their moderate commitment to the Church. The thrust of these patterns is much the same for Hispanic and non-Hispanic Catholics alike, and while there is some variation across generations, for the most part, there are few polarizing divides in the attitudes expressed. The general predictability in Catholic attitudes, however, masks women's changing relationship to the Church.

Catholic women today are less likely than their peers in 1987 to go to weekly Mass, to say that the Church is among the most important parts of their lives, and to say that they would never leave the Church (see chapter 5). Women's commitment today is such that, while in the past there were significant differences in the attitudes and practices of Catholic women and men, that gender gap no longer exists. Women have reduced their commitment along key dimensions and have done so in ways that put them currently on a par with men's historically lower and relatively unchanging patterns of commitment.

Many factors are likely contributing to the decline we observe in women's commitment, including, for example, the generational change represented by the dwindling of pre–Vatican II Catholics. Lived experience would, again, also seem to be highly relevant. Increasingly today, women live in a society where the institutional barriers to their full participation in all domains of life other than the Church are eroding. This disjuncture is coupled with women's everyday/every night experiences of church prohibitions regarding contraception, marriage, and divorce. The disjuncture between church officials and ordinary Catholics is further encapsulated in the church hierarchy's opposition to dialogue about the possibility of women's ordination even in a time when the everyday reality of the shortage of priests poses a significant threat to the accessibility of the Eucharist and the attendant sustainability of Catholic theology, tradition, and community. Our findings suggest that Catholic women, and especially younger cohorts, are less willing than in the past to live with the tension posed by loyalty to the Church while simultaneously being excluded from full participation in its practices. This is a major development. And given women's anchoring role in motivating family religious participation, the ramifications of an ongoing decline—if the patterns we observe were to continue over the next 25 years—do not portend well for the future vitality of the Church.

The Growing Presence of Hispanic Catholics

The continuities in American Catholicism also belie the flux in the composition of its members. Paralleling the transformative demographic shift in the American population as a result of Hispanic immigration, Catholics are experiencing a significant increase in their Hispanic composition. In 1987, Hispanics accounted for approximately 1 in 10 American Catholics; today they compose more than a third. This demographic change has important consequences for American Catholicism: it is changing its face and its geography and mediating its culture and practices. Hispanic Catholics as a whole are, in general, more devout and more deferential to the church hierarchy's authority. Larger percentages of Hispanic than non-Hispanic Catholics say, for example, that various aspects of the Catholic tradition including belief in the resurrection, Mary, the sacraments, and the Church's concern for the poor are personally very important to them. Similarly, Hispanic Catholics are less likely to take a permissive view of what is entailed in being a good Catholic and are also less likely than other Catholics to rely on their own individual judgment in making up their minds about some issues including abortion and remarriage without an annulment. The contours of Hispanics' Catholicism, however, follow the same lines as those of American Catholics as a whole. Thus, Hispanic and non-Hispanic Catholics alike attach greater personal importance to core theological beliefs than to aspects of the Church's structure including the Vatican's claims to authority and the celibacy requirement for priests, as well as to its teachings opposing contraception and same-sex marriage. By the same token, there is a consensus across Catholics irrespective of ethnicity regarding the aspects of Catholicism they find personally meaningful. Given these patterns, the increased presence of Hispanics in American Catholicism is unlikely to change the overarching character of American Catholicism as it is practiced and lived, though certain aspects of Hispanic belief, such as their greater tendency to believe in nonchurch spirituality and to combine these beliefs with the Church's sacramental tradition may alter somewhat the tenor of Catholicism.

Some observers note that American Catholicism would be much weaker numerically if it were not for the flow of Hispanic immigrants into the Church. This is true. This comment, however, is typically made in the same context in which Catholics' "market share" of the American population is being scrutinized in tandem with the often-repeated line that one in three Catholics leave the Church (Pew Forum 2009a). The implicit message conveyed is that the Catholic Church is not really in as good a numerical shape as it seems because it would be losing its share of the population if it were not for Hispanics. The tacit message is that Catholicism is really on the decline and is being propped up by Hispanic immigration.

Whether or not market share concepts facilitate a greater understanding of how religion works or matters in the United States is not at issue here. And we do not dispute the fact that large numbers of Catholics no longer practice their faith. What the line of argument betrays, however, is the presumption that religion is static, set once and for all time as it once was (once upon an imagined time). This framing ignores the historical and sociological fact that American Catholicism would not be what it was in the 1940s and 1950s, or indeed what it is in 2013, if it were not for the immigration of the mid- and late 19th century. Successive waves of Irish, Italian, Polish, and German Catholics, among others, made or, more accurately, reshaped American Catholicism, just as Hispanic Catholics are reshaping American Catholicism today. Clearly, the kind of Church that was built in the late 19th and early 20th century might have been different had immigration not occurred, or had it occurred earlier or later, or had originated in Asia or South America. Immigration, in short, is one of the engines of religious change (and of societal change more generally). We should not be surprised that the nature and extent of immigration at a particular point in time can push the Church along certain tracks and not others, and that it can switch and realign certain tracks. In sum, immigration is an added dimension of Catholic life that is as relevant to the narrative of a dynamic Catholicism today as it has been in the past. Nor should we be surprised that immigration trends are, and will increasingly be, accompanied by other changes including some losses within Catholicism. Some changes will stem from the demographic and cultural characteristics of Hispanic Catholics, and some will coincide with other changes, including the cycle of generational succession bookended by the passing of the pre–Vatican II generation and the rising prominence of the millennial generation. As we documented, young Hispanic women who are part of the millennial generation are far more devout and attached to Catholicism than their same gender, non-Hispanic peers (see chapter 8). It is the former rather than the latter who are more likely to continue to maintain the vitality of the Catholic traditions (e.g., frequent Mass attendance) and beliefs (e.g., importance of social justice concerns) that have been important to American Catholics over the last several decades.

New Infrastructural and Mission Challenges

The growing Hispanic presence among American Catholics puts in sharp relief the structural and infrastructural challenges currently facing the Church. The changing demography is intensifying the geographical redistribution of American Catholics that has been occurring over the last 50 years. At the same time that younger Catholics were abandoning the old ethnic neighborhoods in the inner cities of the Northeast in favor of the suburbs and moving off the farms and villages of the upper Midwest to follow jobs in the South and the West, many Catholic immigrants from Latin America were also seeking opportunities in the fast-growing suburbs around major cities, particularly in the South and the Southwest. This dispersed the geographical locus of Catholicism away from the Northeast, from the traditional bastions of urban Catholic concentrations in Boston, New York, Buffalo, Detroit, and Philadelphia, to the suburbs in and around Los Angeles, Phoenix, Houston, Dallas, Atlanta, and Miami. Dioceses in the Rustbelt of the Northeast and upper Midwest struggled to maintain churches and schools in areas of declining population and still meet the demand for new parishes and schools in the suburbs. Dioceses in the South and the Southwest faced increasing demand to build new parishes and to add Masses in Spanish in existing parishes. The combination of this geographic transition, a rapidly aging and declining priest population, and financial pressures brought on by a sluggish economy and clergy sexual abuse settlements culminated in many dioceses in the Northeast and upper Midwest closing and consolidating parishes and schools, while dioceses in the South and Southwest are building "megaparish" churches that can accommodate 1,500 at a single liturgy and offering multiple Masses in Spanish as well as other languages.

On the other hand, while megaparishes may not be the "one size fits all" solution to the problem of more Catholics and fewer priests, many Catholics are exploring the benefits of small Christian faith communities, such as RENEW, small Christian communities, and Hispanic faith groups. We noted that these groups, first promoted among pre–Vatican II and Vatican II Catholics, are also popular among millennial Hispanic Catholics: 1 in 5 Catholics has participated in one of these groups. And rather than diminishing parish connections, participants in these groups actually identify more strongly with their Catholic faith and are more strongly attached to parish life than those who do not participate in them.

As we have also noted, large proportions of Hispanic Catholics, as is true of Hispanics in general in the United States, have very low household incomes, and many do not graduate from high school or go to college. This socioeconomic gap is particularly evident among the millennial generation: 29 percent of Hispanic millennial Catholics have some high school or less, whereas this is true for only 3 percent of non-Hispanic millennial Catholics. At the other end of the spectrum, whereas 35 percent of non-Hispanic millennial Catholics are college graduates, only 9 percent of Hispanic Millennials have a college degree. This stark educational differential translates into stark income differentials. A majority of Hispanics (52 percent) report income of $25,000 or less, compared to 15 percent of non-Hispanics; in fact, the modal income of non-Hispanic Millennials is $100,000 or more.

Hispanics' glaringly visible economic and educational disadvantage poses significant public policy challenges and, more immediately within the Church, begs for action at the local parish, diocesan, and national level through for, example, the U.S. conference of bishops' Catholic Campaign for

Human Development (CCHD). Such outreach may be hindered, however, by the bishops' combative opposition to any Catholic alliances that they see as contradicting church teachings on other issues (e.g., gay rights, contraception services). Thus, Compañeros, a small nonprofit organization that helps rural Hispanic immigrants in Colorado, had its funding cut by the CCHD due to its alliance with a gay rights advocacy group (Frosch 2012). Immigration and poverty, however, do not preclude same-sex attraction, and in rural America in particular, young gay immigrants may be especially vulnerable to harassment and social isolation.

Hispanics' poor socioeconomic situation also presents a challenge to Catholic colleges and universities. These institutions, such as Boston College, which is celebrating its sesquicentennial in 2013, played a strong role in assuring the post–World War II upward mobility of cohorts of Catholics who were the children and grandchildren of European immigrants. Many of these universities today are among the elite of American higher education. And while they and their alumni have done very well financially, the question is whether they will commit significant resources to make a college education and preparation for a college education affordable and accessible to poor Hispanic Catholics (and others in poverty). This would surely be work that, while requiring considerable investment, would allow Catholic colleges and universities to re-energize their Catholic mission and identity, a core dimension of their identity that many Catholic colleges struggle to realize while balancing their other institutional goals (cf. Cernera and Morgan 2002).

The Dwindling of the Pre–Vatican II Generation

Our 2011 survey marks the dwindling of the stalwart generation of pre–Vatican II Catholics (those currently age 71 and over). Today they account for 10 percent of American Catholics, down from a third 25 years ago. They are the ones who with their non-Catholic peers lived the American century: some experiencing World War I; more the Great Depression, World War II, and the postwar economic, social, and cultural boom; and who in their final decades are experiencing a world dominated by high-speed digitalized media, terrorism and its risk, and globalizing economic, political, and cultural forces. As Catholics, they witnessed an equally transformative century of difference. This is the generation whose lived experience of Catholicism is one that knows firsthand both the pre–Vatican II Church and the transformations following Vatican II. Before Vatican II, they dutifully prayed, paid, obeyed—or when disobeying, they kept it to themselves. And after Vatican

II, they embraced the changed understanding of the Church with an energy and discernment that exemplified for successor generations the many ways in which Catholicism is a living, pluralistic tradition.

The dwindling of the pre–Vatican II generation is surely dampening some aspects of American Catholicism. We already see its impact in the general decline in weekly Mass attendance among Catholics; the pre–Vatican II generation is the only group where more than half (54 percent) attends weekly Mass, the same proportion of them (57 percent) who did so in the late 1980s. For other Catholics, monthly Mass has become the new norm. We also see its impact in the declining importance given by Catholics to the priority of helping the poor, although as with any trend, other factors too are most likely also contributing to this shift (e.g., an accentuation in Catholics' own economic constraints due to the recession). The dwindling of pre–Vatican II Catholics is also contributing to a dilution of the cultural strand in Catholicism that has long managed to hold together disagreement with church teachings on sexuality and gender with a committed loyalty to the Church and Catholicism. Approximately two-thirds of pre–Vatican II non-Hispanic women and men, compared to close to half of all other groups (with the exception of post–Vatican II women who similarly endorse the pre–Vatican II generation's sentiment), say that it is personally meaningful to them that Catholics can disagree with aspects of church teaching and still remain loyal to Catholicism.

Moving Forward

Cardinal Dolan has spoken of his great desire and intent to revive interest among Catholics in the Mass and the Catholic tradition. Dismayed by reports of the numbers of Catholics who do not marry in the Church and of those who leave the Church, Dolan has committed the Church to reinvigorating appreciation among Catholics for Catholicism (Goodstein 2010). He has singled out the quality of Catholic sermons as a weak factor, and indeed there is much anecdotal support for this view. Yet in our survey, Catholics were more likely to cite family responsibilities and general busyness as well as a certain religious indifference (e.g., it's not a mortal sin to miss Mass; "I'm just not a religious person") as important reasons why they do not go to Mass more frequently. By the same token, three-quarters of the respondents said that poor sermons was not an important reason why they didn't go more often (see chapter 6). These responses suggest that Catholic disaffection is not fueled simply by weak preaching, but by a larger indifference toward the Church. This indifference is particularly evident in the attitudes of young non-Hispanic women. As we documented, they are the least connected to, and appreciative of, various aspects of the Catholic tradition, the least attached to Catholicism, and the most skeptical of the church hierarchy's teaching authority and its teachings on sexual issues (see chapter 8).

Church leaders may be able to look to millennial Hispanic women to anchor a more tradition-bound Catholicism and to uphold a certain deference toward the hierarchy. Their Catholicism too, nonetheless, is not without its tensions. Over two-thirds (68 percent) of Hispanic millennial women say, for example, that a person can be a good Catholic without obeying church teaching on contraception, and less than a third (30 percent) say that the Church's teachings that oppose same-sex marriage are personally very important to them as Catholics. Hispanics as a whole are also strong supporters of immigration reform, and they look to the bishops to take an activist role on this issue. If the bishops are seen to be wavering in their commitment to immigration reform and to other social justice goals, this may dampen Hispanic Catholics', including millennial Hispanic women's, regard for the bishops.

Additionally, notwithstanding the personal importance that Hispanic millennial women give to the Eucharist, many of them—like other Millennials and Catholics more generally—also embrace nonchurch spiritual beliefs, such as belief in reincarnation, spiritual energy, and in yoga as a spiritual practice (see chapter 3). Clearly, there is a search for spiritual enrichment in American society today. Many look beyond church walls for this nourishment, and many too explore the possibilities for spiritual renewal within a given religious tradition; the popularity of small Christian and intentional Eucharistic communities and other groups (e.g., RENEW), are examples of this spiritual ferment within Catholicism (see chapter 6). Although church leaders are wary of spiritual beliefs and practices that they see as undermining the centrality of a Jesus-centered theology, there are many spiritual traditions within Catholicism, including the Taize prayer or the Ignatian and Benedictine Rules, for example, and other traditional Catholic devotions that are attractive to many young Catholics and that could be revived as part of mainstream Catholic church devotions. This could possibly strengthen the appeal of the Church as a spiritual venue. On the other hand, if the main way that young Catholic cohorts encounter the Church is through bishops' insistence on proclaiming opposition to contraception and same-sex marriage, for example, and especially if they do so without also giving sustained attention to socioeconomic justice issues and the structural problems in the Church, including the ramifications of the priest shortage, it is unlikely that the Church's stature among the millennial generation will grow as these Catholics move through the course of their lives.

Losses and Gains

A dominant view in sociology since its founding in the late 19th century is that as societies become more economically modernized, they become more secularized, with religion readily losing its relevance. Given the steady march of economic and social change over the past century, it is understandable that social scientists look for evidence of attendant religious decline. Our disciplinary short-sight, however, is that we tend to equate change with decline. Further, we tend to equate decline in one set of indicators as evidence of an across-the-board decline more generally in the field of religious activity as a whole. Yet as we discussed (see chapter 4), a decline in Catholics' deference toward the church hierarchy may on the one hand be taken as evidence of declining religious authority, but on the other hand, as evidence of Catholics' deference to the larger Catholic tradition and specifically to the Church-sanctioned obligation to take personal conscience seriously. Nostalgia for earlier (sometimes imagined) forms of religion—and frequently, too, a nostalgia for a more authoritarian and a more homogeneous style of religion—frequently shadows narratives of decline or of subtraction. Such narratives frame change as if something has been lost, rather than as is empirically more accurate: some things get lost and some things get added.

Religion is not the only sociological subject of inquiry that falls prey to narratives of decline. Community is another; scholarly and popular commentary is replete with analyses of the "decline of community," and there is much commentary too about the "decline of family." But social life, and institutional and social processes, are dynamic, not static. Change happens. With societal change, there are inevitable losses in how, for example, community is structured and how people experience community. But there are also gains—new ways of creating and experiencing community, as is demonstrated by a large body of empirical studies.

So, too, with religion, and specifically Catholicism. It is not just that society as some external force changes. Religion itself as a domain of activity, and any given religious tradition, changes and develops new understandings and new institutional practices. Many of these changes are typically in line with already existing strands within the tradition even though their selective manifestation may vary over time and across different sociocultural contexts. Indeed, as Pope Benedict XVI (2007) himself has affirmed: "The Second Vatican Council neither changed nor intended to change [the Catholic doctrine on the Church], rather it developed, deepened and more fully explained it." Further, we should never lose sight of David Tracy's (1987) insistence on the plurality that exists within all major traditions—religious, political, philosophical—and the continuities and discontinuities that get entangled within any tradition. The history of the Catholic Church is a history that exemplifies doctrinally reflexive change and underscores the centrality of change to its own self-maintenance as a living tradition. Our surveys, spanning 25 years of American Catholics' attitudes on the broad range of dimensions of Catholic life, and the patterns evident in the data speak to both the resilience and the dynamism of Catholicism.

APPENDIX

~

The 2011 Survey

We selected Knowledge Networks, a highly respected research polling firm that conducts scientifically valid polls of selected audiences through an online research panel for our 2011 survey of American Catholics. Panel members are recruited through national random samples and households that agree to participate are provided with access to the Internet and hardware if needed. Unlike Internet convenience panels, also known as "opt-in" panels that include only individuals with Internet access who volunteer themselves for research, Knowledge Networks uses dual sampling frames that include both listed and unlisted telephone numbers; telephone, nontelephone, and cellphone-only households; as well as households with and without Internet access. Only persons sampled through these probability-based techniques are eligible to participate in the panel. This ensures that the sample is statistically valid and nationally representative of the population—in our case, adult, self-identified Catholics.

Knowledge Networks also recruits a nationally representative Hispanic sample and offers the survey in both English and Spanish. This helps to further ensure that we have accurately sampled the full extent of the Catholic population in the United States. As is standard practice in national polls, statistical weighting adjustments, calculated from the Current Population Survey of the U.S. Census Bureau, are then applied to the data to offset known selection deviations.

For this survey, we needed a nationally representative sample of U.S. Catholics in various age groups because we wanted to be able to compare by generation and by ethnicity. Therefore, the panel was divided into Hispanics and non-Hispanics and also into four age groups:

Pre–Vatican II Catholics (ages 71 and older in 2011)
Vatican II Catholics (ages 51–70)
Post–Vatican II Catholics (ages 32–50)
Millennial Catholics (ages 18–31)

Because U.S. Catholics of the pre–Vatican II generation are nearly all (96 percent) white, non-Hispanic and because the numbers of panel members in this group proved to be too small to provide a statistically meaningful subgroup, only non-Hispanic Catholics of the pre–Vatican II generation were included in the survey. The data collection took place from April 25, 2011, to May 2, 2011. A total of 1,442 questionnaires were completed, resulting in an overall margin of sampling error of ± 2.6.

The survey questions are presented in full below with corresponding frequencies (i.e., the actual responses of the people taking the survey). The numbers shown in the tables below are weighted percentages, rounded to the next whole integer. DK/RE = don't know or refused to answer. Some tables do not sum to 100 percent, due to rounding. Question items that are not preceded by a number are either demographic characteristics of panel members that are provided by Knowledge Networks or constructed variables that we calculated.

Frequencies

1. What is your religion?

Catholic
Other.... (TERMINATE)

2. As a Catholic, how important is each of the following to you? Would you say the following is or are very important, somewhat important, or not important at all?

	Very Important	Somewhat Important	Not at all Important	DK/RE
A. The sacraments, such as the Eucharist	63	26	10	1
B. The Catholic Church's teachings about Mary as the Mother of God	64	28	8	<1
C. Church involvement in activities directed toward social justice	34	49	15	1
D. The teaching authority claimed by the Vatican	31	45	23	1
E. A celibate male clergy	23	32	45	1
F. Having a regular daily prayer life	47	38	15	1
G. Helping the poor	68	28	3	1
H. Belief in Jesus' resurrection from the dead	73	20	6	1
I. Participating in devotions such as Eucharistic Adoration or praying the rosary	37	41	21	1
J. The Catholic Church's teachings that oppose the death penalty	30	41	28	1
K. The Catholic Church's teachings that oppose same sex marriage	35	26	38	<1
L. The Catholic Church's teachings that oppose abortion	40	30	29	1

3. Please indicate whether you strongly agree, somewhat agree, somewhat disagree, or strongly disagree with each of the following statements.

	Strongly Agree	Somewhat Agree	Somewhat Disagree	Strongly Disagree	DK/RE
A. How a person lives is more important than whether he or she is Catholic	55	31	9	4	<1
B. Catholicism contains a greater share of truth than other religions do	26	37	25	11	1

	Strongly Agree	Somewhat Agree	Somewhat Disagree	Strongly Disagree	DK/RE
C. Being a Catholic is a very important part of who I am	41	34	17	7	1
D. The sacraments of the Church are essential to my relationship with God	41	34	17	8	<1
E. It is important to me that younger generations of my family grow up as Catholics	40	37	16	7	1
F. I cannot imagine being anything but Catholic	39	31	21	9	1

4. Next, we are interested in your opinion on several issues that involve the moral authority in the Catholic Church. In each case we would like to know who you think should have the final say about what is right or wrong. Is it the Church leaders such as the pope and bishops, individuals taking Church teachings in account and deciding for themselves, or both individuals and leaders working together?

	Church Leaders	Individuals	Both	DK/RE
A. A divorced Catholic remarrying without getting an annulment	21	45	33	1
B. A Catholic practicing contraceptive birth control	10	66	23	1
C. A Catholic advocating free choice regarding abortion	18	52	29	1
D. A Catholic who engages in homosexual activity	16	56	27	1
E. Sexual relations outside of marriage	15	55	29	1

5. Please indicate whether you strongly agree, somewhat agree, somewhat disagree, or strongly disagree with the following statements.

	Strongly Agree	Somewhat Agree	Somewhat Disagree	Strongly Disagree	DK/RE
A. Most priests don't expect the laity to be leaders, just followers	10	45	33	11	2
B. Most Catholics don't want to take on leadership roles in their parish	10	52	31	6	<2

	Strongly Agree	Somewhat Agree	Somewhat Disagree	Strongly Disagree	DK/RE
C. Catholic parishes are too big and impersonal	9	33	41	15	2
D. Catholic Church leaders are out of touch with the laity	15	43	30	11	<2
E. On the whole, parish priests do a good job	31	55	11	1	<2

How satisfied are you with . . .

	Very Satisfied	Somewhat Satisfied	Only a Little Satisfied	Not At All Satisfied	DK/RE
6. ...the leadership of the bishops of the United States	15	55	23	7	1
7. ...the leadership of your local bishop	25	49	19	6	1

8. Catholic bishops often speak out about politics and elections, as well as about policy issues like health care, abortion, immigration, and foreign affairs. Which one of the following best describes how you typically respond to bishops' statements in these areas?

A. The bishops' views are irrelevant to my thinking about politics and public policy	32
B. I consider what the bishops have to say about politics and public policy, but ultimately I make up my own mind	59
C. I try to follow the bishops' guidance and instructions on political and public policy matters	8
D. DK/RE	1

9. Please indicate whether you strongly agree, somewhat agree, somewhat disagree, or strongly disagree with the American bishops on each of the following issues.

	Strongly Agree	Somewhat Agree	Somewhat Disagree	Strongly Disagree	DK/RE
A. Opposition to health care reform legislation	21	31	28	19	<2
B. Support for immigration reform	38	37	15	9	1
C. Opposition to same-sex marriage	30	20	25	24	1

10. Do you support or oppose women in the following roles in the Church?

	Support	Oppose	DK/RE
A. Altar server	91	8	1
B. Reader at Mass (Lector)	95	4	1
C. Eucharistic minister (Extraordinary Minister of Communion)	89	10	1
D. Director of religious education	95	4	1
E. Youth minister	92	7	<2
F. Deacon	75	23	2
G. Parish administrator	92	6	1
H. Priest	60	38	2

11. Following are some questions about social and political issues. Please indicate whether you strongly agree, somewhat agree, somewhat disagree, or strongly disagree with each of the following.

	Strongly Agree	Somewhat Agree	Somewhat Disagree	Strongly Disagree	DK/RE
A. More government funds to provide health care for poor children	44	37	14	3	1
B. More government funds for the military	17	34	34	14	1
C. Stiffer enforcement of the death penalty	26	34	24	14	<2
D. Reduced spending on nuclear weapons	41	41	12	5	1
E. Further cutbacks in welfare programs	18	35	27	19	1

12. The following statements deal with what you think it takes to be a good Catholic. Please indicate if you think a person can be a good Catholic without performing these actions or affirming these beliefs. Can a person be a good Catholic:

	Yes, Can Be a Good Catholic	No, Cannot Be a Good Catholic	DK/RE
A. Without going to church every Sunday	76	22	<2
B. Without obeying the Church hierarchy's teaching on birth control	77	21	1
C. Without obeying the Church hierarchy's teaching on divorce and remarriage	69	29	<2

	Yes, Can Be a Good Catholic	No, Cannot Be a Good Catholic	DK/RE
D. Without obeying the Church hierarchy's teaching regarding abortion	59	39	<2
E. Without believing that in the Mass, the bread and wine actually become the body and blood of Jesus	37	62	<2
F. Without their marriage being approved by the Catholic Church	71	28	<2
G. Without donating time or money to help the poor	59	40	<2
H. Without donating time or money to help the parish	72	27	1
I. Without believing that Jesus physically rose from the dead	30	69	1

13. For each of the following areas of Church life, please indicate whether you think the Catholic laity should have the right to participate in:

	Should	Should Not	DK/RE
Deciding how parish income should be spent	78	20	<2
Deciding how diocesan income should be spent	70	28	2
Selecting the priests for their parish	70	28	2
Deciding about parish closings	73	25	2
Deciding whether women should be ordained to the priesthood	59	40	2

14. How important is the Catholic Church to you personally?

A. The most important part of my life	9
B. Among the most important parts of my life	28
C. Quite important to me, but so are many other areas of my life	40
D. Not terribly important to me	17
E. Not very important to me at all	5
F. DK/RE	1

15. How meaningful is each of these aspects of Catholicism to you personally?

	Very Meaningful	Somewhat Meaningful	Only a Little Meaningful	Not At All Meaningful	DK/RE
A. The Church's emphasis on the importance of the sacraments and the grace they bestow	48	33	12	5	<2

	Very Meaningful	Somewhat Meaningful	Only a Little Meaningful	Not At All Meaningful	DK/ RE
B. The fact that the Church today is part of an unbroken tradition going back to the apostles	47	33	13	6	<2
C. The fact that the Church is universal (i.e., across the world and with much the same rituals wherever you go)	51	33	9	5	2
D. The sense of having a shared community with other Catholics	43	37	13	5	<2
E. The Church's active concern for the poor	53	34	8	3	2
F. The Church's willingness to stand up for the right to life of the unborn	44	29	14	11	2
G. The papacy	35	35	20	7	<3
H. The fact that Catholics can disagree with aspects of church teaching and still remain loyal to the Church	50	35	9	4	2
I. The Mass	54	30	10	4	2

16. Aside from weddings and funerals, about how often do you attend Mass?

A. At least once a week	32
B. Two or three times a month	14
C. About once a month	9
D. A few times a year	24
E. Seldom or never	21
F. DK/RE	<1

17. How regularly do you pray, apart from Mass?

A. More than once a day	15
B. Daily	37
C. Occasionally or sometimes	38
D. Seldom or never	9
E. DK/RE	1

18. Which of the following statements best describes the Catholic teaching about the bread and wine used for communion?

A. The bread and wine really become the body and blood of Jesus Christ	50
B. The bread and wine are only symbols of the body and blood of Jesus Christ	49
C. DK/RE	<2

19. People go to church for different reasons. Please indicate whether or not each of the following is an important reason you go to church.

	Yes, Important Reason	Not an Important Reason	DK/ RE
A. The church requires that I attend	37	63	<1
B. Mainly, it's a habit	32	68	<1
C. I want to please or satisfy someone close to me, like a spouse or parent	24	75	1
D. I enjoy being with other persons in our church	58	41	1
E. I enjoy taking part in the service itself and experiencing the liturgy	85	14	1
F. I feel a need to receive the sacrament of Holy Communion	82	18	1

20. Please indicate whether or not each of the following is an important reason you don't attend church more often.

	Yes, Important Reason	Not an Important Reason	DK/ RE
A. It's boring	27	72	1
B. It's not a mortal sin to miss Mass	29	70	<2
C. Sermons are poor	25	73	<2
D. Family responsibilities	45	53	2
E. I'm too busy	31	68	1
F. Health reasons	26	73	<2
G. Conflict with Mass schedule	29	69	2
H. Just not a religious person	41	58	1

21. Do you now serve, or have you ever served, in any of the following roles at a Catholic parish?

	Yes	No	DK/RE
A. Reader at Mass (Lector)	22	76	2

	Yes	No	DK/RE
B. Eucharistic minister (Extraordinary Minister of Communion)	10	87	2
C. Greeter/usher	17	81	2
D. Altar server	20	79	2
E. Music ministry	12	86	2
F. Member of a parish committee	19	79	2

22. Are you now, or have you ever been, a member of any of the following religious groups?

	Yes	No	DK/RE
A. RENEW	7	90	3
B. A Small Christian Community (or Faith Sharing Group)	15	83	2
C. An Intentional Eucharistic Community	4	93	3
D. A Hispanic/Latino religious community	11	87	2
E. Other (specify)_____	7	74	19

23. Are you currently registered as a member of a Catholic parish?

Yes	No	DK/RE
60	39	1

24. How would you describe yourself? Would you say you are . . .

A. Religious and spiritual	47
B. Religious but not spiritual	14
C. Spiritual but not religious	28
D. Not religious and not spiritual	9
C. DK/RE	1

25. Which, if any, of the following do you believe in? Do you believe . . .

	Yes, Believe	No, Don't Believe	DK/RE
A. ... in reincarnation, that people will be reborn in this world again and again	37	61	<2
B. ... in spiritual energy located in physical things, such as mountains, trees or crystals	41	58	<2
C. ... in yoga, not just as exercise, but as a spiritual practice	32	67	<2
D. ... that at the Consecration during a Catholic Mass, the bread and wine really become the body and blood of Jesus Christ	61	37	<2

26. Many dioceses have been experiencing a shortage of priests that has resulted in some changes in parish life. I am going to read a list of changes that some dioceses have made to address this shortage. Would you tell me after each if you would be willing to accept it in your parish? Would it be very acceptable, somewhat acceptable, or not at all acceptable to you?

	Very Acceptable	Somewhat Acceptable	Not At All Acceptable	DK/ RE
A. Reducing the number of Saturday evening and Sunday Masses	17	52	29	2
B. Bringing in a priest from another country to lead the parish	39	47	12	2
C. Not having a priest available for visiting the sick	8	30	60	2
D. Not having a priest available for administering last rites for the dying	6	19	72	2
E. Having a deacon or lay person run the parish, with visiting priests for sacraments	26	51	21	2
F. Sharing a priest with one or more other parishes	45	46	7	2
G. Sharing lay staff with one or more other parishes	39	51	9	2
H. Having a Communion service instead of a Mass some of the time	18	46	34	<3
I. Merging two or more nearby parishes into one parish	32	53	12	2
J. Closing the parish	6	29	62	2

27. Now here are four statements about the priesthood. After each, please indicate whether you strongly agree, somewhat agree, somewhat disagree, or strongly disagree.

	Strongly Agree	Somewhat Agree	Somewhat Disagree	Strongly Disagree	DK/ RE
A. It would be a good thing if priests who have married were allowed to return to active ministry	38	33	13	14	2
B. It would be a good thing if married men were allowed to be ordained as priests	36	32	14	17	2
C. It would be a good thing if celibate women were allowed to be ordained as priests	26	28	19	26	2

	Strongly Agree	Somewhat Agree	Somewhat Disagree	Strongly Disagree	DK/ RE
D. It would be a good thing if married women were allowed to be ordained as priests	27	22	18	31	<2

28. On a scale from one to seven, with "1" being "I would never leave the Catholic Church," and "7" being "Yes, I might leave the Catholic Church," where would you place yourself on this scale?

Point	1	2	3	4	5	6	7	DK/RE
Percentage	42	15	8	14	8	6	6	1

The Catholic Church has received a great deal of publicity over its handling of allegations of sexual abuse against minors by clergy.

	Yes	No	DK/RE
29. Do you personally know anyone who was abused by a priest?	6	92	1
30. Do you personally know any priest who was accused of child sex abuse?	11	88	1

How much, if at all, has the issue of sexual abuse of young people by priests hurt . . .

	A Great Deal	Some what	Only a Little	Not At All	DK/ RE
31. ...the credibility of Church leaders who speak out on social or political issues?	46	34	12	6	2
32. ...the ability of priests to meet the spiritual and pastoral needs of their parishioners?	37	38	15	9	2

	Excellent	Good	Fair	Poor	DK/RE
33. Overall, how would you rate the job the Catholic bishops as a whole have done in handling accusations of sexual abuse by priests?	5	25	38	30	<2
34. How would you rate the job your local bishop has done in handling accusations of sexual abuse by priests?	9	33	39	18	2

Now a few questions for statistical purposes:

MARITAL STATUS:

Married	54
Living with partner	10
Separated	<2
Divorced	9
Widowed	5
Never married	20

35. If married, was your current marriage approved by the Catholic Church as a valid marriage?

Yes	69
No	30
DK/RE	<2

36. If married, is your spouse Catholic?

Yes	78
No	20
DK/RE	<2

EDUCATION:

Less than high school graduate (0-11)	14
High school graduate (12)	32
Some college	19
Associate degree	7
Bachelors degree	18
Masters degree	7
Professional or Doctorate degree	3

37. Did you ever attend a Catholic school or college for any of your education?

	Yes	No	DK/RE	If Yes, Total Years
A. Attended Catholic elementary school	37	62	1	AVG=6
B. Attended Catholic high school	19	79	2	AVG=4
C. Attended Catholic college or university	8	89	3	AVG=3

RACE:

White, non-Hispanic	63
Hispanic	32
Black, non-Hispanic	1
Other, non-Hispanic	3
2+ races, non-Hispanic	<2

GENDER:

Male	50
Female	50

AGE:

Years	18–24	25–34	35–44	45–54	55–64	65–74	75+
Percentage	10	16	21	19	19	9	6
				Mean Years of Age			47
				Median Years of Age			46

GENERATION:

Pre–Vatican II (71+)	10
Vatican II (51–70)	31
Post–Vatican II (32–50)	37
Millennial (18–31)	23

COMMITMENT:

Low	14
Medium	66
High	19

REGION:

Northeast	27
Midwest	22
South	27
West	24

POLITICAL PARTY (7 categories):

Strong Republican	12
Not strong Republican	10
Leans Republican	18
Undecided/Independent/Other	<3
Leans Democrat	21
Not strong Democrat	18
Strong Democrat	18

POLITICAL PARTY (3 categories):

Republican	22
Independent	42
Democrat	36

POLITICAL PARTY (3 categories):

Republican and leans Republican	40
Undecided/Independent/other	<3
Democrat and leans Democrat	57

HOUSEHOLD INCOME:

Under $25,000	24
$25,000 to 34,999	11
$35,000 to 49,999	15
$50,000 to 74,999	16
$75,000 to 99,999	13
$100,000 to $149,999	16
$150,000 or over	6

~

Notes

Introduction

1. See Patrick McNamara, *Conscience First, Tradition Second*, 1992; Kenneth Briggs, *Holy Siege*, 1992; Gene Burns, *The Frontiers of Catholicism*, 1992; Andrew Greeley, *The Catholic Experience*, 1967, and *Faithful Attraction*, 1991; and Richard Schoenherr and Lawrence Young, *Full Pews and Empty Altars*, 1993.

Chapter 2

1. This figure is calculated from the proportion of the U.S. adult population who self-identify as Catholic, based on survey data from several highly respected polls, such as Gallup and Pew.

2. According to the 2010 U.S. Census, Hispanics now make up 16.4 percent of the overall population.

3. We do not intend to imply by this statement that Hispanic Catholics are of one mind in their attitudes, beliefs, and practices. We recognize that intra-Hispanic variation is equally as diverse as variation between Hispanics and other ethnic groups.

4. These numbers, from *The Official Catholic Directory*, report the number of parish-identified Catholics, for example, those who are registered in a parish or receiving sacraments from a parish (including children as well as adults). This number is always lower than the number of self-identified Catholics reported from survey data, which includes Catholics who may attend Mass infrequently and are typically not registered in a parish.

5. According to data reported by the National Catholic Educational Association.

6. Data from school censuses conducted by the National Catholic Educational Association suggest that more than 13 percent of the children enrolled in Catholic high schools are not Catholic.

Chapter 4

1. The quote from Cardinal Dolan is on the occasion of his election as President of the U.S. Conference of Catholic Bishops (see Goodstein 2010: A16). The second quote is from a letter to the editor, published in the *New York Times*, from Merle Molofsky (2012) recalling the independence of a faculty colleague, a nun, with whom she taught in the 1970s. The third is from an interview conducted on NPR's *Fresh Air* with Sister Pat Farrell on July 17, 2012, in the context of the Vatican's reprimand of the LCWR (e.g., Goodstein 2012a).

2. As explained in chapter 3, highly committed Catholics are those who go to Mass at least weekly, who say that the Church is the most important or among the most important parts of their life, and who place themselves at either 1 or 2 on a 7-point scale measuring their sense of whether they would ever leave the Church. Based on these criteria, 19 percent of our respondents are highly committed Catholics.

Chapter 5

1. The percentages given here are based on our calculations derived from the Pew Forum (2009a: 24) report that provides numbers and percentages separately for defecting Catholics who are currently unaffiliated, and defecting Catholics who are currently Protestant. Our calculations are based on combining both groups.

Chapter 6

1. Data from *The Official Catholic Directory*, compiled from parish sacramental records, indicate that about a quarter of the marriages celebrated in the Church are between a Catholic and a non-Catholic. This proportion has remained quite stable in recent decades.

2. Although the data we present here come from surveys with similar questions conducted at five different points in time, these data are not a panel study because we did not reinterview the same people for each survey in this series. Therefore, we cannot assume that the changes we document are due to the fact that each generational cohort is moving through time into a different stage in their life-cycle. The only scientific way to distinguish between life-cycle and cohort effects is through a longitudinal panel study.

Chapter 7

1. In 2010, Catholics were elected to the House from 33 different states, 7 of them Southern, another sign of the changing geography of the Catholic population. All elected from the 7 southern states are Republicans.

2. The phrase "social justice" receives much less support than the phrase "concern for the poor." Does the latter phrase suggest a local, subsidiarity concern, or is it that Catholics are just not attracted to the phrase "social justice"? In a values study of American Jews, *PRRI*, April 2012, Jones and Cox found that 80 percent said that "social justice" was one of their core values. Catholics frequently use the phrase "social teachings" of the Church to mean a broad national commitment. Perhaps that phrase would receive more support.

3. In May 2012 in Hartford, Connecticut, Gov. Daniel Malloy (D) signed into law a bill outlawing the use of the death penalty in the state, making it the 17th overall state and the 5th in the past 5 years to end the use of capital punishment. Hailing the signing as a "historic occasion," Archbishop Henry Mansell of Hartford said, "The Catholic church opposes the death penalty and has been fighting for its elimination for many years" (*National Catholic Reporter*, May 11–24, 2012, 3). The Connecticut Catholic Public Affairs Conference is quoted saying that "[j]ustice can be served and society can be protected from violent criminals without the death penalty. These goals can easily be met by replacing the death penalty with a lifetime sentence without the possibility of release" (ibid.).

References

Abbott, Walter. Ed. 1966. *The Documents of Vatican II*. New York: Herder and Herder.

Adams, Lucy A. 2012. Letter. Commonweal (February 24): 2.

Albergo, Giuseppe. 2006. *A Brief History of Vatican II*. Translated by Matthew Sherry. Maryknoll, NY: Orbis Books.

Allen, John. 2012. "Loose Canon on Annulments May Get Tighter." *National Catholic Reporter* (May 1).

Ammerman, Nancy. 1997. "Golden Rule Christianity: Lived Religion in American Mainstream." In David Hall, ed. *Lived Religion in America*, 196–216. Princeton, NJ: Princeton University Press.

Archibold, Randal, and Victoria Burnett. 2012. "Cuban Official Rules Out Reforms Urged by Pope." *New York Times* (March 28), A8.

Baggett, Jerome. 2009. *Sense of the Faithful: How American Catholics Live Their Faith*. New York: Oxford University Press.

Bartkowski, John, Aida Ramos-Wada, Chris Ellison, and Gabriel Acevedo. 2012. "Faith, Race-Ethnicity, and Public Policy Preferences: Religious Schemas and Abortion Attitudes among U.S. Latinos." *Journal for the Scientific Study of Religion* 51: 343–358.

Bender, Courtney. 2010. *The New Metaphysicals: Spirituality and the American Religious Imagination*. Chicago: University of Chicago Press.

Benedict XVI, Pope. 2007. "Responses to Some Aspects Regarding Certain Aspects of the Doctrine on the Church." Vatican City: The Congregation for the Doctrine of the Faith (July 10).

Blaire, Stephen E., Bishop. 2012. "Bishop Blaire Reflects on the Human Costs and Moral Challenges of a Broken Economy in U.S. Bishops' Labor Day Statement." U.S. Council of Catholic Bishops (August 24).

Briggs, Kenneth. 1992. *Holy Siege: The Year That Shook Catholic America*. San Francisco: HarperCollins.

Bruni, Frank. 2012. "Many Kinds of Catholic." Column. *New York Times* (March 20): A23.

Burns, Gene. 1992. *The Frontiers of Catholicism: The Politics of Ideology in a Liberal World*. Berkeley: University of California Press.

Burns, Gene. 2005. *The Moral Veto: Framing Contraception, Abortion, and Cultural Pluralism in the United States*. New York: Cambridge University Press.

Carroll, Michael. 2007. *American Catholics in the Protestant Imagination*. Baltimore, MD: Johns Hopkins University Press.

Carty, Thomas J. 2008 "White House Outreach to Catholics." In Kristin Heyer, Mark J. Rozell, and Michael A. Genovese, eds., *Catholics and Politics: The Dynamic Tension between Faith and Power*, 184–187. Washington, DC: Georgetown University Press.

Casanova, Jose. 1994. *Public Religions in the Modern World*. Chicago: University of Chicago Press.

Catechism of the Catholic Church. 1994. Dublin: Veritas.

Catechism of the Catholic Church. 1995. New York: Doubleday.

Cernera, Anthony, and Oliver Morgan. 2002. *Examining the Catholic Intellectual Tradition: Issues and Perspectives*. Fairfield, CT: Sacred Heart University.

Chaves, Mark. 1994. "Secularization as Declining Religious Authority." *Social Forces* 72: 749–774.

Cohn, D'Vera, Jeffrey Passel, Wendy Wang, and Gretchen Livingston. 2011. *Barely Half of U.S. Adults Are Married—A Record Low*. Washington, DC: Pew Research Center.

Congar, Yves. 1967. *Tradition and Traditions: An Historical and Theological Essay*. New York: Macmillan.

Congregation for the Doctrine of the Faith. 1977. "Vatican Declaration: Women in the Ministerial Priesthood." *Origins* 6 (February 3): 517, 519–531.

Congregation for the Doctrine of the Faith. 1995. "Inadmissibility of Women to Ministerial Priesthood." *Origins* 25 (Nov. 30): 401, 403–405.

"Connecticut Ends Death Penalty." 2012. *National Catholic Reporter* (May 11–24): 3.

Dawkins, Richard. 2008. *The God Delusion*. Boston: Houghton Mifflin.

deTocqueville, Alexis. 1835/1984. *Democracy in America*. New York: New American Library.

Diaz-Stevens, Ana Maria. 1994. "Latinas and the Church." In Jay Dolan and Allan Figueroa Deck, eds., *Hispanic Catholic Culture in the U.S.: Issues and Concerns*, 240–277. Notre Dame, IN: University of Notre Dame Press.

D'Antonio, William, James Davidson, Dean Hoge, and Mary Gautier. 2007. *American Catholics Today: New Realities of Their Faith and Their Church*. Lanham, MD: Rowman & Littlefield.

D'Antonio, William, James Davidson, Dean Hoge, and Katherine Meyer. 2001. *American Catholics: Gender, Generation, and Commitment*. Lanham, MD: Rowman & Littlefield.

D'Antonio, William, James Davidson, Dean Hoge, and Ruth Wallace. 1996. *Laity American and Catholic: Transforming the Church*. Kansas City, MO: Sheed and Ward.

D'Antonio, William, James Davidson, Dean Hoge, and Ruth Wallace. 1989. *American Catholic Laity in a Changing Church*. Kansas City, MO: Sheed and Ward.

Dillon, Michele. 1999. *Catholic Identity: Balancing Reason, Faith, and Power*. New York: Cambridge University Press.

Dillon, Michele. 2009. "Diverse Spiritualities: Results from the IEC Survey." Paper presented to the IEC Assembly. Washington, DC.

Dillon, Michele, and Paul Wink. 2007. *In the Course of a Lifetime: Tracing Religious Belief, Practice, and Change*. Berkeley: University of California Press.

Dionne, E.J. 2012. "Agree to Disagree? Not Before Engaging in Vigorous Debate." *Catholic Health World* (May 1): 1.

Donadio, Rachel. 2008. "Pope, Visiting France, Speaks about Role of Faith." *New York Times* (September 13): A8.

Donadio, Rachel. 2009. "For Vatican, Spain Is a Key Front in Church-State Battle." *New York Times* (January 6): A6.

Donadio, Rachel. 2010a. "Pope Issues Forceful Statement on Sexual Abuse Crisis." *New York Times* (May 12): A4.

Donadio, Rachel. 2010b. "Vatican Sets New Rules on Responding to Sex Abuse." *New York Time* (July 15): A1.

Donadio, Rachel. 2012a. "Papal Mass in Mexico Offers Message to Trust God." *New York Times* (March 26): A10.

Donadio, Rachel. 2012b. "Pope Rebukes Priests Who Advocate Ordaining Women and Ending Celibacy." *New York Times* (April 6): A10.

Douglas, Ann. 1977. *The Feminization of American Culture*. New York: Doubleday.

Duffy, Eamon. 2011. "The Diplomat: The Tragic Silence of Pius XII." *Commonweal* (November 4): 13.

Durkheim, Emile. 1912/2001. *The Elementary Forms of Religious Life*. Translated by Carol Cosman. Oxford: Oxford University Press.

Ellis, John Tracy. 1956. *American Catholicism*. Chicago: University of Chicago Press.

Ellison, Chris, Gabriel Acevedo, and Aida Ramos-Wada. 2011. "Religion and Attitudes toward Same-Sex Marriage among US Latinos." *Social Science Quarterly* 92: 35–56.

England, Paula. 2005. "Emerging Theories of Care." *Annual Review of Sociology* 31: 381–399.

Fichter, Joseph, S.J. 1973. *One Man Research: Reminiscences of a Catholic Sociologist*. New York: John Wiley & Sons.

Fischer, Claude, and Michael Hout. 2006. *Century of Difference: How America Changed in the Last One Hundred Years*. New York: Russell Sage.

Fisher, Ian, and Larry Rohter. 2007. "The Pope, Addressing Latin America's Bishops, Denounces Capitalism and Marxism." *New York Times* (May 14), A10.

Froehle, Bryan T., and Mary L. Gautier. 2000. *Catholicism USA: A Portrait of the Catholic Church in the United States*. Maryknoll, NY: Orbis Books.

Frosch, Dan. 2012. "Catholic Fund Cuts Off Groups Over Ties Unsettling to Church." *New York Times* (April 6): A1.

Gallup Report. 2012. "Religiousness: A Key Factor for Romney and Obama Support," (April 25). Princeton, NJ: The Gallup Organization.

Gautier, Mary L., Mary E. Bendyna, RSM, and Anna C. Buck. 2008. *Issues Concerning Retirement for Diocesan Priests: A Report for Laity in Support of Retired Priests, Inc.* Washington, DC: Center for Applied Research in the Apostolate.

Gautier, Mary L., Paul M. Perl, and Stephen J. Fichter. 2012. *Same Call, Different Men: The Evolution of the Priesthood since Vatican II.* Collegeville, MN: Liturgical Press.

Goldscheider, Calvin, and William D. Mosher. 1991. "Patterns of Contraceptive Use in the United States: The Importance of Religious Factors." *Studies in Family Planning.* March/April.

Goodstein, Laurie. 2010. "Catholic Bishops Pick New Yorker as Their Leader." *New York Times* (November 17): A1, 16.

Goodstein, Laurie. 2011. "Priests Challenge Vatican on Ordaining Women." *New York Times* (July 23): A1.

Goodstein, Laurie. 2012a. "Vatican Reprimands a Group of U.S. Nuns and Plans Changes." *New York Times* (April 19): A16.

Goodstein, Laurie. 2012b. "Bishops Sue Over Mandate to Provide Birth Control." *New York Times* (May 22): A13.

Grace, Gerald, and Joseph O'Keefe, SJ, eds. 2007. *International Handbook of Catholic Education: Challenges for School Systems in the 21st Century, Part I.* Dordrecht, Netherlands: Springer.

Gray, Mark M. 2012. *Perspectives from Parish Leaders: U.S. Parish Life and Ministry.* Washington, DC: Center for Applied Research in the Apostolate.

Gray, Mark, Mary Gautier, and Melissa Cidade. 2011. *The Changing Face of U.S. Catholic Parishes.* Washington, DC: Center for Applied Research in the Apostolate.

Gray, Mark M., and Paul M. Perl. 2008. *CARA Catholic Poll.* Washington, DC: Center for Applied Research in the Apostolate.

Greeley, Andrew. 1967. *The Catholic Experience: A Sociologist's Interpretation of the History of American Catholicism.* New York: Doubleday and Co.

Greeley, Andrew. 1972. *The Catholic Priest in the United States: Sociological Investigations.* Washington, DC: United States Catholic Conference.

Greeley, Andrew. 1977. *The American Catholic: A Social Portrait.* New York: Basic Books.

Greeley, Andrew. 1985. *American Catholics since the Council.* Chicago: Thomas More Press.

Greeley, Andrew. 1989. "On the Margins of the Church: A Sociological Note." *America* (March 14).

Greeley, Andrew. 1991. *Faithful Attraction: Discovering Intimacy, Love, and Fidelity in American Marriage.* New York: Tor Books.

Habermas, Jurgen. 1975. *Legitimation Crisis.* Boston: Beacon Press.

Habermas, Jurgen. 2008. "Notes on a Post-Secular Society." *New Perspectives Quarterly* 25:4.

Hastings, Adrian, ed. 1991. *Modern Catholicism: Vatican II and After.* New York: Oxford University Press.

Hochschild, Arlie, with Anne Machung. 1990. *The Second Shift.* New York: Avon Books.

Hoge, Dean R., and Aniedi Okure. 2006. *International Priests in America: Challenges and Opportunities.* Collegeville, MN: Liturgical Press.

Hout, Michael. 2005. "Educational Progress for African Americans and Latinos in the United States since the 1950s to the 1990s." In Glenn Loury, Tariq Madood, and Steve Teles, eds., *Ethnicity, Social Mobility and Public policy*. Cambridge: Cambridge University Press.

Hout, Michael. 2012. "Social and Economic Returns to College Education in the United States." *Annual Review of Sociology* 38: 1–22.

Hout, Michael, and Claude Fischer. 2002. "Explaining the Rise of Americans with No Religious Preferences: Politics and Generations." *American Sociological Review* 67: 165–190.

Hout, Michael, and Andrew Greeley. 1987. "The Center Doesn't Hold: Church Attendance in the United States, 1940–1984." *American Sociological Review* 52: 325–345.

Humphreys, Joe. 2012. "Dawkins Calls for Catholic Honesty." *Irish Times* (June 6).

John Paul II, Pope. 1994. "*Ordinatio Sacerdotalis*," *Origins* 24 (June 9): 49–52.

Jones, Robert, and Daniel Cox. 2011. *Catholic Attitudes on Gay and Lesbian Issues*. Washington DC: Public Religion Research Institute.

Kennedy, Sheila Rauch. 1998. *Shattered Faith: A Woman's Struggle to Stop the Catholic Church from Annulling Her Marriage*. New York: Henry Holt.

Klinenberg, Eric. 2012. *Going Solo: The Extraordinary Rise and Surprising Appeal of Living Alone*. New York: Penguin.

Kristof, Nicholas. 2012. "We Are All Nuns." Column. *New York Times* (April 29): SR11.

Laurentin, Rene. 1973. "Peter as the Foundation Stone in the Present Uncertainty." In Edward Schilebeeckx and Bas van Iersel, eds., *Truth and Certainty*, 95–113. New York: Herder and Herder.

Leege, David C., et al. 2002. *The Politics of Cultural Differences*. Princeton: Princeton University Press.

Lee, SM, Bernard, and William D'Antonio. 2000. *The Catholic Experience of Small Christian Communities*. New York: Paulist Press.

Lenski, Gerhard. 1961. *The Religious Factor: A Sociologist's Inquiry*. New York: Doubleday, Anchor Books.

Luker, Kristen. 1984. *Abortion and the Politics of Motherhood*. Berkeley: University of California Press.

Matovina, Timothy. 2012. *Latino Catholicism: Transformation in America's Largest Church*. Princeton: Princeton University Press.

McClory, Robert. 1995. *Turning Point*. New York: Crossroad.

McDonald, PBVM, Dale, and Margaret M. Schultz. 2012. *United States Catholic Elementary and Secondary Schools 2011–2012*. Washington, DC: National Catholic Educational Association.

McElwee, Joshua J. 2012. "LCWR 'Stunned' by Vatican's Latest Move." *National Catholic Reporter* (April 19).

McGuire, Meredith. 2008. *Lived Religion: Faith and Practice in Everyday Life*. New York: Oxford University Press.

McNamara, Patrick. 1992. *Conscience First, Tradition Second*. Albany: SUNY Press.

Merton, Thomas. 1952. *The Seven Story Mountain*. San Francisco: Harper.

Moen, Phyllis, and Kelly Chermack. 2005. "Gender Disparities in Health." *Journal of Gerontology* 60B: 99–108.

Molofsky, Merle. 2012. "A Nun's Reply: 'No One Can Tell Me What to Think.'" Letter. *New York Times* (May 18): A26.

Morris, Charles R. 1997. *American Catholic: The Saints and Sinners Who Built America's Most Powerful Church*. New York: Random House/Time.

National Catholic Reporter. 2012. Editorial (November 23–December 6): 28.

National Conference on Citizenship. 2010. *Civic Life in America*. Washington, DC: National Conference on Citizenship/Corporation for National and Community Service.

Navarro-Rivera, Juhem, Barry A. Kosmin, and Ariela Keysar. 2010. *U.S. Latino Religious Identification, 1990–2008: Growth, Diversity & Transformation*. Hartford, CT: Trinity College Program on Public Values.

Newport, Frank. 2012. "Catholics' Presidential Pick Differs by Ethnicity, Religiosity." Gallup Daily Tracking Poll (May 2).

O'Dea, Thomas F. 1958. *American Catholic Dilemma: An Inquiry into the Intellectual Life*. New York: Sheed and Ward.

Ospino, Hosffman. 2011. *Hispanic Ministry in the 21st Century: Present and Future*. Miami, FL: Convivium Press.

Otterman, Sharon. 2012. "Complex Emotions with Naming of First American Indian Saint." *New York Times* (July 25): A18.

Parrott, Jeff. 2012. "Where 20,000 or 30,000 Are Gathered: Life in a Catholic Megaparish." *U.S. Catholic* 77:4 (April 2012).

Parsons, Talcott. 1971. *The System of Modern Societies*. Englewood Cliffs, NJ: Prentice Hall.

Paul VI, Pope. 1968/1983. *Humanae Vitae: Encyclical Letter of His Holiness Pope Paul VI*. San Francisco: Ignatius Press.

Perl, Paul M., and Mark M. Gray. 2000. *CARA Catholic Poll*. Washington, DC: Center for Applied Research in the Apostolate.

Perl, Paul M., Jennifer Z. Greely, and Mark M. Gray. 2006. "What Proportion of Adult Hispanics Are Catholic? A Review of Survey Data and Methodology." *Journal for the Scientific Study of Religion* (September) 45: 419–436.

Pew Forum on Religion and Public Life. 2007. *Changing Faiths: Latinos and the Transformation of American Religion*. Washington, DC: Pew Research Center.

Pew Forum on Religion and Public Life. 2008. *The U.S. Religious Landscape Survey: Religious Beliefs*. Washington, DC: Pew Research Center.

Pew Forum on Religion and Public Life. 2009a. *Faith in Flux: Changes in Religious Affiliation in the U.S.* Washington, DC: Pew Research Center.

Pew Forum on Religion and Public Life. 2009b. "GOP Seen as Friendlier to Religion than Democrats." Washington, DC: Pew Research Center.

Pew Forum on Religion and Public Life. 2010. *Religion among the Millennials*. Washington, DC: Pew Research Center.

Pew Forum on Religion and Public Life. 2011. "Most say Homosexuality Should be Accepted by Society." Washington, DC: Pew Research Center.

Pew Forum on Religion and Public Life. 2012. "Nones on the Rise." Washington, DC: Pew Research Center.

Pius XI, Pope. 1930. *Casti Connubii*. Papal Encyclical promulgated by Pius XI on December 31, 1930.

Pius XII, Pope. 1951. "Counsel to Teaching Sisters: An Address by His Holiness Pius XII to the First International Congress of Teaching Sisters" on September 15, 1951.

Putnam, Robert. 2000. *Bowling Alone: The Collapse and Revival of American Community*. New York: Simon and Schuster.

Quiñonez, Lora Ann, and Mary Daniel Turner. 1993. *The Transformation of American Catholic Sisters*. Philadelphia, PA: Temple University Press.

Roof, Wade Clark. 1999. *Spiritual Marketplace: Baby Boomers and the Remaking of American Religion*. Princeton: Princeton University Press.

Rowe, Brian, and Michael Sean Winters. 2012. "Ryan Budget Faces Catholic Pushback." *National Catholic Reporter* (May 11–24): Nation 5.

Schoenherr, Richard A., and David Yamane. 2002. *Goodbye Father: The Celibate Male Priesthood and the Future of the Catholic Church*. New York: Oxford University Press.

Schoenherr, Richard, and Larry Young. 1993. *Full Pews and Empty Altars*. Madison, WI: University of Wisconsin Press.

Seidler, John, and Katherine Meyer. 1989. *Conflict and Change in the Catholic Church*. New Brunswick, NJ: Rutgers University Press.

Smelser, Neil. 1968. *Essays in Sociological Explanation*. Englewood Cliffs, NJ: Prentice Hall.

Smith, Christian, and Melinda Denton. 2005. *Soul Searching: The Religious and Spiritual Lives of American Teenagers*. New York: Oxford University Press.

Smith, Christian, with Patricia Snell. 2009. *Souls in Transition: The Religious and Spiritual Lives of Emerging Adults*. New York: Oxford University Press.

Smith, Kristin. 2008. *Working Hard for the Money: Trends in Women's Employment, 1970 to 2007*. University of New Hampshire: Carsey Institute Report.

Sullivan, Francis A. 1991. "The Theologian's Ecclesial Vocation and the 1990 CDF Instruction." *Theological Studies* 52: 51–68.

Sullivan, Francis A. 1995. "Guideposts from Catholic Tradition." *America* (December 9): 5–6.

Tentler, Leslie Woodcock. 2004. *Catholics and Contraception: An American History*. Ithaca, NY: Cornell University Press.

Tierney, Brian. 1971. "Origins of Papal Infallibility." *Journal of Ecumenical Studies* 8: 841–864.

Tracy, David. 1987. *Plurality and Ambiguity*. San Francisco: Harper & Row.

Wallace, Ruth. 1992. *They Call Her Pastor: A New Role for Catholic Women*. Albany: State University of New York Press.

Walsh, Michael J. 1991. "Pius XII" in *Modern Catholicism*: 20–26. New York: Oxford University Press.

White, John K., and W. V. D'Antonio. 2007. "Catholics and the Politics of Change: The Presidential Campaigns of Two JFKs." *Religion and the Bush Presidency*. New York: Palgrave MacMillan.

Wilde, Melissa. 2001. "From Excommunication to Nullification: Testing and Extending Supply-Side Religious Marketing with The Case of Catholic Marital Annulments." *Journal for the Scientific Study of Religion* 40: 235–249.

Wilde, Melissa. 2007. *Vatican II: A Sociological Analysis of Religious Change.* Princeton, NJ: Princeton University Press.

Wooden, Cindy. 2007. "Pope Says Eucharist Essential for Christians in Often-Hostile World." *The Pilot* (June 16), p. 7.

Wuthnow, Robert. 1998. *After Heaven: Spirituality in America since the 1950s.* Berkeley: University of California Press.

Ye, Cong, Jenna Fulton, and Roger Tourangeau. 2011. "More Positive or More Extreme? A Meta-Analysis of Mode Differences in Response Choice." *Public Opinion Quarterly* 75: 349–365.

Index

41, 100–1, 103, 114–15, 118; politics
and, 103; as priests, 20, 22–23, 30,
41, 52, 111, 114–19, 163–64, 166,
18–-85, 190; declining commitment
to Church of, 89–92, 96–97, 103–11,
169–70

women's equality, 20, 80, 89, 97, 102, 105
women's ordination, 101–4
women religious, 15, 16

yoga, as spiritual practice, 63–66, 94,
162, 17

About the Authors

William V. D'Antonio (PhD 1958, Michigan State University) is a research fellow in the Institute for Policy Research and Catholic Studies at The Catholic University of America. He is coauthor of nine books and coeditor of four, including *American Catholics Today* (2007) and *Voices of the Faithful* (2007). Dr. D'Antonio served on the faculty of the University of Notre Dame from 1959–1971, and served as professor and chair of the department from 1966–1971. He served as professor and chair of the department at the University of Connecticut from 1971–1976 and received emeritus professor status there in 1986. He also served as executive officer of the American Sociological Association from 1982 until his retirement in 1991. Since 1993 he has been a visiting research professor in sociology at Catholic University. In 2004 he was awarded an honorary Doctor of Humane Letters from St. Michael's College, and served as a Fulbright Senior Fellow in Italy. In 2008, The Center for the Study of Religion and Society, Department of Sociology, University of Notre Dame named its annual award to the center's outstanding graduate student in his honor. In 2009 he received the Rev. Louis J. Luzbetak Award for Exemplary Church Research from the Center for Applied Research in the Apostolate.

Michele Dillon (PhD 1989, University of California, Berkeley) is professor and chair of sociology at the University of New Hampshire. Her publications include *In the Course of a Lifetime: Tracing Religious Belief, Practice and Change* (coauthor Paul Wink; 2007), *Catholic Identity: Balancing Reason, Faith, and*

Power (1999), *Debating Divorce: Moral Conflict in Ireland* (1993), *Handbook of the Sociology of Religion* (editor; 2003), *Introduction to Sociological Theory* (2010), and over fifty research articles, essays, and book chapters. Dr. Dillon is the current president of the Society for the Scientific Study of Religion. She has also served as chair of the American Sociological Association section on the sociology of religion, and as president of the Association for the Sociology of Religion. In 2011–2012, she was the JE and Lillian Byrne Tipton Distinguished Visiting Professor in Catholic Studies at the University of California, Santa Barbara.

Mary L. Gautier (PhD 1995, Louisiana State University) is a sociologist and senior research associate at the Center for Applied Research in the Apostolate (CARA) at Georgetown University. Before coming to CARA, Dr. Gautier taught in the sociology department at LSU and at Texas Christian University in Fort Worth, Texas, and served as a lay pastoral associate at a parish in Baton Rouge, Louisiana, for six years. At CARA Dr. Gautier specializes in Catholic demographic trends in the United States, manages CARA databases on Church information, and conducts demographic projects. She also edits *The CARA Report*, a quarterly research publication, as well as other CARA publications. She is coauthor of six books on Catholicism, most recently *Same Call, Different Men: The Evolution of the Priesthood Since Vatican II* (2012).